T0285528

FREUD'S PATIENTS

FREUD'S PATIENTS
A BOOK OF LIVES

MIKKEL BORCH-JACOBSEN

REAKTION BOOKS

Published by
Reaktion Books Ltd
Unit 32, Waterside
44–48 Wharf Road
London NI 7UX, UK
www.reaktionbooks.co.uk

Thirty-one of the 38 vignettes collected here were originally published in French as *Les Patients de Freud: Destins* in 2011. Published by special arrangement with Éditions Sciences Humaines in conjunction with their duly appointed agent, 2 Seas Literary Agency

Translation by Andrew Brown
© Sciences Humaines 2011
English translation © Reaktion Books 2021
Additional material © Mikkel Borch-Jacobsen 2021

Printed and bound in Great Britain
by TJ Books Ltd, Padstow, Cornwall

A catalogue record for this book is available from the British Library

ISBN 978 1 78914 455 0

CONTENTS

PREFACE

We all know the characters described by Freud in his case studies: 'Emmy von N.', 'Elisabeth von R.', 'Dora', 'Little Hans', the 'Rat Man', the 'Wolf Man', the 'Young Homosexual Woman'. But do we know the real people behind these illustrious pseudonyms – respectively, Fanny Moser, Ilona Weiss, Ida Bauer, Herbert Graf, Ernst Lanzer, Sergius Pankejeff, Margarethe Csonka? More generally, do we know all those many patients on whom Freud never wrote anything, or at least not directly: Pauline Silberstein (who committed suicide by throwing herself from the top of her therapist's building), Olga Hönig (the mother of 'Little Hans'), Bruno Veneziani (the novelist Italo Svevo's brother-in-law), Elfriede Hirschfeld, Albert Hirst, the architect Karl Mayreder, Baron Victor von Dirsztay, the psychotic Carl Liebmann and so many others? Do we know that Bruno Walter, the great conductor, was one of Freud's patients, as was Adele Jeiteles, the mother of Arthur Koestler? And that Freud also hypnotized his own wife, Martha Bernays, before analysing his daughter Anna?

In what follows I have tried to reconstruct the sometimes comical, most often tragic and always captivating stories of these patients who have long been nameless and faceless: in total, 38 sketchy and necessarily incomplete portraits, drawn from the documents available today and told without prejudging revelations that, in the future, might emerge from those which are still closed to researchers within the Freud Collection at the Library of Congress in Washington, DC. Thirty-eight portraits, and that is it: I have selected only those of Freud's patients on whom we already have enough information to justify a biographical note, however brief. Those about whom we know little apart from their names or initials have been excluded – for now. This collection therefore does not claim to be exhaustive, merely representative. As partial as it is, this sample should at least allow the reader to get an idea of Freud's actual clinical practice, over and above the fabulous narratives he himself drew from it.

I have limited myself to Freud's *patients*, without including the many people who lay down on Freud's couch mainly to train as analysts (such as Anna Guggenbühl or Clarence Oberndorf, for example) or out of simple intellectual curiosity (such as Alix and James Strachey, or Arthur Tansley). This survey includes only people who came to see Freud for symptoms from which they sought to be cured or existential difficulties from which they could not extricate themselves. It is for this reason that I have included Anna Freud, Horace Frink and Monroe Meyer, even if it is clear that in their cases the analysis was also a training one. All three of them were, first and foremost, in need of care, and it is as therapy that their treatments should be evaluated, as in the case of the other patients cited here.

Finally, I have refrained as far as possible from taking into account Freud's interpretations, which are what make his case histories so fascinating and interesting. By comparison, the stories the reader will find here are prosaic and quotidian. No theory, no commentary: I have kept to the surface of the facts, documents and testimonies available, without speculating on the motivations, conscious or unconscious, of any of the people involved. Those who seek in these stories a confirmation of Freud's stories may therefore be disappointed, as they will not find 'their' Freud here. On the other hand, they *will* find another Freud, the Freud of his patients and their entourage. I am not sure whether we can reconcile these two Freuds, or these two ways of telling stories. I apologize in advance to those whom this history-based approach will confuse or shock. The reader will find the sources on which I have relied at the end of the volume. Some are primary, as historians say, others are secondary.

An earlier incarnation of this book came out in French ten years ago and has been significantly augmented and updated, based on new material that has emerged in the meantime. Errors and omissions have been rectified (at least those that were detected), a number of biographical vignettes have been fleshed out with fresh information, and seven newly identified patients have been added to the 31 that featured in the French edition. These additions do not, however, change much the overall conclusion that can be drawn from these informal follow-up studies: with a few ambiguous exceptions, such as the treatments of Ernst Lanzer, Bruno Walter and Albert Hirst, Freud's cures were largely ineffectual, when they were not downright destructive.

Motor-cars came shooting out of deep, narrow streets into the shallows of bright squares. Dark patches of pedestrian bustle formed into cloudy streams. Where stronger lines of speed transected their loose-woven hurrying, they clotted up – only to trickle on all the faster then and after a few ripples regain their regular pulse-beat. Hundreds of sounds were intertwined into a coil of wiry noise, with single barbs projecting, sharp edges running along it and submerging again, and clear notes splintering off – flying and scattering. Even though the peculiar nature of the noise could not be defined, a man returning after years of absence would have known, with his eyes shut, that he was in the ancient capital and imperial city, Vienna.

Robert Musil, *The Man without Qualities*

1
BERTHA PAPPENHEIM
(1859–1936)

Bertha Pappenheim, always presented under the name of 'Anna O.' as the original patient of psychoanalysis, was actually never treated by Freud himself but by his friend and mentor Josef Breuer. If we are to believe Freud, however, she rightfully belongs in the history of psychoanalysis. In 1917 he recalled how 'Breuer did in fact restore his hysterical patient Anna O., that is, freed her from her symptoms . . . This discovery of Breuer's is still the foundation of psycho-analytical therapy' (18th *Introductory Lecture on Psychoanalysis*). Whether Bertha Pappenheim can be reduced to Anna O. is another story.

She was born on 27 February 1859 in Vienna to Jewish parents. Her father, Siegmund Pappenheim, was a millionaire who had inherited a grain trading company. Her mother, Recha Goldschmidt, came from an old Frankfurt family. The Pappenheims were strictly Orthodox and Bertha received the traditional education of a *höhere Tochter* (a girl of the upper middle class waiting to enter the 'marriage market'): religious education (the study of Hebrew and biblical texts), foreign languages (English, French, Italian), needlepoint, piano, horse riding. Bertha, who was a lively and energetic young girl, felt suffocated in this confined life, which she was later to denounce in the article 'On the Education of Young Women in the Upper Classes' (1898). As Breuer was to reveal in a medical report sent to his colleague Robert Binswanger, she was also secretly in revolt against her religious upbringing: 'She is not at all religious; the daughter of very orthodox, religious Jews, she has always been accustomed to carry out all instructions meticulously for her father's sake and is even now disposed to do so. In her life religion serves only as an object of silent struggles and silent opposition.'

So Bertha took flight, first in a fantasy world she called her 'private theatre' and then in illness. The earliest symptoms appeared in the autumn of 1880, at a time when Bertha looked after her beloved father, who had fallen ill with a pleurisy that was to prove fatal. Bertha had a persistent cough, and at the end of November Josef Breuer was called upon. Breuer, a well-respected internist, was the physician of the Jewish high bourgeoisie and aristocracy in Vienna. He diagnosed a hysteria, upon which Bertha took to her bed and developed 'in rapid succession' an impressive array of symptoms: pain in the left side of the occiput, blurred vision, hallucinations, various contractures and anaesthesias, trigeminal (or facial) neuralgia, 'aphasia' (from March 1881 onwards she spoke only in English), split personality and altered states of consciousness ('absences') during which she threw tantrums that she could not remember afterwards.

Breuer, who came to see her every day, noticed that her condition improved each time he let her tell, during her 'absences', the sad stories of her private theatre – a process she termed (in English) a 'talking cure' or again 'chimney sweeping'. However, her condition worsened after the death of her father on 5 April 1881. She refused to eat and told no more fairy tales à la Hans Christian Andersen, but instead related morbid 'tragedies'. She also had negative hallucinations: she did not see the people around her and recognized only Breuer. On 15 April Breuer called upon his colleague the psychiatrist Richard von Krafft-Ebing for a second opinion. Unconvinced of the authenticity of the patient's symptoms (she claimed to be unaware of his presence), Krafft-Ebing blew into her face the smoke of a piece of paper that he had ignited. This caused an explosion of anger on the part of Bertha who began to beat Breuer violently. Finally, on 7 June, Breuer forcibly placed her in an annexe to a clinic for nervous disorders run by his friend Dr Hermann Breslauer at Inzersdorf. There she was quieted with the help of large doses of chloral hydrate, the sedative of choice at the time. As a result, Bertha developed an addiction to chloral.

Once the patient was stabilized, the talking cure could resume. Bertha's stories had changed. During her altered states, she no longer told imaginary tales or tragedies: 'What she reported was more and more concerned with her hallucinations and, for instance, the things that had annoyed her during the past days.'

When she told of a frustration that had been the source of a particular symptom, it would disappear miraculously. Breuer therefore set out to eliminate her countless symptoms one by one (for example, the 303 instances of hysterical deafness). What followed was a therapeutic marathon that resulted – if we are to believe the case history published thirteen years later by Breuer in *Studies on Hysteria*, which he co-wrote with Freud – in complete recovery by 7 June 1882, the anniversary of her admission at the Inzersdorf clinic. This followed a final narration during which Bertha relived a scene at the bedside of her father that was supposed to have triggered her illness: 'Immediately after its reproduction, she was able to speak German. She was moreover free from the innumerable disturbances which she had previously exhibited. After this she left Vienna and travelled for a while, but it was a considerable time before she regained her balance entirely. Since then she has enjoyed complete health.' Freud would also always describe Anna O.'s talking cure as a 'great therapeutic success' (1923).

As the research of historians Henri Ellenberger and Albrecht Hirschmüller has established, the reality was quite different. Bertha Pappenheim's treatment had in fact been a veritable 'ordeal' for Breuer, as he wrote later to his colleague the psychiatrist August Forel. The treatment had never shown any real progress and as early as the autumn of 1881 Breuer was thinking of placing Bertha in another clinic, the Bellevue Sanatorium run by the psychiatrist Robert Binswanger in Kreuzlingen, Switzerland. Moreover, as we know from a letter sent on 31 October 1883 by Freud to his fiancée Martha Bernays, Mathilde Breuer had become jealous of her husband's interest in his attractive young patient and rumours had begun to circulate. So when Breuer terminated the treatment in June 1882, it was not because Bertha Pappenheim had recovered (in mid-June she was still suffering from a 'slight hysterical madness'), but because he had decided to throw in the towel and transfer her to Bellevue. She was admitted there on 1 July 1882 after having 'travelled' briefly to visit relatives in Karlsruhe.

Founded in 1857 by Ludwig Binswanger (the grandfather of Ludwig Binswanger Jr, the promoter of existential psychoanalysis), the Bellevue Sanatorium was a renowned institution. Located in an idyllic park on Lake Constance the sanatorium hosted, with discretion and for a high fee, the elite of the mentally ill. It was a place where, as the Viennese novelist Joseph Roth wrote in *The Radetzky March*, 'spoiled lunatics from rich homes receive onerous and cautious treatment, and the staff is as caring as a midwife.' There was an orangery, chaises longues, a bowling alley, an outdoor kitchen, tennis courts, a music room and a billiard room. One could also go hiking and horse riding nearby (Bertha took advantage of this daily). Bellevue patients stayed in comfortable villas scattered throughout the park.

Bertha Pappenheim had a two-room apartment and brought with her a lady companion who spoke English and French. Indeed, she was still partly 'aphasic' in German and plagued by more or less the same symptoms as before. In addition to her addiction to chloral hydrate, she was now also addicted to morphine due to Breuer's efforts to calm her painful facial neuralgia. Her stay in Kreuzlingen lasted four months and brought little progress as far as her neuralgia and her dependence on morphine were concerned. The register at the time of Bertha's release on 29 October 1882 mentions that she was 'improved', but a letter she sent to Robert Binswanger on 8 November tells a different story: 'As for my health here, I can tell you nothing which is new or favourable. You will realize that to live with a syringe always at the ready is not a situation to be envied.'

Bertha Pappenheim in riding costume during her stay at the Bellevue Sanatorium.

Breuer declined to resume treatment when Bertha returned to Vienna in early January 1883 after a detour in Karlsruhe. From 1883 to 1887 Bertha was readmitted to Breslauer's clinic three times. Each time the diagnosis by doctors was the same: 'hysteria'. This is confirmed by the correspondence between Freud and his fiancée Martha Bernays. Bernays knew Bertha personally (Bertha's father had been her legal guardian after the death of Bernays's own) and Freud kept her informed of her friend's condition. On 5 August 1883 he wrote: 'Bertha is once again in the sanatorium in

Gross-Enzensdorf, I believe [Inzersdorf, in fact]. Breuer is constantly talking about her, says he wishes she were dead so that the poor woman could be free of her suffering. He says she will never be well again, that she is completely shattered.' In two letters to her mother, dated January and May 1887, Martha wrote that her friend Bertha continued to suffer from hallucinations in the evening. Thus, five years after the end of Breuer's treatment and multiple stays at clinics, Bertha Pappenheim had still not recovered.

In 1888 Bertha moved to Frankfurt, where most of her relatives on her mother's side lived. There, probably at the instigation of her cousin the writer Anna Ettlinger, she published anonymously a collection of some of the same fairy tales she had narrated to Breuer during her 'hypnoid' states, under the title *Short Stories for Children*. This writing cure seems to have been far more therapeutic than the talking cure. Two years later Bertha published a second collection of stories, *In the Second-hand Shop*, under the pseudonym P. Berthold. In addition to these early literary essays, she began to get involved in Jewish social work in Frankfurt, volunteering in soup kitchens for immigrants from Eastern Europe and at an orphanage for Jewish girls, of which she became house-mother in 1895.

In this, Bertha Pappenheim was playing her role as a prominent member of the Jewish community. It seems that she had eventually reconciled with religion (when and why, we don't know), and she clearly conceived of her social work as a *mitzvah*, a good deed. (This is why she was always opposed, in the organizations to which she belonged, to any remuneration for their members.) However, she did not limit herself to traditional charities. She not only participated in practical tasks, which was unusual for a lady of the upper middle class, but applied to Jewish social work the principles and methods of the German feminist movement, to which she had been introduced by Helene Lange's periodical *Die Frau*.

In 1899 she translated into German Mary Wollstonecraft's *A Vindication of the Rights of Woman* (1792) and published a play entitled *Women's Rights*, in which she criticized the economic and sexual exploitation of women. From a severely disturbed hysteric and addict, Bertha Pappenheim had morphed within a few years into a writer and a leader of Jewish feminism. In 1900 she wrote *The Jewish Problem in Galicia*, a book in which she attributed the poverty of the Jews of Eastern Europe to their lack of education.

Bertha Pappenheim dressed as her ancestor Glückel von Hameln.

In 1902 she set up the Women's Relief (Weibliche Fürsorge), which provided shelter, counselling, job training and referral services for Jewish women. She also launched a campaign to denounce prostitution and white slavery in the Jewish communities of Russia and Eastern Europe, an undertaking which drew criticism from the rabbis who feared that bringing these practices into the open would strengthen antisemitic stereotypes. Bertha Pappenheim was not impressed (little appears to have been likely to impress her). In her view, defending the rights of Jewish women amounted to defending Judaism as such by bringing these alienated women back into the fold of the community.

In 1904 she founded the League of Jewish Women (Jüdischer Frauenbund, or JFB), of which she was elected president. It was to become under her leadership the largest Jewish women's organization in Germany (in 1929 it had no fewer than 50,000 members). The JFB opened centres offering vocational guidance and training to encourage women to work and gain independence.

In addition to her work as head of the JFB, which led her to travel in North America, the Soviet Union, the Balkans and the Middle East, Bertha Pappenheim created in 1907 a home for unwed mothers and illegitimate children at Neu-Isenburg, which she considered the work of her life. She also found time to translate from Yiddish the *Tsenerene* (a seventeenth-century women's Bible comprising the Pentateuch, the *Megillot* and the *Haftarot*), the *Mayse Bukh* (a collection of medieval Talmudic tales and stories for women) and the famous diary of Glückel von Hameln (1646–1724), a distant ancestor of hers. To this should be added countless articles, poems, stories and plays for children, as well as some beautiful prayers that were published after her death in 1936 to comfort Jewish women under Nazism: 'My God, you are not a god of mellowness, of the word and of incense, not a god of the past. An all-present God you are. A demanding God you are to me. You have sanctified me with your "You shall." You expect my decision between good and evil; you demand that I prove to be strength of your strength, to strive upwards to you, to carry others away with me, to help with everything in my power. Demand! Demand! So that with every breath of my life I feel in my conscience: there is a God' ('Anruf', 14 November 1934).

In 1920 she was recruited by Martin Buber and Franz Rosenzweig to teach at the Freies Jüdisches Lehrhaus, a centre for Jewish studies that the two men had founded in Frankfurt, where she mingled with Siegfried Kracauer, Shmuel Yosef Agnon and Gershom Scholem.

Meanwhile, Bertha Pappenheim pursued a parallel career as First Patient of Psychoanalysis under the name of Anna O. Publicly, Freud continued to present the talking cure of Anna O. as the origin of psychoanalytic therapy. Privately, though, he confided to his disciples that Breuer's treatment had in fact been a fiasco, all the while adorning this revelation with an even more sensational story. In 1909 his disciple Max Eitingon had proposed in a lecture to interpret Anna O.'s symptoms as an expression of incestuous fantasies towards her father, including a fantasy of pregnancy that she supposedly transferred onto Breuer, taken as a father figure. Freud, who had long since broken with Breuer and was irritated that opponents such as August Forel and Ludwig Frank invoked his former mentor against him, took up this interpretation and ended up presenting it to his audience as fact. After the end of Anna O.'s treatment, he claimed, Breuer had been called back and found her in the throes of a hysterical childbirth, 'the logical termination of a phantom pregnancy' (Ernest Jones) for which he was supposed to be responsible. Unnerved by the sudden revelation of the sexual nature of his patient's hysteria, Breuer then fled hurriedly, taking his wife on a second honeymoon to Venice, where he made *her* pregnant with a real child.

Bertha Pappenheim presumably never heard of this wicked tale, which was long confined to the inner circle of Freud's followers. No doubt she would have rejected it with horror, as she rejected psychoanalysis as a whole. According to her friend and close collaborator

Dora Edinger, she had 'destroyed all documents referring to her early breakdown and requested her family in Vienna not to give out information after her death'; 'Bertha never spoke about this period of her life and violently opposed any suggestion of psycho-analytic therapy for someone she was in charge of, to the surprise of her co-workers.'

Bertha Pappenheim, who opposed Zionism and the emigration of Jews out of Germany, only belatedly realized the seriousness of the Nazi threat. It was discovered that she had a tumour in the summer of 1935, just before the promulgation of Hitler's Nuremberg Race Laws. In the spring of 1936, already very ill, she was sum-moned by the Gestapo regarding some anti-Hitler statements made by one of the residents at her Neu-Isenburg home. Upon her return, she took to her bed and never left it. She died at Neu-Isenburg on 28 May 1936, just in time to escape the Nazis. In her will, she asked those who would visit her grave to leave a small stone 'as a quiet promise . . . to serve the mission of women's duties and women's joys, unflinchingly and courageously'.

In 1953 Ernest Jones revealed the identity of Anna O. in the first volume of his Freud biography, adding for good measure the story of Bertha Pappenheim's alleged hysterical pregnancy, which Freud had told him. Bertha's relatives were shocked. On 20 June 1954 *Aufbau*, the newspaper of German-speaking immigrants in New York, published a letter from Paul Homburger, Bertha

German postage stamp issued in 1954 in honour
of Bertha Pappenheim.

Pappenheim's executor: 'Much worse than the revelation of her name as such is the fact that Dr. Jones on page 225, adds on his own account a completely superficial and misleading version of Bertha's life after the conclusion of Dr. Breuer's treatment. Instead of informing us how Bertha was finally cured and how, completely mentally reestablished, she led a new life of active social work, he gives the impression that she was never cured and that her social activity and even her piety were another phase of the development of her illness . . . Anyone who has known Bertha Pappenheim during the decades which followed will regard this attempt at interpretation on the part of a man who never knew her personally as defamation.'

2

ERNST FLEISCHL VON MARXOW
(1846–1891)

Simon Ernst Fleischl Edler von Marxow was born on 5 August 1846 in Vienna. He came from a prominent Jewish family that combined wealth and influence. His father, the banker and businessman Carl Fleischl Edler von Marxow, was ennobled in 1875. His mother Ida, née Marx, was an educated woman who surrounded herself with scientists, artists and journalists such as the archaeologist Emanuel Löwy, the novelist Marie von Ebner-Eschenbach and the poet Betty Paoli. One of his uncles, the famous physiologist Johann Nepomuk Czermak, is known, among other things, for having introduced the use of the laryngoscope.

It was probably to follow his uncle's example that Fleischl studied medicine, with the intention of becoming a researcher. Exceptionally bright and full of original ideas, he obtained his doctorate in medicine in 1870 at the age of 24 and became assistant to the eminent Carl von Rokitansky in anatomopathology. The following year, however, he injured himself during an autopsy and his right thumb, which became infected, had to be amputated. This resulted in extremely painful neuromas that made his life unbearable, and for which the surgeon Theodor Billroth operated on him several times with no lasting result. Unable to continue his work in anatomopathology, he turned to physiology and in 1873 became assistant to Ernst Wilhelm von Brücke at the Institute of Physiology. There, despite his persistent pain, he conducted experimental research on the excitability of nerves and was able to show that the stimulation of the sensory organs causes variations in electrical potential on the surface of the corresponding areas of the cerebral cortex, a discovery that would eventually make possible the electroencephalogram. He also invented various optical measuring instruments, such as the spectropolarimeter and the hematometer.

Fleischl was not only an outstanding researcher, but, according to all who knew him, an exceptional personality. Handsome, charming, witty, slightly eccentric, he was a brilliant conversationalist who was able to talk about literature and music as well as about the latest advances in physics. He was very close to his colleague Sigmund Exner and to Josef Breuer, and his circle of friends also included the psychiatrist Heinrich Obersteiner, the philologist Theodor Gomperz, the writer Gottfried Keller, the urologist Anton von Frisch (the father of the Nobel Prize winner Karl von Frisch), the composer Hugo Wolf, the gynaecologist Rudolf Chrobak and the physician Carl Bettelheim. Through Breuer and Gomperz he entered the fashionable circle of the wealthy Todesco, Wertheimstein and Lieben families, and was for a while informally engaged to Franziska (Franzi) von Werheimstein (see 'Elise Gomperz'). Drawing on experiments carried out by his uncle Czermak, he made at a party at the Wertheimsteins' a demonstration of hypnosis on a hen that deeply impressed the audience and contributed to the renewed interest in hypnotic states among scientists in Vienna in the early 1880s. With his friend Obersteiner, he also carried out hypnotic experiments on himself.

At Brücke's Institute of Physiology, Fleischl made the acquaintance of a research assistant, the young Sigmund Freud, who had started working there in 1876. Freud greatly admired Fleischl, who represented for him a sort of ideal, and the two men gradually became very close, despite the difference in age and status. Through Fleischl, Freud also became acquainted with the physician Josef Breuer. Together, Fleischl and Breuer financially supported their young protégé, who regularly ran out of money.

Ernst Fleischl von Marxow.

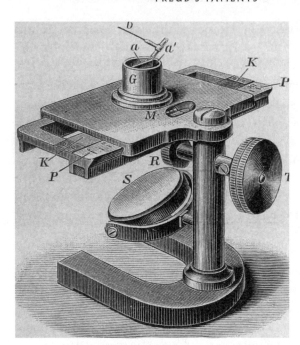

Fleischl's
hematometer.

Having become closer to Fleischl after leaving the Institute of Physiology in 1882, Freud discovered the misery that lay behind his mentor's brilliance. Few people knew it but Fleischl was psychologically fragile and subject to nervous breakdowns. In a letter to Martha Bernays, Freud even described him as a neurotic: 'How terrible it is to be a nervous person!' (21 May 1885). To calm his excruciating pain, which often kept him up all night, Fleischl was taking morphine and had developed an addiction to it, like so many others at the time. His friends worried for him and were trying to find ways to help him. Theodor Gomperz consulted the famous French neurologist Jean-Martin Charcot about Fleischl's phantom limb pain on the occasion of a stay that his niece Franzi von Wertheimstein had made in the spring of 1884 in one of the Master's private clinics. Charcot recommended 'repeated igni-puncture . . . on the cervicodorsal spine region', but that does not seem to have helped.

It is in this context that in late 1883 Freud read an article by the army surgeon Theodor Aschenbrand on cocaine, an alkaloid synthesized from coca leaves in 1860 by Albert Niemann. Aschenbrandt had added a little cocaine to the water served to his Bavarian recruits and found that the soldiers had become unusually resistant to fatigue and hunger (a well-known effect of the coca leaf among the indigenous peoples of Peru). Intrigued, Freud had inquired further and came upon a series of articles in the *Detroit Therapeutic Gazette* extolling the many virtues of cocaine, including its use in morphine detoxification. According to the *Gazette*, cocaine really seemed to be a universal panacea: 'One feels like trying coca with or without the opium [morphine] habit. A harmless remedy for the blues.'

Freud does not seem to have noticed that the *Gazette* was actually a piece of promotional literature published by the pharmaceutical company Parke-Davis in Detroit, whose main product since 1875 had been cocaine. (George S. Davis, one of the two founders of the company, was the *Gazette*'s editor.) Eager to attach his name to a great scientific discovery that would bring him fame and fortune, Freud bought some cocaine from the manufacturer Merck in Darmstadt and began to trial the product in oral doses on himself and a few people around him: Martha Bernays, Josef Breuer and his wife Mathilde (for her migraines), and Fleischl. Excited about the euphoriant properties of cocaine, Freud published in July 1884 an article 'On Coca', in which he basically took up all the *Gazette*'s selling points. Cocaine, he announced, was a stimulant and an aphrodisiac. It was good for dyspepsia,

cachexia, sea-sickness, hysteria, neur-asthenia (what we would call today depression or chronic fatigue), melancholia (the depressive pole of manic depression), facial neuralgia (trigeminal neuralgia), asthma and impotence. At the end of his article, Freud also suggested that cocaine had anaesthetic properties that ought to be explored. His friend Carl Koller did exactly that and discovered that cocaine could be used as local anaesthetic in ophthalmology, thus beating Freud to it and becoming instantly famous in his place.

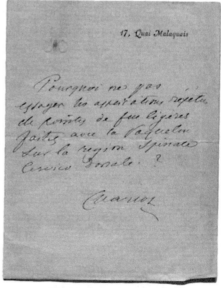

Charcot's prescription for
Fleischl's neuroma.

Freud's article also contained a section on the use of cocaine in the detoxification of morphine. Freud relied almost exclusively on cases of successful demorphinization alleged in Parke-Davis's promotional *Gazette*, but he also claimed to have been able to detoxify a case of this kind himself. The weaning had been a success. The patient had not been depressed; he 'was not bedridden and could function normally. During the first days of the cure he consumed [orally, that is] 3 dg of *cocaïnum muriaticum* daily, and after ten days he was able to dispense with the coca treatment altogether.'

As Carl Koller was to reveal in 1928, the patient in question was none other than Ernst Fleischl von Marxow. The cocaine treatment, which began on 7 May 1884, did not go exactly as Freud claimed in his article. Although it had seemed promising during the first days, Freud wrote as early as 12 May to his fiancée: 'With Fleischl things are so sad that I cannot enjoy the cocaine successes at all.' Cocaine, which Fleischl took 'continuously', did not prevent him from suffering extreme pain and having 'attacks' that left him nearly unconscious. Freud added: 'Whether in one of these attacks he took morphia, I do not know, he denies it, but a morphinist, even if it is Ernst Fleischl, cannot be believed.' On 19 May, cocaine having suppressed neither the pain nor the withdrawal symptoms, Theodor Billroth attempted at Freud's and Breuer's request a new operation on the thumb's stump and recommended that Fleischl 'take considerable amounts of morphia . . . and he was given he does not know how many injections' (23 May 1884). The next day, Gomperz wrote to his wife Elise that during the surgery their friend 'had suffered terribly despite the narcosis [the morphine injection], so that he had to be anesthetized again after a while, just to relieve the pain' (20 May 1884).

The detoxification had been an utter failure. Yet Freud set out to write his article 'On Coca', despite Breuer's reservations (on 12 June 1884, he wrote to Martha Bernays: 'Breuer absolutely does not want to tell me anything good about it'). The article was submitted to the printer on 18 June and appeared on 1 July. It quickly aroused great interest in the United States, especially from Parke-Davis. The company made a point to mention in a brochure the interesting work of 'Professor Fleischl and Dr. Sigm. Freud of Vienna', which confirmed its own promotional literature. (Parke-Davis also offered Freud $24 to compare the company's cocaine to that of Merck. Like a modern-day pharmaceutical 'Key Opinion

Leader', Freud was glad to endorse Parke-Davis's product and predicted that it 'should have a great future'.)

The odd mention of 'Professor Fleischl' comes from the fact that Freud had anonymously published reviews and abstracts of his own article in various American medical journals, using his prestigious patient and 'collaborator' as scientific backing. In an article published in December 1884 in the *St Louis Medical and Surgical Journal*, he wrote: 'Prof. Fleischl of Vienna confirms the fact that muriate of cocaine is invaluable subcutaneously injected in *morphinism* (0.05–0.15 grm. dissolved in water)... a sudden abstinence from morphine requires a subcutaneous injection of 0.1 gram. of cocaine... in 10 days a radical cure can be effected by an injection of 0.1 gram. of cocaine 3 times a day.'

The dosage was the same as that indicated in the original article, but the method of administration was different (subcutaneous injection rather than oral administration). Behind this little detail hid the fact that Fleischl had not only continued injecting morphine, in spite of his 'radical cure', but had begun to inject cocaine. On 12 July 1884, shortly after the publication of his article 'On Coca', Freud mentioned in passing to his fiancée that his friend was taking cocaine 'regularly'. It is clear from Freud's American articles that Fleischl had already switched to the syringe by October 1884. Whether or not he did this initially against Freud's advice, as the latter would claim in veiled terms in Chapter Two of *The Interpretation of Dreams*, it is clear that Freud also adopted this pharmacologically much more aggressive method of administration at some point. In January 1885 he announced to his fiancée that he wanted to see if one could relieve facial neuralgia by injecting cocaine directly into the nerve, adding: 'and maybe even Fleischl can be helped... If only I could take away his pain' (7 January 1885). In a lecture published in early April 1885, in which he again claimed that he had cured a morphine addict by giving him cocaine, Freud explicitly recommended injection: 'I have no hesitation in recommending the administration of cocaine for such withdrawal cures in subcutaneous injections of 0.03–0.05 g per dose, without any fear of increasing the dose.'

As any drug addict knows, the combination of an 'upper' such as cocaine and a 'downer' such as morphine or heroin is one of the most euphoriant and dangerous (the cause of the death of the painter Jean-Michel Basquiat and the actor John Belushi, among many others). It is also the most irresistibly addictive combination. Once hooked, Fleischl constantly increased the doses of cocaine to get the famous 'rush'. On his return from a trip to his summer residence in St Gilgen in October 1884, his cocaine use had already become so significant that the manufacturer Merck asked Fleischl to inform him of the effects he observed. In June of the following year, Freud wrote to Martha: 'Since I have given him the cocaine, he has been able to suppress the faints and he could better control himself, but he took it in such monstrous quantities (1,800 Marcks for cocaine in three months, about a gram a day) that in the end he suffered from chronic intoxication' (26 June 1885). Yet in his article of April 1885 Freud had written about his morphine patient: 'No cocaine habituation set in; on the contrary, an increasing antipathy to the use of cocaine was unmistakably evident.'

Fleischl was in a state beyond description. He veered constantly from 'the clearest despair up to the most exuberant joy over bad jokes' (10 April 1885). Breuer, Exner and Freud took turns spending the night with him. Freud took cocaine himself to stay awake: 'His talk, his explanations of all kinds of difficult things . . . his manifold activities interrupted by states of the most complete exhaustion relieved by morphia and cocaine: all that makes an *ensemble* that cannot be described' (21 May 1885). Fleischl's friends felt the end approaching. Freud, who had asked him once again for help financially, wrote to Martha: 'I wonder if he will lend me anything. If so, he may no longer be there when we need to think about paying back' (10 March 1885). In June Fleischl began developing hallucinations characteristic of cocaine addiction, but which Freud, in his ignorance, compared to delirium tremens: Fleischl had the creepy sensation of insects or snakes crawling on his skin, a phenomenon known today as 'formication' or, more colloquially, 'coke bugs'.

In early August Fleischl went to the family home in St Gilgen, accompanied by his younger brother Paul. Freud wrote to him from Paris, where he was attending Jean-Martin Charcot's lectures on hysteria, asking for money. Fleischl did not answer. Upon his return to Vienna, Freud told Martha that 'Fleischl looks miserable, more like a corpse' (5 April 1886); 'he hallucinates constantly and it will probably not be possible to let him remain in society for much longer' (7 April 1886). Freud resumed his night watches at

Fleischl's apartment, at least until the end of May 1886. We do not know if he continued beyond that point, for his correspondence with Martha stopped shortly thereafter due to their marriage.

In July 1887 Freud published a reply to Albrecht Erlenmeyer, a morphine addiction specialist who had tested cocaine on his own patients. Erlenmeyer's results contradicted those of Freud: not only had the patients continued taking morphine, but they had developed an addiction to cocaine. Dr Freud, concluded Erlenmeyer, had added to morphine and alcohol a 'third scourge of humanity, cocaine'. Stung, Freud responded by again invoking 'the surprisingly favourable results of the first morphine withdrawal by means of cocaine carried out on the Continent. (It is perhaps well to mention at this point that I do not speak of experiments carried out on myself, but of another whom I advised on the matter.)' As for the negative results obtained by Erlenmeyer, they were due, according to Freud, to his administering the cocaine subcutaneously, not orally as Freud had prescribed – a 'serious experimental error' for which Erlenmeyer's patients had paid the price. After that Freud forgot his articles about cocaine, including the one in which he recommended the syringe.

Ernst Fleischl von Marxow seems to have lived his last years removed from 'society'. Did he ever manage to wean himself off cocaine? This is what Freud claimed in a letter he wrote in 1934 to the Viennese professor of ophtalmology Josef Meller: 'After a surprisingly easy morphia withdrawal, he [Fleischl] became a cocainist instead of morphinist, developed bad psychic disturbances and we were all happy when later on he returned to the earlier and milder toxic.' However, we may do well to have some doubts about this, for Freud's mention of hallucinations in his letter to Martha of 7 April 1886 seems to indicate that Fleischl was at that date still taking cocaine (morphine very rarely causes this type of effect).

After that? In a letter written in 1891 to Franzi von Wertheimstein, Fleischl's former love interest, Breuer seemed to suggest that towards the end Fleischl had substituted chloral for morphine to relieve his pain: 'Aside from the pain, Ernst wasn't even deeply unhappy when made drunk and half-stupid by the chloral he completely lost consciousness of everything and of himself. Then there was the ongoing fight against his proclivity to excessive intake of chloral, in which he fell steadily, the terrifying hangover which

resulted and which lasted one week, and then again the repetition'
(28 October 1891). Breuer doesn't mention cocaine, but it seems
unlikely that the human wreck that Fleischl had become would
have found the strength to escape its grip.

Ernst Fleischl von Marxow died at last on 22 October 1891 in
Vienna. Breuer wrote to Franzi von Wertheimstein: 'I bemoan
Ernst, as I have done for years, but I cannot say that I bemoan his
death . . . We all owe a death to Nature, but not suffering, not this
pathetic crumbling of such a brilliant personality.'

3

MATHILDE SCHLEICHER
(1862–1890)

Mathilde Schleicher, Freud tells us in a case report written in 1889, came 'from a distinguished family but [was] prone to nervous illnesses'. Her father, Carl (Cölestin) Schleicher, was a well-known genre painter and she herself was a singer. She had always been very impressionable and suffered from migraines. Her 'nervous illness' broke out in February 1886. According to Freud, the triggering event had been the breaking off of an engagement by her fiancé. According to another case report written later by Dr Hanns Kaan, the fiancé, a 'weak character', had instead broken off the engagement after she had become depressed and developed 'hysterical facial changes'. Whatever the case, she fell into a severe melancholic state that was characterized by self-accusations and delusional ideas.

Freud had just set up private practice as a 'nerve doctor' in April 1886, and Mathilde Schleicher was among his very first patients. Presumably it is Breuer who had referred her in his capacity as the Schleichers' family doctor, for it is to him that Freud later turned when Mathilde developed the clearly somatic disease from which she would die. The treatment, Freud wrote in his report, had a 'changing course' – in other words, ups and downs. What we know is that the young nerve doctor made use of hypnosis to recover and erase traumatic memories (he had started to use this 'Breuer method', as he called it, towards the end of 1887). Dr Kaan, in his report, notes indeed that the patient 'worshipped the doctor who had treated her by hypnosis during her melancholic condition'. By spring 1889 it seemed that the hypnotic treatment had been successful. Mathilde's depression eased up gradually and in June she presented to her doctor-hypnotist a history book – *Germania*:

Two Millennia of German Life – with the following inscription: 'To the excellent Dr. Freud, with my affectionate memory. As a token of the deepest gratitude and the deepest respect. Mathilde Schleicher, June [1]889'.

The respite was short-lived. The following month the patient developed full-blown mania. She was exuberant, agitated, could not sleep. She spoke constantly of the brilliant concert career for which she was destined and of the millions she was going to earn. She would take over from Bianchi (Bianca Bianchi, the lead singer of the Vienna Opera). She had grandiose wedding plans. At the slightest provocation, she would fall into violent convulsions that Freud considered 'clearly hysterical in nature, which moreover also occurred during the melancholia and multiplied during her recovery from it'.

Overwhelmed, Freud committed her on 29 October 1889 to the private clinic of Dr Wilhelm Svetlin with a diagnosis of 'cyclical mood alteration' (what Kraepelin was to call ten years later 'manic depressive psychosis'). In his case report, Freud wrote coyly: 'A more serious violation of the limits that her gender and education should assign to her did not occur, although here and there attempts were made.' Medical records held at the Svetlin clinic were less prudish. Two days after Mathilde's arrival at the clinic, the attending physician noted: 'Nymphomaniac, half naked rolls on the ground while masturbating, calls on Dr. Freud whose slave she wants to be.' A week later, it was Dr Kaan, Svetlin's assistant, who became the object of her 'erotic arousal'. On 12 November 'the manic delirium concerns almost exclusively sexual things: she thinks herself pregnant, every bowel movement is a birth, the faeces are her baby, the "jewel of her crown", which she tries to hide from the orderly under a pillow.'

Doctors at the clinic seem to have been of the opinion that the worsening state of the patient, notably her convulsions, were due to Dr Freud's hypnotic treatment (the medical file mentions that she 'simulates hysterical convulsions'). For seven months she was given all kinds of hypnotics and sedatives, as was customary at the time with agitated patients: morphine, chloral hydrate, bromide, opium, cannabis, valerian and so forth. Occasionally she was also given sulfonal, a new hypnotic introduced in 1888 by Alfred Kast that had been described in medical journals as completely harmless and non-addictive, unlike other products in use. The manic state having abated, she was released on 25 May 1890.

'Healed?' wondered the clinic physician in his file. Evidently not. As might be expected, the melancholic cycle resumed, with depression, apathy and insomnia. Did Freud again use hypnosis, as he was wont to do at the time? We do not know. What is certain is that he prescribed a treatment alternating chloral hydrate and sulfonal (2 grams per day every other week), presumably to overcome the insomnia. Back from holiday in early September, Freud found Mathilde 'anaemic'. She was still 'melancholic'. Then there was vomiting, urinary retention and abdominal pain. The urine collected by catheter was a strange red. Neither Freud nor Breuer, whom he had called to the rescue, understood what was going on. On 24 September 1890 Mathilde Schleicher died 'fully conscious' with horrible abdominal cramps. She was buried two days later in the Jewish section of Vienna's Central Cemetery.

The enigma of her death was resolved a few weeks later when an article appeared under the signature of Hermann Breslauer (a friend of Breuer's and one of Bertha Pappenheim's doctors), who warned for the first time against the dangers of sulfonal: taken at too high a dose or over too long a period, this product might cause acute porphyria, a liver damage signalled by the red colour of the urine. But the article came too late. Mathilde Schleicher had died, poisoned by the medication prescribed by her doctor.

A couple of months later, Freud reported on her case in the *Internationale Klinische Rundschau* (6 December 1891): 'During the summer, report of urine retention. Vomiting once, soon over with. Back [home] after 3 months, anaemic, otherwise still melancholic. A few days later: vomiting, retention of urine, abdominal pains, no fever. A few days later, urine with catheter, red colour. (Examination by Dr. Jolles laboratory.) Never before protein and renal elements. Abdominal pains, anxiety, gloomy, clear consciousness, vomiting, persistent constipation, cyanosis finger tips. After that, weak pulse, racing [pulse], diaphragm paralysis. Death while fully conscious – complete picture 5–6 days.'

4

ANNA VON LIEBEN
(1847–1900)

Anna von Lieben, née Baroness Anna von Todesco, came from an aristocratic Jewish family in Vienna. Her father, the banker Eduard von Todesco, was descended from Ahron Hirsch Todesco, a silk merchant in the Pressburg ghetto who had made his fortune at the end of the eighteenth century before coming to settle in Vienna. On her mother Sophie's side, Anna was related to the Gomperz, Auspitz and von Wertheimstein families, who were also part of the Viennese Jewish upper bourgeoisie.

The Todescos lived in style. Sophie von Todesco, née Gomperz, held a salon in the luxurious palace that she and her husband had built on the Ring opposite the new Vienna Opera (the palace still exists). Just as in the salon of her sister Josephine von Wertheimstein, also née Gomperz, it was a place where you could meet everyone who was anyone in the Viennese world of politics, finance and the arts: Johannes Brahms, Franz Liszt, the two Strausses, the painters Hans Makart and Franz von Lenbach, the sculptor Viktor Tilgner and many more. Close friends included the philologist Theodor Gomperz (Sophie and Josephine's brother), his wife Elise, the philosopher Franz Brentano, the poets Ferdinand von Saar and Hugo von Hofmannsthal, the psychiatrist Theodor Meynert, the physiologist Ernst Fleischl von Marxow, and Josef Breuer, the family doctor of the Todesco, Gomperz, von Wertheimstein and von Lieben families. In the summer, when Vienna became too hot, the family took refuge in the Villa Todesco, a large and no less luxurious house in the Brühl. Everywhere there was an army of uniformed servants.

The children were surrounded by governesses and tutors. Anna, like her brother and sisters, studied French and English, as well as painting and music. Very early on she began to paint and write poems (a collection was published by her relatives and friends after her death). From an early age, too, she showed signs of psychological instability, as did other members of her maternal family (her great-grandmother Rosa Auspitz, her uncle Theodor Gomperz and his wife Elise, Josephine von Wertheimstein and her daughter Franzi all presented signs of neurosis, even of overt psychosis). From the age of sixteen, she was afflicted with all kinds of 'nervous' disorders. Her condition improved somewhat after her marriage to the banker Leopold von Lieben in 1871, as well as during her five pregnancies, but soon the symptoms returned: facial neuralgia (like Bertha Pappenheim, whom she probably knew through Theodor and Elise Gomperz), migraines, fainting, mood swings and attacks of nerves. Like Josephine, her 'Aunt Pepi' whom she adored, she had pains in her legs and feet which confined her to her chaise longue. Hugo von Hofmannsthal, who in 1895 had started a 'Novel of inner life' (never finished) on the Todesco family, wrote that Anna von Lieben was 'animal', 'sensitive' and 'half mad'.

Due to her lack of exercise and her love of delicacies, she became obese. To lose weight, from time to time she followed a strict diet of champagne and caviar. She led a nocturnal existence, and no one in the family ever knew when she would emerge during the day. She was very accomplished at chess and she had hired a professional player to be constantly available at night in case she felt like a game or two. (Breuer noted, in the *Studies on Hysteria* published in 1895 in collaboration with Freud, that she liked to play two games simultaneously.) She sometimes raided fabric stores, forcing them to stay open after closing time so that she could satisfy her passion for fine materials. She had also been a morphine addict since adolescence, and had nervous attacks when she did not get her dose. Her husband tired of her and took a mistress, the novelist Molly Filtsch.

Palais Todesco.

After living for a time in the Palais Todesco, the von Lieben family moved in 1888 to a palace built for the Auspitz family, where their brother-in-law, the philosopher Franz Brentano, who had married Leopold's younger sister Ida von Lieben, also lived. They had to install a lift to take the corpulent Anna up and down. The Palais Lieben-Auspitz, located at 6 Oppolzergasse, was barely five minutes by horse-drawn carriage from 8 Maria Theresienstrasse where Freud lived, which was convenient when he was summoned urgently to calm down one of Anna's attacks of nerves.

Indeed, in the autumn of 1887 Freud had become Anna von Lieben's 'nerve doctor' on the advice of her two personal physicians, Breuer and the gynaecologist Rudolf Chrobak. Anna von Lieben had previously been treated in Paris by Jean-Martin Charcot, the 'Napoleon of neuroses', and the fact that the young Freud could have mentioned the latter as a referee, or even been directly recommended by him, had undoubtedly played in Freud's favour (in February 1888 he wrote to his friend Wilhelm Fliess that his clientele, 'which as you know, is not very considerable, has recently increased somewhat by virtue of Charcot's name'). It is clear, moreover, that the treatment took place under the distant supervision of the Master, since the patient returned regularly to see Charcot in Paris while Freud in Vienna kept him informed of developments in the case. Henriette Motesiczky von Kesseleökeö, Anna's daughter, told Kurt Eissler, the Secretary of the Freud Archives, that each time her mother returned from a visit to Charcot, she spoke only in French.

The treatment began on 17 October 1887, one day after the birth of Freud's first child, Mathilde. On 23 October Freud reported to his sister-in-law Minna Bernays: 'While Martha was in the throes of childbirth, I was summoned to appear on the Monday at a consultation with Chrobak at Mrs Lieben's. Mrs Anna Lieben is a daughter of the late Baron Todesco and has been duly handed over to me by Breuer and Chrobak. Since then I have spent my evenings ingratiating myself with her.'

Anna von Lieben quickly became Freud's most important female patient – his 'prima donna', as he wrote in a letter to Wilhelm Fliess – as well as his main source of income. Anna demanded constant attention and Freud was, so to speak, on permanent call, including during the holidays when he would visit her at the

Villa Todesco in the Brühl. Once
or twice a day (that is to say also in
the evenings, because of Anna's
sleeping pattern), he had to jump
into a carriage and hurry to the
Palais Lieben-Auspitz to calm an
umpteenth attack. He would stay
there for thirty to sixty minutes
at a time. When she had a particularly acute crisis he would even
spend the night with her, sleeping
on the floor.

It seems that Anna von Lieben
was one of the first patients, if not
the very first, to benefit from the
new therapeutic method that Freud
had started to use at the same time.
On 28 December 1887, just two
months after Anna's treatment

Anna von Lieben, c. 1865.

began, Freud reported to his friend Wilhelm Fliess that 'the past
weeks I have thrown myself into hypnosis and have achieved all
sorts of small but noteworthy successes' – an allusion to what
Freud, in an encyclopaedia article on 'Hysteria' written at the same
time, reverentially called the 'Breuer method.'

This method, inspired by Charcot and contemporaneous
experiments made by Pierre Janet and Joseph Delboeuf, was in
fact very different from Bertha Pappenheim's 'talking cure', which
Freud knew very well had been a fiasco. Back in 1881–2 Breuer
had used Bertha Pappenheim's self-hypnotic states to have her
remember the events that were supposed to have been triggering
her symptoms (this is what he himself would subsequently name
the 'cathartic method' in *Studies on Hysteria*). Freud, on the other
hand, initially induced hypnosis in his patients to have them relive
and *forget* their traumas, 'deleting' them from their memories by
way of suggestion as if they had never taken place. As late as 1891,
in a letter to Minna Bernays, he compared his treatment of Anna
von Lieben to the fanciful method of electrical 'extirpation' of
unpleasant memories imagined by Edward Bellamy in his science-
fiction novel *Dr Heidenhoff's Process* (1880).

Anna von Lieben was happy to oblige. From 1887 to 1893 she relived under hypnosis 'several hundred' traumas, mostly psychical, that she had endured during her lifetime: frights, shameful events, slights, anxieties, sexual peccadillos. Over the years, the quest for traumas led ever further into the past. Breuer, who followed Freud's treatment closely, would later tell his colleague August Forel how they had both been 'filled with doubt and surprise when the analysis of a severe case of hysteria (e.g. of "Cäcilie M." in the book) led us further into childhood' (27 November 1907). In *Studies on Hysteria*, Freud writes that Cäcilie M. – the pseudonym Breuer and he gave to Anna von Lieben – 'once again relived through all the traumas of her life – long forgotten, as they seemed to her, and some, indeed, never remembered at all – accompanied by the acutest suffering and by the return of all the symptoms she ever had. The "old debts" which were thus paid covered a period of thirty-three years.' Counting backwards from the last year of treatment (1893), the first traumas experienced by Anna would therefore have taken place at the age of twelve or thirteen.

These revivifications of traumas, which were accompanied by screams and violent movements, must have made a great impression on those around Anna. According to Henriette Motesiczky, the von Lieben children called Freud 'der Zauberer': he was the 'magician' who appeared at all hours of the day and night to put their mother into a trance and perform strange rituals. Freud, in *Studies*, mentions that sometimes he 'hastened the end of the attack by artificial means' – a discreet allusion to the injections of morphine he administered to satisfy her addiction. According to Henriette Motesiczky, this was the explanation for the constant attacks her mother suffered and the temporary effectiveness of the memories summoned up by her doctor: 'Come on, the only thing she expected from him was morphine. And when he had given her enough he'd probably be in her good graces.' The famous cathartic cure of Cäcilie M. – Anna von Lieben was in fact a morphine cure.

The results were disappointing, for the crises would always come back as the craving made itself felt again. Once the trauma had been relived under hypnosis and the attack had been ended by the usual 'artificial means', Freud writes, 'her troubles disappeared as though by magic and she felt well once again – till the next attack, half a day later.' Freud thought it was because he was unable to put the patient into deep hypnotic somnambulism with post-hypnotic amnesia, a prerequisite, according to him, for the complete 'de-suggesting' of the traumatic reminiscence. In July 1889 he invited Anna von Lieben to join him in Nancy, where he intended to study under Hippolyte Bernheim, the great master of 'suggestive' psychotherapy, in order to perfect his hypnotic technique. Perhaps Bernheim would manage to put Anna in a state of deep somnambulism? Sadly not. Anna was as insufferable as ever. From Nancy, where he went every day to Anna's hotel to calm her down, Freud wrote to Minna Bernays: 'Every effort to have her adopt a purely human relationship with other people fails on account of the fact that the colossus thinks only of her nerves and simply doesn't listen to anything else' (28 July 1889).

Back in Vienna, Freud and 'She' (as he referred elliptically to Anna in his correspondence with Minna Bernays) resumed their routine. In August 1890, in the middle of his holiday, Freud wrote to Fliess that he had to cancel a meeting with him because of an emergency at the Villa Todesco: 'My most important patient is just now going through a kind of nervous crisis and might go well in my absence' (1 August 1890). To Minna Bernays, the year after: 'She still in Döbling . . . Thirty friends in time of need [thirty florins] have been provided by L.[ieben] for the summer, I hope not the main troops but only the outposts' (7 July 1891); 'She is going this week to the Brühl, is of course still not done. I count on six more months of income from her' (28 July 1891).

And then: 'She is definitely waning' (27 April 1893). The von Lieben family had indeed become increasingly sceptical of Freud, who in their opinion worsened the patient's condition rather than helping her. To Eissler, who asked her in 1972 if the family members liked Freud, Henriette Motesiczky replied bluntly: 'No . . . We all hated him . . . They [my sisters] always said: "He doesn't do her any good."' This sentiment was echoed by her uncle Theodor Gomperz, who for his part could observe the effects of Freud's hypnotic treatment of his wife, Elise, and it is easy to imagine what people were saying in the family. In the spring of 1893 it was Anna herself who started to have qualms about her 'magician': 'She just had an episode during which she could not stand me, for she suspected me of not treating her out of friendship but just for the money' (to Minna Bernays, 17 April 1893). In the autumn, or shortly before, Leopold von Lieben finally decided to end her treatment with Freud, which had spanned almost six years and had produced no lasting improvement.

Anna von Lieben was subsequently tended to by the neurologist Paul Karplus, who would soon marry her daughter Valerie, then by the physician and poet Josef Winter, and finally by her friend Julie Schlesinger. Apart from a few temporary remissions, her condition did not change. 'On the whole,' the poet Ferdinand von Saar reported to her cousin Franzi von Wertheimstein, 'a depressing picture, and I am gripped by a deep melancholy when I see her like that, lying before me covered with plaids on the chaise longue' (25 August 1894). On 31 October 1900 Anna von Lieben died in her bath from a cardiac arrest. She was 53 years old.

Much later, her grand-daughter, the expressionist painter Marie-Louise von Motesiczky, brought to her analyst Paul Federn a diary kept by Anna during her youth. Federn showed it in turn to Freud, who was 'very amused' by it. Another diary kept by Anna during her treatment with Freud was burned by Karplus, presumably because of its revealing contents.

In a poem entitled 'That's The Way It Is', Anna had written:

We seek love as celestial poem
And dare never look at it
When it speaks with loving human eyes
To us poor, respectable women.

For between us and the sweet face
Press shadows full of dread,
Iron duty, that master, wins
Among us poor, respectable women.

In another poem, 'Case History', we find this:

Youth that was buried too early
Must have life once again,
Once again to gulp breath,
In order to sink away forever.

5

ELISE GOMPERZ

(1848–1929)

Elise von Sichrovsky was a childhood friend of Anna von Lieben, whose milieu she shared (her father, Heinrich von Sichrovsky, was the founder of the Kaiser Ferdinands-Nordbahn railway company financed by the Rothschild bank in Vienna). In 1869 she also became Anna's aunt by marrying Theodor Gomperz, who was sixteen years older than she was, and who had known her since she was a child. She thus entered one of the oldest and most distinguished Jewish families in Vienna, which dated back to the beginning of the seventeenth century. One of Gomperz's ancestors was Aaron Emmerich Gumpetz, an *Aufklärer* who had been the mentor and friend of Moses Mendelssohn. The son of a banker and as such a wealthy man, Theodor was a renowned philosopher and Hellenist, a member since 1882 of the Academy of Sciences and the author of many scholarly works (including *The Interpretation of Dreams and Magic*, published in 1866, 34 years before Freud's own *Interpretation of Dreams*). In 1879, on the recommendation of his friend Franz Brentano, he asked the young Sigmund Freud to translate the twelfth volume of the complete works of John Stuart Mill of which he was the editor (Elise Gomperz had translated another, on 'Auguste Comte and Positivism'). Subsequently, the two men had other opportunities to cross paths, as Gomperz was very close to Ernst Fleischl von Marxow and Josef Breuer, who was also his family doctor.

While adopting a very traditional paternalistic attitude in private, Theodor Gomperz was an ardent defender of the rights of women and in particular their right to higher education. His wife, likewise, was close to the pioneering feminist Marianne

Hainisch and helped her with the Frauenvereinigung für soziale Hilfstätigkeit (Women's Association for Social Assistance).

By entering the Gomperz family, Elise had also entered what Charcot called at the time a 'neuropathic family'. Theodor's grandmother, Rosa Auspitz, was very pious and had been interned after trying to sacrifice her children to the Lord with a knife. Theodor's sister, Josephine von Wertheimstein, had also suffered a psychotic episode after the death of her young son Carl and spent four years in seclusion under the supervision of psychiatrist Theodor Meynert. Theodor himself had suffered from severe depression in his youth after being spurned by the stepdaughter of his intellectual idol, John Stuart Mill. His two nieces, Anna von Lieben and Franziska (Franzi) von Wertheimstein, were severely neurotic. Whether by mimicry or boredom, Elise had very quickly developed nervous disorders very similar to those of her nieces (and contemporaries): migraines, insomnia, sciatica, hyperaesthesia and various types of neuralgia. She would also make huge scenes during which she broke dishes, hit her children and yelled at the servants. (This seemed to run in the family, for the same was said of her sister, Elise von Sichrovsky.)

Theodor Gomperz, 1869.

Elise herself attributed her 'nervousness' to the emotions aroused in 1876 by a family crisis, when Ernst Fleischl von Marxow, whom everyone thought was courting his lady friend Franzi von Wertheimstein, had inexplicably changed his mind and had asked for the hand of Elise's younger sister, Sophie von Sichrovsky, even though she was, by all accounts, far less gracious and brilliant than Franzi. Outraged, the von Wertheimsteins accused Elise and Theodor of having manoeuvred in favour of Sophie, which, according to her son Heinrich, had put Theodor 'in the most painful situation of his life'. Sophie's family, meanwhile, disapproved of this marriage with the 'arrogant' Fleischl, and the engagement

Elise Gomperz,
1869.

was eventually broken off. Sophie gave back her engagement ring and Fleischl remained a bachelor, to the puzzlement of his friends. (Clearly not fully informed, Freud would write six years later to his fiancée: 'I believe [Fleischl] has been engaged for ten or twelve years to a girl of his own age, who was prepared to wait for him indefinitely, but with whom he has now fallen out, for reasons unknown to me' (18 June 1882). Did Freud mean Franzi von Wertheimstein, who was indeed about the same age as Fleischl?)

According to Heinrich Gomperz, his mother's nervous disorders had actually appeared a year after her marriage, much earlier than this painful episode. No doubt because of the age difference, the relations between the two spouses do not seem to have been particularly passionate – it was, said their granddaughter Monika Meyer Holzapfel, a 'paper marriage'. They slept in different bedrooms, and in every respect Theodor adopted an attitude closer to that of a father than a lover. (In 1891 he was to have an affair with a woman the same age as Elise, which continued in epistolary form until his death.)

In 1886 Theodor Gomperz decided that his wife's nerves definitely needed treatment. In a letter to his sister Josephine and his niece Franzi dated 23 August 1886, he explained: 'Elise . . . has suffered so much lately from her nerves that she had me worried and I realized that something lasting had to happen in her case also. Looking at our family circle, there are not too many bright spots. Almost everywhere, at the very least, irritable and excited nerves – the heritage of a very ancient civilized people and urban life.' (Charcot spoke at the time of 'Jewish neuropathy', and the agitation of the big cities was the explanation proposed by the American neurologist George Miller Beard to explain modern 'neurasthenia'.)

What was Gomperz alluding to when writing that Elise 'also' (*auch*) needed treatment? Most likely to the fact that both Franzi and her cousin Anna von Lieben had already gone to Paris to see Charcot. In any case, it was Charcot to whom Gomperz turned for advice, owing to their previous contact. Charcot prescribed a 'cure' (*Cur*) and recommended the young Dr Freud, who had just opened a practice in April upon returning to Vienna from Paris, where he had studied under him. On 27 August Gomperz wrote to his wife: 'As far as Charcot is concerned, here is what I think: he orders a cure (for you) and his disciple, Freud, will continue it in Vienna under Chrobak's supervision.'

Did Elise go to Paris to take the cure under Charcot's super-vision in one of his private clinics, like her two nieces? Probably, since the plan was for Freud to 'continue' the treatment 'in Vienna'. What we do know is that Freud became the physician in charge of Elise Gomperz's nerves around that time. He was to hold that position for eight years. In his edition of his father's correspon-dence, Heinrich Gomperz writes that Freud 'treated not without success E.[lise] G.[omperz]'s nervous pains from around the end of the 1880s to the middle of the 1890s'. It is likely, therefore, that Elise Gomperz benefitted from the whole panoply of treatments with which Freud experimented during those years: electrotherapy, isolation in a private clinic, hydrotherapy, hypnotic suggestion *à la* Bernheim, the 'Breuer method' and the 'cathartic method'.

An exchange of letters dating from 1892–3 allows us to recon-stitute with some precision one of the sequences in Elise's treatment. On 2 July 1892 Freud was summoned to treat a very painful facial neuralgia (Freud to his wife, 1 July 1892). He administered hypnosis, but it does not seem to have been successful, for six days later Freud wrote to Elise on a correspondence card that he was confident that the pain would eventually disappear, 'for there is nothing wrong with this hypnosis, it is as good as any other' (8 July 1892). On 25 July the pain was still there, and Freud wondered whether it was not in fact due to a toothache. On 30 July mention is made on another correspondence card of a mysterious secret about which Freud had written a long letter to Breuer without being able to give him 'a full explanation since I am bound by my promise . . . We are not going to do hypnosis [Freud was scheduled to visit Elise the next day], but we should talk about this matter all the same.' Then everyone went on their summer holidays.

Elise's facial neuralgia returned as soon as she went back to Vienna on 10 October. On 23 October Theodor Gomperz wrote to his son Heinrich: 'Nothing new here as Freud, because of the failure of the electrical treatment, predicts a definite recovery through hypnosis, which however did not prevent Mama from having an attack last night, which, though delayed by several hours, was no less severe.' The next day, Freud suggested Elise have another 'dose' of hypnosis in order to overcome the 'resistance' against what was hidden behind the pain (we are in late 1892, precisely at the moment when Freud started theorizing hysteria in terms of psychical conflict and 'counter-will'): 'I think we need to repeat the dose and explain the situation by considering that the thing resists because it must not be expressed' (24 October 1892).

The dose brought some respite. On 8 November Theodor wrote to Franzi von Wertheimstein: 'Thanks to a hypnosis, Elise today had the first peaceful night after a long time. It remains to be seen if that keeps up or if a moderate repeat of this unpleasant remedy has a more lasting effect than the previous application of two weeks ago.' To Heinrich: 'Thanks to hypnosis, Mama really seems on the way to recovery' (13 November 1892). Then the pain came back. Theodor began to have serious doubts about the benefits of the cathartic treatment advocated by Breuer and Freud.

At the very beginning of January 1893, Elise was sent to the neurologist Wilhelm Winternitz's private clinic in Kaltenleutgeben to undergo a course of hydrotherapy. Away from her husband and her therapist, her condition improved significantly. However, Elise

and Freud continued to communicate, which irritated Theodor: 'I
am glad to see that . . . you are starting to feel better, I only regret
that you also keep consulting Freud from afar . . . Nothing but
auricular confessions and hypnosis – from which we have not seen
any miracles; I was able only to observe an increasing deterioration. All sensible people – with the exception of Breuer and Freud
– continuously warn against the continuation of these hitherto
worse than ineffective experiments . . . I regard the hypnosis as a
newly discovered medication that cannot be properly dosed and
that, like other more directly effective medications, has the effect
of a poison if used inappropriately' (8 January 1893).

The letter promptly caused a return of Elise's pain. As a result,
on 13 January, Freud recommended that Elise stop writing to her
husband.

On 22 January Freud acknowledged receipt of a message in which
Elise announced that hydrotherapy had finally got the better of her
neuralgia: 'I am delighted for you at the well-being that henceforth
awaits you and heave a sigh of relief after the happy conclusion of
this torment.' The reprieve was short-lived. Two months later, Elise
developed hyperaesthesia, like her niece Franzi. Freud hypnotized
her again before she left for a cure in Meran. Exasperated, Theodor
dispatched a stern letter from the seaside resort of Abbazia where
he was enjoying spring's first rays of sun in the company of his
friend, the surgeon Theodor Billroth: 'I have a strong conviction,
which by the way is shared by Billroth, that the hypnotic treatment
is responsible for your hyperaesthesia. You have never been so
irritable and sensitive . . . generally speaking, each idea manifests
itself immediately as pain, which of course is the natural tendency
of all ideas, however moderated and frustrated by inhibitions. The
[hypnotic] suggestion, which for a few moments deactivates the
functioning of the inhibition apparatus, actually seems to me
(hopefully without being unfair) *the school of hallucination.*'

The treatment continued nevertheless, which seems to indicate
that Elise was relatively independent of her husband – and also
very 'stubborn', as her son Heinrich described her. Much later, in
a letter sent on 5 May 1931 to an ageing Freud, Heinrich Gomperz
alluded to a 'family secret' that he had found in his mother's correspondence: 'it is only recently that I came across letters that you
wrote to my mother in 1893, which I found in her estate and that

enlightened me about a family secret that I was in any case already on the track of.' What secret could this be, if not the one that Freud had promised Elise to keep at the time? Freud replied on 17 May: 'I seem to remember the "family secret" your discovery relates to . . . If it really is about this episode – but I may be wrong in this – it was important for me too. On that occasion, something happened that enlightened me on the therapeutic value of hypnosis and led me to try a new technique.'

Anyone familiar with Freud's writings will have immediately recognized the famous episode evoked by him in his 1925 *Auto-biographical Study*: one day when one of his female patients was awakening from hypnosis, she had suddenly thrown her arms around his neck, thereby making him understand 'the nature of the mysterious element that was at work behind hypnotism [that is, the transference of a desire of a sexual nature onto the person of the therapist]. In order to exclude it, or at all events to isolate it, it was necessary to abandon hypnotism.' Freud had already described the same episode in *Studies on Hysteria*, although in less dramatic terms: 'In one of my patients the origin of a particular hysterical symptom lay in a wish, which she had had many years earlier and had at once relegated to the unconscious, that the man she was talking to at the time might boldly take the initiative and give her a kiss. On one occasion, at the end of a session, a similar wish came up in her about me. She was horrified at it, spent a sleepless night, and at the next session, though she did not refuse to be treated, was quite useless for work.'

The last mention of the treatment in Theodor's extant correspondence is to be found in a letter dated 13 February 1894. Elise was again suffering from facial neuralgia and Theodor kept Heinrich informed: 'Mama . . . [hopes] to find relief through a Freudian hypnosis, which took place yesterday.' Did the treatment last beyond that date? What we know is that Elise Gomperz continued to maintain an affectionate relationship with her therapist over the years. At his request and in conjunction with her friend the Baroness Marie von Ferstel, in 1901 she lobbied the Minister of Education (a colleague of Theodor's) in support of Freud's candidacy to the position of Professor extraordinarius. Her condition does not seem to have been much changed, for her son was to describe her later as generally 'nervous' and subject to mood swings.

Theodor Gomperz died in 1921. In his will, written in 1887, he proposed a therapy for his wife: 'I urgently desire – as a matter of fact, I demand – that my melancholic wife, whose innately delicate nervous system was unhinged by frights, sicknesses, etc. and gives cause for great concern, should cease as soon as possible to exhibit deep mourning and should find distraction and recreation by being sociable, attending concerts, going on journeys, etc.' We do not know if Elise followed this excellent advice. She passed away on 16 March 1929, at the age of 81.

6
FRANZISKA VON WERTHEIMSTEIN
(1844–1907)

L ost in the vast Freud Collection of the Library of Congress in Washington, DC, is a holographic letter from Jean-Martin Charcot sent in March 1888 to Theodor Gomperz. The library catalogue indicates that this manuscript is part of a donation made in 1960–63 by the Sigmund Freud Archives, the organization created in the early 1950s by the psychoanalyst Kurt Eissler to collect all documents and testimony relating to Freud. Charcot's letter indeed deals with a patient about whom his young colleague Freud had sent a report, evidently because he had her in treatment: 'I have taken note of the information given to me concerning the current state of Mlle X's health and I think that in the present state of affairs it is absolutely necessary that Mademoiselle come and stay in one of our hydrotherapy establishments to do the cure there [pour y faire la cure], in the most favorable conditions. Despite the current eating difficulty, the trip seems to me to be possible without inconvenience and without great difficulty. The notes and explanations communicated to me by my honored colleague Dr. Freund [sic] have been very helpful to me in assessing the case. Paris 18 March 1888, Charcot.'

So who was Mademoiselle X? It must have been someone close to Gomperz for Charcot to send this confidential letter to him and also someone about whom they had both been in contact before, otherwise why would Charcot speak of 'the current state' of her health? Yet it could not be *Madame* Elise Gomperz, of course. Nor could it be *Mademoiselle* Bettina Gomperz, Theodor and Elise's only daughter, who was only nine at the time. It must therefore have been *Mademoiselle* Franziska von Wertheimstein, the unmarried niece whom Theodor had been taking care of since

Portrait of the young
Franziska von Werheimstein
by Riccard.

her father, Leopold, had died in 1883 and who was going through a serious nervous crisis in that very year, 1888 (she had fits of uncontrollable anxiety when she came into contact with certain objects). Franzi, as she was called, had 'done the cure' with Charcot four years earlier, from April to mid-July 1884, and he was therefore already familiar with the case.

None of the reports Freud sent to Charcot about members of the extended Gomperz family have survived, so nothing is known about Franziska von Wertheimstein's treatment, or about how long it lasted. One can reasonably assume that Freud had been called to the rescue by Breuer, the Wertheimstein and Gomperz families' physician, but for how long? What we do know is that Franzi did not 'do the cure' with Charcot but instead went in June to Bad Gastein, a spa town in the Austrian Alps. Josephine von Wertheimstein, her mother, confided to her friend the poet Eduard von Bauernfeld that 'the doctors' – most likely Breuer and Freud – 'made in June the experiment of separating her from all her relatives, in order to implement isolation for a while and thus succeed in calming her nerves' (27 October 1888). In the autumn, Franzi's condition having hardly improved in Bad Gastein, 'the doctors' decided to send her for treatment at Mariagrün, the psychiatrist Richard von Krafft-Ebing's private clinic where Breuer used to place some of his wealthy 'nervous' patients. Patients there were treated to hydrotherapy, therapeutic conversation and hypnotic suggestion, in a grand hotel atmosphere. Franzi remained at Mariagrün until the summer of 1889, completely isolated from her mother and friends. Did Freud continue to follow her case after her return to Vienna, as he was to do a little later with other patients sent by Breuer to Krafft-Ebing? We do not know.

It was not the first time that Franzi suffered from her nerves, far from it. The burden of her 'neuropathic heredity', as Charcot would have it, was heavy, as was that of her relatives Anna von Lieben and Elise Gomperz. Her mother already had a long history of nervous disorders. Married at 23 to the banker Leopold von Wertheimstein, Salomon Rothschild's right-hand man in

Vienna, she soon presented symptoms of distress characteristic of the 'poor, respectable women' of whom Anna von Lieben spoke – depression, inhibitions, asthenia, insomnia and various other ailments. Still in her twenties, Josephine had developed mysterious contractures and pain in her knees that forced her to walk on crutches. Dragging behind her Franzi and her son Carl, both of whom suffered from the same knee and leg pains, she went from spa town to spa town – Ischl, Meran, Bad Gastein, Bad Aussee – in order to undergo cures that sometimes lasted up to a year. A knee operation performed by the famous surgeon Friedrich von Esmarch did not bring relief.

Infatuated with the attaché at the British embassy in Vienna, Robert Bulwer-Lytton, Josephine had nonetheless refrained from acting on her feelings ('The iron duty, this master, wins') and had transferred all her love to her two children, whose artistic gifts she encouraged. Franzi was a talented musician who also wrote poems (just like her mother) and studied painting and drawing with the Viennese artist August Eisenmenger. Carl, despite his young age, was already a promising sculptor. When Carl succumbed within 24 hours to a misdiagnosed case of scarlet fever, Josephine literally collapsed. Mad with grief, she developed a delirium in which she blamed herself for having killed her son and dreaded doing the same to Franzi. She had to be isolated. For four years, she remained completely cut off from reality.

When she awoke from her mental confusion in 1870, she found herself in a beautiful villa that her husband had bought in Döbling, an outlying neighbourhood north of Vienna, to help her to forget the past. Still crippled with pain in her legs and assisted by Franzi, she resumed her social activities there. The Villa Wertheimstein, surrounded by a vast park, became the meeting place for the Viennese liberal elite. Every Sunday, Josephine and Franzi held a salon and hosted the same mix of artists, scientists and politicians as Sophie, their sister and aunt, respectively, in the Palais Todesco. Josephine's sister-in-law, the opera singer Caroline Gomperz-Bettelheim, would come to

Rudolf von Alt, *Villa Wertheimstein*, undated watercolour.

sing, accompanied on the piano by Franz Liszt or Anton Rubinstein. The poets Eduard von Bauernfeld and Ferdinand von Saar, later Hugo von Hofmannsthal, were regular guests (Bauernfeld ended his days in a small outbuilding located in the park).

Everyone loved Franzi, so beautiful, so talented, so good and generous. But Franzi lived in the shadow of her mother and her illnesses, which she faithfully emulated: contractures in the legs and knee pain that likewise forced her to sometimes walk with crutches, migraines, depressive states, hyperaesthesia, touch phobia, eating disorders. Like Josephine, she suffered above all from what their friend Bauernfeld called 'gomperzitis', a chronic indecision bordering on *folie du doute*. (In a late letter to her daughter, Josephine wistfully noted: 'Between my will and implementation there is an abyss that I cannot cross – how many things have collapsed because of my lead inaction!', 10 October 1893). Over the years, Franzi had been courted by the Dutch lawyer and banker Gustav Sichel, the chemist Adolf von Lieben, the legal scholar Joseph Unger and many more, but she could never make up her mind, discouraged by her mother who jealously guarded her happiness and always found fault with suitors, all the while lamenting that her daughter remained single. Franzi had even let go of her dear Ernst Fleischl von Marxow, with whom she got along so wonderfully and who everyone thought was in love with her. No one understood why he abruptly announced his engagement to Sophie von Sichrovsky, with whom he had far less affinity. Neither Franzi nor Fleischl ever explained what had happened between them or why they had separated on bad terms, but it is easy to imagine that Fleischl had turned to Sophie out of spite after his advances had been rejected by Franzi or because she had left him too long in uncertainty, like so many others before him.

Franzi was 32 when she broke up with Fleischl and after that there were no more suitors. 'Unfit for life,' as Hugo von Hofmannsthal described her, she gradually shut herself up in the beautiful Villa Wertheimstein, in complete symbiosis with her mother – suffocated by her love, overcome with solicitude for her. There were occasions when she could not stand being with her, sometimes for weeks on end, but the rest of the time they did not leave each other. After the death of Leopold von Wertheimstein in 1883 and the deterioration of their health, it became increasingly difficult for them to hold salons. Josephine and Franzi now spent most of their time taking cures in Bad Aussee or Meran, at least when Franzi did not have to be isolated in some sanatorium or private clinic, which happened with increasing frequency.

Franzi walked inexorably into the void of existence, accompanied by her mother's lamentations: 'Her life is so incomplete, so provisional; and so goes time and with it life. – She, who could be so happy, is not at all . . . She has the feeling that her talent for painting, her musical sense, her desire for culture, her aspiration to enjoyment, all this remains fallow . . . What I suffer from this fact is beyond words' (Josephine

Portrait of Franziska von Wertheimstein by Emil Orlik, 1900.

to Adalbert Wilbrand, 21 April 1881). 'Because of the pain caused by her failed, useless and sad life, by the fallowing of all energies, the dark background that is always in her heart obscures her entire existence . . . She has no pleasure in life' (to Wilbrand, 13 July 1889). 'Franzi . . . feels very weak and miserable – always talks about death, says she won't survive the next night, next hour; she looked so bad that I almost died of anguish and despair' (to Wilbrand, 30 November 1890). 'Franzi is ailing again and has been tortured by this frightful carebaria (*Kopfdruck*) which robs her of all joy of living' (to Theodor Gomperz, 10 March 1891).

Josephine von Wertheimstein died on 16 July 1894, leaving Franzi helpless and distraught: 'I am like in a dream, cannot think, feel: nothing but a void, a desert, an excruciating nostalgia. My life was hanging by those two eyes, everything I did, thought, saw, everything was for her. I am an orphan, like a little child, lost in this deserted world, in the void of the future . . . I remain like a shadow without its light' (Franzi to Wilbrand, 4 August 1894). Franzi had to be placed in the sanatorium of neurologist

Alexander Holländer (a colleague and ex-collaborator of Freud). Back in the Villa Wertheimstein, she went on with her solitary life. She who had been at the centre of one of Vienna's most brilliant salons no longer saw anyone. Only Ferdinand von Saar, who had long harboured a secret and impossible love for her, continued to visit her. Suffering from an incurable cancer, he shot himself in the head with his service pistol in July 1906. Franzi died soon thereafter, on 20 January 1907. She had begun to show, Breuer said, signs of insanity. In her will, Franzi bequeathed the Villa Wertheimstein to the city of Vienna, 'on condition that the park be made accessible to the public for all eternity'.

Twelve years earlier, in the *Studies on Hysteria*, published jointly with Breuer, Freud had mentioned in a footnote the case of a certain Fräulein Mathilde H. She was, he said, a 'good-looking, nineteen-year-old girl. When I first saw her she was suffering from a partial paralysis of the legs. Some months later, however, she came to me for treatment on account of a change in her character. She had become depressed to the point of a tedium vitae, utterly inconsiderate to her mother, irritable and inaccessible . . . One day she became talkative in her hypnosis and told me that the cause of her depression was the breaking off of her engagement, which had occurred several months earlier. Closer acquaintance with her fiancé had brought out more and more things that were unwelcome to her and her mother. On the other hand, the material advantages of the connection had been too obvious for it to be easy to decide to break it off. So for a long time they had both wavered and she herself had fallen into a state of indecision in which she regarded all that happened to her with apathy. In the end her mother uttered the decisive negative on her behalf. A little later she had woken up as though from a dream and began to occupy her thoughts busily with the decision that had already been made and to weigh the pros and cons. This process, she told me, was still going on: she was living in the period of doubt, and every day she was possessed by the mood and thoughts which were appropriate to the day in the past with which she was occupied. Her irritability with her mother, too, had its basis only in the circumstances which prevailed at that time. In comparison with these activities of her thoughts, her present life seemed like a mere appearance of reality, like something in a dream. – I did not succeed in inducing the girl to talk again. I continued to address her while she was in deep somnambulism and saw her burst into tears each time without ever answering me; and one day, round about the anniversary of her engagement, her whole state of depression passed off – an event which brought me the credit of a great therapeutic success by hypnotism.'

A good-looking woman, a partial paralysis of the legs, a depressive state, an engagement broken off because of a 'state of indecision' and the intervention of the mother, the retrospective rumination of the pros and cons, the irritability with the mother: how can we not recognize, behind the disguise of the 'nineteen-year-old girl' of *Studies*, Fräulein Franziska von Wertheimstein and the constant crises caused by the failure of her marriage plans, perhaps more precisely the one that had followed Fleischl's departure? By the time Freud had this patient in treatment and practised the 'Breuer method' with her, in other words towards the end of the 1880s or the beginning of the 1890s, Franzi's break with Fleischl went back much further in time than the few 'months' alleged by Freud. But if Mathilde H., Franziska von W. and Mlle X. are indeed one and the same person, this would only confirm that Franzi had remained stuck in the past, reliving endlessly the fatal hesitation, the apathy, the impossibility of moving from will to action. Hypnosis, it seems, only reinforced this tendency to 'reminisce'.

Freud tells us that Mathilde H.'s depression disappeared at the end of this reviviscence. That of Franziska von W., as we know, always came back.

7

FANNY MOSER
(1848–1925)

Fanny Moser was said to be the richest woman in Central
Europe. She was born on 29 July 1848 and belonged to an old
Swiss patrician family, the von Sulzer-Wart of Winterthur.
Her grandfather, Johann Heinrich von Sulzer-Wart, had been
raised to the peerage by the Bavarian king and the young Baroness
Fanny Luise von Sulzer-Wart was therefore part of the aristocracy
that evolved in the Germanic principalities and grand duchies.
At 23 she married Heinrich Moser, a 65-year-old industrialist. The
son and grandson of watchmakers from Schaffhausen, Moser had
amassed an immense fortune by selling Swiss watches in Russia
and the rest of Asia. (The company H. Moser & Cie still exists,
and it is said that the expensive 'Moser-Soviet' watches were very
popular among the *nomenklatura* of the former Soviet Bloc.) Back
in Schaffhausen, Moser had also founded a railway company and
had built himself a palatial residence overlooking the Rhine, the
Villa Charlottenfels.

The marriage was happy, despite the age gap between the
spouses and tensions with Heinrich Moser's children from a previous marriage. The couple had two daughters, Fanny Junior
and Luise Junior, nicknamed Mentona after the French town of
Menton where Heinrich and Fanny liked to spend their holidays.
In his correspondence, however, Moser did mention his wife's
constant 'nervousness'. On 23 October 1874, just four days after
the birth of their second daughter, Heinrich Moser collapsed,
felled by a heart attack. He left the bulk of his fortune to his wife
and their daughters. Furious, his son Henri spread the rumour
that Fanny had poisoned his father. She was finally cleared after
her husband's body had been exhumed twice for autopsy and

toxicological analysis, but the scandal had been such that she was permanently snubbed by the royal and aristocratic circles in which she aspired to evolve.

In 1877 she sold the Moser watch company to the industrialist Paul Girard on the condition that he did not change its name and from then on lived on her income in a castle that she had acquired at Au, near Lake Zurich. There she established a kind of parallel court, entertaining distinguished guests from all over Europe. She practised patronage and philanthropy, supporting, for example, the anti-alcohol campaigns of August Forel and Eugen Bleuler, the two successive directors of the Burghölzli psychiatric hospital in Zurich. She also donated 10,000 Swiss francs – a considerable sum at the time – to build a mental hospital in Schaffhausen. She was known in the neighbourhood for her eccentricities and numerous lovers, among whom were often her doctors. Her 'nervousness' had indeed worsened, probably due to the social ostracism of her peers, and she made a high consumption of doctors, psychiatrists and psychotherapists. Forel and Bleuler, whose signatures appear on the castle's guest book, knew her as a patient. When she did not hold court, she would take the waters in the posh spas of Europe.

Yet the 'nervousness' would not subside, and there was always a new doctor to consult, a new cure or a new private clinic to try.

In the spring of 1889, after spending the winter in the resort of Abbazia on the Adriatic coast, Fanny Moser went to Vienna with her daughters in order to consult Josef Breuer. She had most likely been referred by Forel, who knew Breuer well (they had studied together in Vienna). She was depressed and suffered from sleeplessness, pain and various tics. Every two minutes, her face assumed an expression of disgust and she would make a gesture as if to repel an imaginary assailant:

Marble bust of Fanny Moser.

'Don't move! Don't say anything! Don't touch me!' After having had her in treatment for six weeks, Breuer decided to send her to his young friend and colleague Sigmund Freud. In her memoirs, Mentona Moser would reminisce about Breuer's 'first assistant': 'He was short and thin, had jet black hair and black eyes, he looked very young and shy.'

The treatment began on 1 May 1889, at the hotel where Fanny Moser was staying. Freud's first decision was to send her to a private clinic in Vienna, the Löw Sanatorium, where he came to see her daily. Having found that she was easily hypnotizable, probably because she had previously been hypnotized by Forel, he decided to apply the 'Breuer method', which consisted of having the patient re-experience past traumas under hypnosis and 'deleting' them by suggestion before the awakening. (In *Studies on Hysteria*, where Fanny is pseudonymized as 'Frau Emmy von N., from Livonia', Freud oddly claims that 'this was my first attempt at handling that therapeutic method,' whereas we know that he had been using it since the end of 1887.) He immediately got from Fanny a veritable avalanche of traumatic memories. In the space of nine days, from 8 May to 17 May 1889, she recalled nearly forty traumas, ranging from the most dramatic (witnessing the sudden death of her husband) to the most trivial (being frightened by a toad). After seven weeks of treatment Fanny Moser returned to Au with her daughters, her condition apparently having improved.

The following month, on 19 July 1889, Freud paid Frau Moser a visit on his way to Nancy, where he was going to see Hippolyte Bernheim with a letter of recommendation from Forel. Presumably it was on this occasion – and not two years later, as he writes for the purpose of concealment in *Studies on Hysteria* – that he was asked to examine Fanny Junior (we find no trace of another stay at Au in the spring of 1891 either in his correspondence or in the guest book in which visitors to the castle were asked to register). While in Vienna, Fanny Junior had been treated by a gynaecologist recommended by Freud, most probably Rudolf Chrobak, and she was now in open adolescent revolt against her mother (the relationship between Fanny Moser and her two daughters was to be permanently strained). According to Freud, Fanny Junior 'exhibited unbridled ambitions which were out of proportion to the poverty of her gifts, and she became disobedient and even violent towards her mother'. Considering that 'all her step-brothers and sisters (the children of Herr von N. by his first marriage) had succumbed to paranoia' – a groundless assertion on his part – he diagnosed the onset of a 'neuropathy'. As a result, Fanny Junior was promptly dispatched to a clinic. (Contradicting Freud's dire prognosis, Fanny Junior would eventually leave for Lausanne to pursue formal studies and become a distinguished zoologist before writing a two-volume book on parapsychology.)

Seven months later, Freud learned from Breuer that Fanny Moser considered him and the Viennese gynaecologist responsible for her daughter's 'illness'. As she was accustomed to do when one of her visitors displeased her, she had stuck a small piece of paper over Freud's signature in her guest book. Her condition having again deteriorated, she was placed by Forel and Breuer into a clinic. There she expressed violent opposition to the physician who treated her by hypnosis, following Freud's directions. Finally, she escaped from the clinic with the help of a friend. In May 1890 she was back in Freud's office in Vienna, her 'hysterical' dislike of him notwithstanding.

This second course of hypnotic treatment lasted eight weeks and resulted in some improvement. Fanny Moser returned to Au, from where Freud continued to receive sporadic news. Tensions with Fanny Junior, who wanted to pursue scientific studies against her mother's will, once again caused a worsening of her condition in 1893. The famous Swedish hypnotherapist Otto Wetterstrand, a friend of Forel, was called in specially from Stockholm in late September. (In anticipation, Fanny had sent Freud a note during the summer asking for permission to be hypnotized by another doctor.) Accompanied by Fanny Junior, Fanny then went to Stockholm during the winter of 1893–4 to follow a course of 'prolonged sleep'. This revolutionary treatment, which Wetterstrand had launched in the early 1890s, consisted in placing the patient in hypnosis for several days or even several weeks in a row. Unlike Freud, however, Wetterstrand found it difficult to hypnotize Fanny, and it took him several weeks before he succeeded. Clearly, Fanny was raising the stakes.

In 1899 Wetterstrand was to report on twelve cases of 'difficult hysteria' treated by him using the technique of prolonged sleep. Ten of them had fully recovered, another had hardly changed and the last one had subsequently relapsed, requiring a new treatment. This was most likely a reference to Fanny Moser. In September 1894, at a Congress of German Physicians and Naturalists held in Vienna, Freud had found the opportunity to ask Forel about Frau Moser. With her, Forel told him in confidence, it's always the same thing: first she gives up her symptoms, then she falls out with you, then she gets sick again. We know from Fanny Moser's guest book that Wetterstrand came back to Au in August 1896, very likely for yet another treatment. As for Forel, he was called to the castle in June of the following year.

Late in life, Fanny fell in love with a younger man who took advantage of her and extracted part of her fortune. She had broken with her daughters and cut off financial support to them. Mentona, whom she loathed and who felt the same about her, had become a card-carrying Communist. In 1918 Fanny Junior, who was now married to the composer Jaroslav Hoppe, tried in vain to place her mother under guardianship. She wrote to Freud on 13 July, asking him to write a formal report on the mental state of her mother during her treatment with him.

Freud replied obliquely, justifying himself for having sided at the time with the mother against the daughter: 'It is with great interest that I have learned that you are that little Fanny about whom I was so concerned and was called by Frau Fanny Moser to come to Au. You are right, at that time I did almost nothing for you, I didn't understand anything about you. Please, kindly consider that at that time I also did not understand the case of your mother, although she had been my patient twice for a period of several weeks . . . Especially thanks to this case and its outcome, I understood that the treatment with hypnosis is meaningless and useless, and I got the impulse to invent the more rational psycho-analytic therapy.' A surprising statement, for if this were the case, why did Freud not inform the readers of Studies on Hysteria, published five years later?

Freud then reread the whole episode through the lens of his more recent theories, as if this could be of any help to Fanny Hoppe-Moser and her sister in their conflict with their mother: 'Your mother's behavior towards you and your sister is far from being as enigmatic to me as it is to you. I can offer you the simple explanation that she loved her children just as tenderly as she also hated them bitterly (what we term ambivalence); and that this was so already then – in Vienna.' In 1935 Freud drove the point home when thanking Fanny Hoppe-Moser for the copy of her book on parapsychology that she had sent him: 'I can not blame you for not having yet forgiven my bad diagnostic error of the time. Not only was I still very inexperienced, but our art of reading the hidden psyche was still in its infancy. Ten, maybe five years later, I could not have failed to guess that the poor woman led a difficult struggle against her unconscious hatred for her two children and tried to defend herself by means of over-tenderness. These evil ghosts seem to have surfaced later in reworked form and determined her behaviour. But back then I did not understand anything and just believed in her information.'

Fanny Moser had died ten years earlier, on 2 April 1925, still out of touch with her two daughters and still rich despite the millions siphoned off by her lover. Obituaries saluted the great philanthropist and patron of the arts, who had helped so many talents to bloom.

8

MARTHA BERNAYS
(1861–1951)

For a long time she remained the anonymous 'heroine' of Freud's very first case history, 'A case of successful treatment by hypnotism'. In this text, which he published in two instalments in December 1892 and January 1893 in the psychiatrist August Forel's *Zeitschrift für Hypnotismus*, Freud presented the strange case of 'a young woman between twenty and thirty years of age with whom I happen to have been in contact from her childhood' and who 'remained under my observation for several years' after the treatment. Freud also knew her mother, her younger sister and one brother but was 'not acquainted', he writes, 'with my patient's other relatives'. The patient was happily married, even-tempered, and apart from a transient '*hystérie d'occasion*' that prevented her from breastfeeding her three children, she was not neurotic in any way; nor were her mother and younger sister. However, the brother known to Freud had suffered from neurasthenia due to the 'usual sexual waywardness of puberty'. (The American neurologist George Miller Beard held at the time that neurasthenia could be caused by 'sexual exhaustion'.) This neurasthenia had made the brother into 'the torment of his family' and had 'ruined his life plans'. Freud left open, therefore, the possibility that his patient might be part of a 'neuropathic family' in Charcot's sense.

The young woman had given birth to three children. From the approximate chronology provided by Freud we can infer that the first child was born at the end of 1886 or the beginning of 1887, the second at the end of 1889 or the beginning of 1890 and the third at the beginning of 1891. The birth of the first child was successfully concluded with forceps by the woman's gynaecologist,

Dr Gustav Lott. However, despite her wish to breastfeed the baby, the mother did not have enough milk. In addition to her lactation problems, the mother developed a 'worrying' rejection of food, had physical pain when the child was brought to her chest, was agitated and could not sleep: 'After a fortnight . . . the attempt was abandoned as a failure and the child was transferred to a wet-nurse.'

On the occasion of the birth of her second child, the problem with breastfeeding recurred, along with 'even more distressing symptoms than the first time'. Because 'external circumstances added to the desirability of avoiding a wet-nurse', Lott and the woman's family doctor, Josef Breuer, decided to call in Freud on the fourth day to see if hypnosis could help. Although being 'received with a bad grace' by the patient and her husband, who worried that 'a woman's nerves might be totally ruined by hypnosis,' Freud was able to restore lactation using the kind of hypnotic and post-hypnotic techniques that he had learned from Hippolyte Bernheim during his stay in Nancy in the summer of 1889. Having put the patient in deep somnambulism and given her post-hypnotic amnesia for what had transpired during the session, Freud firmly contradicted her apprehensions and symptoms: 'Have no fear! You will make an excellent nurse and the baby will thrive. Your stomach is perfectly quiet, your appetite is excellent, you are looking forward to your next meal, etc.' That same evening the patient had a meal, went to sleep peacefully and 'fed the baby irreproachably' in the morning. During the day, however, the symptoms returned, so Freud re-hypnotized the patient and told her with even greater vigour that after his departure, she would clamour for food and demand that the family bring her dinner right away – which she did, to the surprise of her husband and mother, who had never seen her being so assertive. When Freud came back the next day, the patient refused to have any further treatment because she was now perfectly well. Oddly enough, no mention was made of what Freud called his 'remarkable achievement'. (Remarkable it was indeed: never again would Freud be able to report on such an unambiguous therapeutic success.)

The same scenario unfolded one year later when a third child was born and Freud was called in again to remove the mother's strange and seemingly insurmountable reluctance to feed her baby. The treatment was successful – again. Still, neither the patient nor her husband expressed gratitude to Freud due to their 'aversion' to hypnosis.

So who was this ungrateful *hystérique d'occasion*? For more than a century, her identity remained shrouded in mystery as scholars scoured in vain for a married woman who had three children in 1892, whom Freud had known from her childhood and whose brother's health and life plans had been ruined by sexual excesses. It turns out that she was indeed married but not to another man: she was Freud's own wife, Martha Bernays. A few Freud scholars had long suspected that this might be the case, but it became obvious with the publication in 2005 of the correspondence between Martha's younger sister, Minna Bernays, and Freud. There we learn from a letter sent by Freud to Minna in the evening of 16 October 1887 to announce the birth of his daughter Mathilde that the delivery had been concluded with forceps by Martha's gynaecologist, Dr Gustav Lott. We also learn from a letter sent three days later that the family was waiting for a wet-nurse who had been called in from Roznau, which indicates that Martha had difficulty breastfeeding the baby – something that must have been a recurrent problem, since we know from other sources that: 1. the Freuds had hired a wet-nurse to breastfeed their second child, Jean-Martin, who nevertheless had to be fired immediately because she had omitted to mention that she had no milk – probably the 'external circumstances' alluded to by Freud in his case history (Martin Freud's memoirs); 2. Sophie Freud, the Freuds' fifth child,

Martha Bernays,
July 1882.

was breastfed by a wet-nurse 'who even has milk' (Freud to Minna Bernays, 15 April 1893); 3. Anna Freud, the sixth child, was treated to Gartner's whole milk, a newly introduced baby formula (Freud to Wilhelm Fliess, 8 December 1895).

The letters sent to Minna in the wake of Mathilde's birth also intimate that Martha had been afflicted by an ailment that was 'worrying' enough to keep her gynaecologist in attendance for several days and that entailed some kind of eating problem from which she recovered after the wet-nurse's arrival (Freud to Minna, 23 October 1887). Two weeks after the delivery, Martha was still in bed and had not yet recovered her strength (Martha to Minna, 31 October 1887). If we add that the Freuds' second and third children were born on 7 December 1889 (Jean-Martin) and 19 February 1891 (Oliver), exactly as the chronology of the case history suggests, we see that the fit between Martha's childbirths and those of Freud's anonymous patient is almost perfect. The few discrepancies – Mathilde's birthdate being off by one year; the patient's first child being transferred to a wet nurse after a fortnight rather than after four days; her being married to a man sceptical of Freud's treatment (!) – can all be put down to Freud's desire to send his readers off track and protect his wife's privacy, as she might otherwise have been too easily recognizable within their circle of acquaintances. And of course, Martha 'remained under [Freud's] observation for several years' after the treatment.

Likewise, Martha's family history matches the few indications that Freud gives us regarding his patient's relatives. Freud tells us that he knew the patient's mother, her younger sister and one of her brothers but not her other relatives, which also holds for Martha's mother Emmeline Bernays, her younger sister Minna and her older brother Eli. As for Martha's other relatives, Freud had never had an opportunity to meet them: three brothers and a sister had all died before he knew her, as did her father, Berman Bernays, who succumbed to a heart attack in 1879. In this respect, Freud's assertion that he had been 'in contact (*in Verkehr*) with her from her childhood' is not altogether straightforward if he is indeed talking about Martha, for he had actually met her for the first time in April 1882, when she was already 21 years old. But he must have heard about her and her family well before through her brother Eli and Ignaz Schoenberg, two friends of his who had been courting, respectively, his own sister Anna and Martha's sister Minna.

Freud had fallen instantly in love with the slim young woman when the two Bernays sisters paid a visit to the Freud sisters and he saw her modestly peeling apples at the kitchen table. Martha reciprocated and the two became secretly engaged only two months later (secretly, for Emmeline Bernays, the mother, took a dim view of the penniless and non-observant young medical student).

Martha was born in Hamburg on 26 July 1861 and was thus five years younger than Freud. Her paternal grandfather, Isaak Bernays, was the Chief Rabbi of Hamburg, and unlike her fiancé she was brought up in a strictly Orthodox home. Two of her paternal uncles, Michael and Jakob Bernays, were distinguished scholars (Michael converted to Christianity in order to become a professor at the University of Munich, which caused grave tensions within the family). Berman Bernays, on the other hand, was the family's black sheep. After running a linen shop in Hamburg, he engaged in dubious financial transactions and was sent to prison for one year after having been convicted for fraudulent bankruptcy. Upon his release from prison in 1869, he moved with his wife and children to Vienna to start a new life and re-establish his reputation. As fate would have it, the company there for which he worked went bankrupt in 1879 and when he died a few months later, probably as a result, he left next to nothing to his widow and children. The Bernays family had to step in to support them and Siegmund Pappenheim, a distant relative (and the father of Bertha Pappenheim), was named legal guardian of the children.

When Freud became engaged to Martha, the financial situation of the Bernays children had improved somewhat due to an inheritance from their uncle Jakob Bernays, who died in 1881. Eli, who in the meantime had become the family's breadwinner, invested Martha and Minna's parts in stocks. Emmeline, who had never been happy in Vienna, decided in early 1883 to move back to Hamburg with Martha and Minna, 'selfishly' tearing them away from their respective fiancés (Freud to Minna, 21 February 1883). Thus started a four-year separation between Martha and Sigmund that ended with their eventual marriage in September 1886 and during which they exchanged more than 1,500 love letters, which became all the more exalted and jealous (on Freud's side) when the object of desire was distant and inaccessible.

As the wedding finally approached and the fiancés needed to recoup Martha's inheritance for her dowry, Freud discovered with dismay that Eli, faced with financial difficulties, had used it to cover debts that he had incurred. Eli was thus repeating a pattern that had led to his father's downfall. Already wary of his brother-in-law since the latter had temporarily broken off the engagement with his sister Anna in 1882, Freud further learned that Eli, who was known to be 'very much interested in women' (Albert Hirst, interview with Kurt Eissler), had before his marriage fathered an illegitimate child with a 'young woman of easy virtue' and had been blackmailed by her into paying large sums of money to hide his 'youthful romance'. Incensed, Freud suspected that this 'immature, stupid, inordinately vain and lazy lad' had squandered Martha's inheritance for that purpose and he told Minna as much (Freud to Minna, 5 June 1886). He also demanded, on pain of ending their relationship, that Martha break off all relations with her brother, an ultimatum that she wisely resisted despite her consternation and resentment.

Eli eventually managed to return the money to Martha, thus assuaging Freud's worst fears, but the financial drain caused by his philandering contributed to his eventual bankruptcy in 1891. Fleeing his creditors, Eli emigrated to the United States, leaving his wife and children behind. Anna, who had given birth to their son Edward in November, only heard from him at Christmas 1891. She eventually joined him in New York with baby Edward in October 1892, leaving her daughters Judith and Lucie temporarily in the care of the Freud family in Vienna. Freud had tried unsuccessfully to convince her to stay in Vienna with him and Martha, which had resulted, according to his niece Hella Bernays, in lasting 'non-friendliness between Father [Eli] and Uncle [Sigmund]'. Despite this acrimony, he generously contributed money to assist the couple in their move to the New World and asked friends and relatives to do the same.

It is evidently this painful sequence of events, which was unfolding at the same time as he was writing his case history, to which he alludes when describing his patient's brother, who had lost his way due to his youthful sexual excesses and had developed as a result a 'typical neurasthenia of early manhood' that had made him into 'the torment of his family' and 'ruined his life plans'. It is difficult not to read Freud's ostensible diagnosis as a hidden and very private jab at his despised brother-in-law (why not indulge in the sweet pleasure of revenge, since no one will ever know?).

Martha was to give birth to three other children – Ernst, Sophie and Anna – each delivery leaving her as exhausted as before. But apart from these *occasions*, she did not display any unusual symptoms and would never again require any psychotherapeutic intervention, hypnotic or otherwise. As Freud writes in his case history: 'Her capability, her quiet common sense and her naturalness made it impossible for anyone, even her family doctor, to regard her as a neurotic.' In fact, Martha was almost hyper-normal, the perfect image of late nineteenth-century bourgeois propriety. People who knew her paint the portrait of a woman who ran the household with non-Viennese, *hamburgerisch* efficiency and was almost obsessive about punctuality and cleanliness. Freud's niece, Judith Bernays-Heller, couldn't help but diagnose her aunt with a housewife's neurosis: 'An analyst would say that there was a kind of obsessional neurosis in her love for order, her punctuality, her reticence and also in her social reserve' (interview with Kurt Eissler). Ernst Hammerschlag, who knew her from childhood, told Eissler that the Frau Professor was diffident and self-effacing to the point of coming out as obsequious and '*überhöflich*', over-polite. Sometimes, he added, she looked like a 'frightened hare'.

Committed to conventional morality, Martha seems to have wilfully ignored her husband's theories and activities, just as the anonymous patient of Freud's case history had refused to acknowledge his hypnotic intervention. In an interview he granted in 1957 to John Billinsky, Carl Gustav Jung reminisced about his encounter with Martha when he first visited the Freuds in Vienna in 1907: 'At Freud's home that evening during the dinner, I tried to talk to Freud and his wife about psychoanalysis and so on, but I soon discovered that Mrs. Freud knew nothing about what Freud was doing. There was a superficial relationship between Freud and his wife.' From other sources, one gets the impression that the marriage was indeed all the more harmonious as husband and wife moved in spheres that seldom intersected, except for punctual meals during which Freud did not say a word. Max Schur, Freud's personal physician, described Martha as 'the typical housewife who made his [Freud's] life comfortable, never asked questions, who, as he said, had never read a word by him, who would say: "If he says so, it must be right. Still, I don't understand it!"' When Schur read in the first volume of Ernest Jones's biography the account of the young Freud's passionate letters to his fiancée, he wrote to Jones: 'As to Martha – here I have my doubts whether at the time I knew them she still was the 'one and only'. As far as I could see it, he spent less and less time with her . . . there was so little left of the great love that I was quite surprised by Volume I' (30 September 1955). Freud himself didn't make a secret of it, bluntly declaring to Emma Jung that his marriage 'had long been amortized' (recalled in a letter from Emma Jung to Freud, 6 November 1911).

For intellectual companionship, Freud looked to Minna, Martha's sister. 'Tante Minna', as she was called, had never married following the death of her fiancé Ignaz Schoenberg from tuberculosis, and she had joined the Freud household in 1896 to help Martha with the children. Although they were very close, the two sisters could hardly have been more different. Martha was small, feminine, even-tempered, retiring. Minna was tall, large, 'masculine' (Ernst Hammerschlag), opinionated, moody, sharp-tongued, 'domineering' (Anna Maastright, Ludwig Jekels). Mrs Max Barsis described to Eissler the dynamic between the two sisters: 'In the household, she [Minna] was more – how should I put it – in the role of the key person (*die Hauptperson*). The Frau Professor was very unassuming, so unassuming that she always receded into the background.' Judith Bernays-Heller confirmed: it is only after Minna's death that she realized 'what a special and distinctive personality she [Martha] had, for as long as Tante Minna was there she was always a little pushed over by her'. According to Ludwig Jekels, the whole family was under Minna's sway: 'Minna's influence over the family was so great that she would have stifled any voice.'

Friends and relatives all agree: Minna was *klug* (bright), *gebildet* (cultivated), *belesen* (well-read), *geistig* (cerebral), *intellektuell* (intellectual). Unlike her sister, she followed Freud's work closely and easily interacted with his colleagues and visitors. After dinner, Freud would bring her with him to the *Kaffeehäuser* where he met acquaintances and followers. According to Max Graf, 'he always went out, in the evening, with his sister-in-law' (interview with Kurt Eissler). During his summer holidays, Freud would also travel alone with Minna to faraway places, leaving Martha behind with the children. On one occasion at least, he even checked in with her at a hotel in the Swiss Alps as 'Dr Sigm Freud u. Frau' (Dr and Mrs Sigm. Freud).

These trips '*de lit à lit en l'Italie*' ('from bed to bed in Italy', Sándor Ferenczi to Freud, 26 December 1912) were of course highly unusual, and rumours about them circulated within Freud's circle of friends and relatives. Judith Bernays-Heller remembers the gossip in her family about Freud's escapades with his 'second wife'. Oskar Rie, a close friend of Freud's, is said to have quipped: 'For children Freud went to Martha, for pleasure he took Minna.' Others were puzzled, disconcerted. Max Graf: 'I had the impression that there was something odd in the relation with his sister-in-law . . . But since things were not very clear, I didn't want to speak publicly about it. – Eissler: Did he have sexual relations with her? – Graf: I don't think so.' Asked about these 'gossips' by Eissler, the psychoanalyst Ludwig Jekels answered that Eduard Hitschmann, another follower of Freud's, 'was of the opinion that there was something between Freud and Tante Minna'. The rumours were apparently so widespread that Freud once told Eva Rosenfeld, who was in analysis with him, that he found it surprising that the Minna topic had never surfaced in her associations of ideas.

The most emphatic testimony, however, is that of Jung. To John Billinsky, he confided: 'Soon [after his first visit to the Freud home] I met Freud's wife's younger sister – she was very good looking, and she not only knew enough about psychoanalysis, but also about everything Freud was doing. When, a few days later, I was visiting Freud's laboratory [office], Freud's sister-in-law asked if she could talk with me. She was very much bothered by her relationship with Freud and felt guilty about it. From her I learned that Freud was in love with her and that their relationship was indeed very intimate. It was a shocking discovery to me, and even now I can recall the agony I felt at the time.' In a long interview he granted Eissler in 1953, Jung was slightly less assertive: 'That much is certain: the younger sister had a huge transference [onto Freud] and Freud *was not insensible* [in English]. – Eissler: You mean, there was a liaison with the younger sister? – Oh, a liaison!? I don't know how much!? . . . So, that I cannot say! I guess that everything was highly correct, in any case on the surface entirely correct . . . Every man has his secrets.'

Whether 'Sigi' and Minna's so-called transference and countertransference remained within the bounds of bourgeois correctness will probably remain forever an open (and in the end irrelevant) question, but that they had Goethean 'elective affinities' to each other – 'that much is certain'. Martha cannot have failed to notice, or sense, that she was the 'one and only' no longer. Kurt Eissler bluntly asked her niece Hella Bernays about it: 'Now how was Frau Professor? Be indiscreet!' – Hella Bernays: 'Well, my heart bleeds for her! Because if I had a husband who had an affair with my sister, I'd die! And I wouldn't put up with it! But apparently she did!'

Martha did indeed ignore the emotional triangle, just as she had ignored her husband's hypnotic intervention and his strange theories. According to Max Schur, she never complained, 'never expressed doubts, never reproached him [Freud] for anything at times when it was probably tough'. She never showed any jealousy towards her sister, instead relying emotionally on her, much more so than on her husband. Bertha Hammerschlag, Breuer's daughter, remembered: 'Frau Fr[eud] was very attached to Minna. Minna's death may have got to her more than Freud's death.' Lilly Freud-Marlé, a niece on the Freud side, quoted the aged Martha's own words: 'I miss her [Minna] very much, I could so beautifully confide everything to her, dump everything on her.'

The first thing Martha Bernays did after Freud's death was to light the Sabbath candles on Friday evenings, something her husband had forbidden her to do since their wedding. She also took to reading again, as she used to do in her youth.

She died on 2 November 1951, ten years after Minna, her dear little *Schnickchen*. We know about her because she was Sigmund Freud's wife.

9

PAULINE SILBERSTEIN
(1871–1891)

Pauline Silberstein was the wife of Eduard Silberstein, a child-hood friend of Freud with whom the latter had exchanged an abundant correspondence during their adolescence. Eduard Silberstein, who throughout his life kept the nickname 'Berganza' that he used with his friend 'Cipión' (the alias of Sigmund), came from a wealthy Orthodox Jewish family from Jassy (Iasi), the former capital of the Romanian region of Moldavia. After study-ing law in Leipzig and Vienna, where he also studied philosophy under Franz Brentano, he settled down as a banker and then as a grain merchant in Braila, another city in Romania. In a letter writ-ten in 1884 to Martha Bernays, Freud reported that their friendship had become more distant since he had tried to dissuade Eduard from marrying 'a stupid rich girl whom he had been sent to have a look at . . . He is prepared to marry the girl so as to establish his independence as a merchant.' In reality, Silberstein had not fol-lowed through with this arranged marriage plan. In the late 1880s he married Pauline Theiler, a girl from Jassy who was fifteen years younger than him, with whom he had fallen in love.

Shortly after her marriage, however, Pauline had developed a deep 'melancholy'. Accompanied by a maid, she had come to Vienna to be treated by Freud. It is not known exactly how long the treatment lasted or what it consisted of (this was the time when Freud used what he called the 'Breuer method'), but the Silberstein family retained a vivid memory of it. In a letter sent in 1988 to Kurt Eissler, who tried to convince her that Pauline Silberstein had not been in analysis under Freud, Rosita Braunstein Vieyra, the granddaughter of Eduard Silberstein, gave firm testimony on this subject: 'I must for the record state that my Mother and three

Pauline Silbertstein,
undated.

cousins (all now dead) spoke about Dr Freud's treatment of Pauline S. They always added that, unfortunately, it had not been successful . . . Thus I must beg to differ and assert with all due respect, that you are in error when you conclude that Pauline Silberstein, née Theiler, was not treated by Dr Freud. She was.'

As Rosita Braunstein Vieyra informed Eissler, Freud's treatment had produced a fatal outcome. On 14 May 1891 Pauline Silberstein turned up at 4.30 p.m. outside the building in which Freud lived at 8 Maria Theresienstrasse, asked her maid to wait downstairs and, after climbing a few floors, threw herself off the building, head first. She was twenty years old.

The following day, several newspapers in Vienna gave differing versions of the event. According to the *Neues Wiener Tagblatt*, a young foreign woman who had come to Vienna for treatment for a 'serious nervous disorder . . . made her way to a medical doctor residing in the rear wing of the Stiftungshaus in Maria Therese St. in order to undergo a treatment'. (The Kaiserliches Stiftungshaus, also called Sühnhaus or 'House of Atonement', was

The House of Atonement.

an impressive neo-Gothic building erected with imperial funding at the site of a theatre which had been destroyed in a fire that claimed 449 victims.) The young lady had climbed three floors and flung herself down from a balustrade. According to the *Neue Freie Presse* 'a young elegantly dressed lady' had thrown herself from the fourth floor down the stairwell. The *Neue Freie Presse* added that, according to the evidence collected, the 'unfortunate woman' had arrived in Vienna that same morning to be treated by a doctor, which allowed Kurt Eissler and Walter Boehlich, the editor of Freud's letters to Eduard Silberstein, to assert that Pauline Silberstein had died before she could even consult with Freud.

The official death certificate drawn up by the Viennese police gave yet another version of the facts: Pauline Silberstein, wife of Dr Eduard S., a merchant in Braila, Romania, had thrown herself down into the courtyard of the building where she lived, 10 Maria Theresienstrasse (most probably a clerical error: the wing of the Sühnhaus where Freud had his office on the mezzanine level was at 8 Maria Theresienstrasse).

It is, however, unlikely that Pauline Silberstein had been staying with Freud, as *Die Presse* mentioned for its part that 'the lady was lately a patient in the sanatorium of Dr [Alexander] Holländer [in Hacking, in the thirteenth district of Vienna] and on this afternoon had gone with her maid . . . to Dr Frey [*sic*], a nerve doctor in the Stiftungshaus, for a consultation.' The *Illustriertes Wiener Extrablatt* specified that 'Frau S.[ilberstein] . . . had come to Vienna some three months ago to seek help here for her nervous troubles,' which definitely excludes that she had arrived in Vienna on that same day. The *Illustrietes Wiener Extrablatt* further noted that she 'intended . . . to see a physician to get electrical treatment [*um sich elektrisiren zu lassen*]'. We know that Freud, at the time, was still using electrotherapy in combination with hypnosis.

The event must have been particularly traumatic for the residents of the building. In that same month, May 1891, Freud gave his notice at the Sühnhaus in order to move to 19 Berggasse, a much less prestigious building. The apartment was refitted in July and the Freud family moved into their new quarters in early September, far from the ghosts of the House of Atonement.

Pauline Silberstein, meanwhile, was buried in the Jewish section of the Central Cemetery in Vienna, Gate 1, Group 19, row 57, number 16. Eduard Silberstein remarried Anna Sachs. One of Anna's first gestures when she moved into her new house was to place a bouquet of flowers under Pauline's painting on the living-room wall.

In a letter sent on 22 April 1928 to the B'nai B'rith in Braila, concerning Eduard Silberstein, who had died three years earlier, Freud briefly mentioned having treated his friend's wife: 'I spent many years of my boyhood and young manhood in intimate friendship, indeed in fraternal fellowship, with him . . . and once had occasion to attend to his first wife.' It is the only time Freud ever made any public reference to Pauline Silberstein.

10

ADELE JEITELES
(1871–1970)

We would probably know nothing about this occasional patient of Freud had she not also been the mother of the novelist and essayist Arthur Koestler. Her name was Adele Jeiteles and she belonged to one of the most distinguished Jewish families of the Austro-Hungarian Empire. Among her ancestors were Rabbi Loeb ben Simon, a holy man who lived in Prague in the seventeenth century, Judah Loeb, who coined the word 'Haskalah' to designate the Jewish Enlightenment, and the successful novelist Julius Seydlitz (Isaac Jeiteles). Her grandfather, businessman Israel Jeiteles, was one of the few Jews to be allowed to place the imperial guarantee on his headed writing paper. We also know from an interview with Marie Paneth (see the Alois Jeitteles vignette) by Kurt Eissler that another Jeiteles, Alois Jeitteles (with two 't's) 'was treated by Freud for melancholy psychosis, and committed suicide in the early 1900s'.

Adele's father, Jacob Jeiteles, was a wealthy importer, and Adele grew up in opulence. Fluent in French and English, she was pretty, witty and courted on all sides. Adele was by no means neurotic, but from time to time she had a tic that was considered 'nervous'. One of her aunts, the educator and feminist Eleonore Jeiteles, knew Freud personally (presumably through her friends Emma Eckstein and Therese Schlesinger-Eckstein) and recommended that Adele see him.

According to an interview granted by Adele to Kurt Eissler in 1953, her visit to Freud took place in the early 1890s, when she was in her twenties. It seems that Freud already had a big reputation at the time: 'In Vienna, you know, it's funny to say it now, but we didn't take him seriously! . . . You were considered half crazy when you went to Dr Freud's. I only went because of my aunt.' Adele's friends, on the other hand, were tickled by her visit to the nerve specialist: 'There was so much written about the fact that everything, nerves, etc., stems from sexual things, right? All this was naturally a source of amusement for young girls . . . All my friends were naturally very curious.'

According to Arthur Koestler, his mother went to see Freud two or three times. She took an immediate dislike to him (*ein ekelhafter Kerl*, she was to confide to Eissler – 'a disgusting guy'). He had big sideburns, which she hated. 'He received me rather coldly, he examined me, started massaging me here [the nape of the neck] and asked me if I had a lover – I still remember it. I was very shocked. I don't think I answered him at all. That much I know. *C'est tout!* [in French]. And then I left.' Freud ordered her to come back, but Adele didn't oblige. Aunt Lore (Eleonore Jeiteles) was 'terribly angry' with her and wanted to know why she refused to return to Dr Freud: 'I told her I thought it was pointless . . . The whole thing, this whole business was very unpleasant to me.'

Adele Jeiteles,
undated.

Later in life, Adele was to change her mind about psycho-analysis. She had moved to Budapest, where she married Heiman Kösztler (a name her son Arthur changed to 'Koestler' one day when he was using a typewriter that lacked an umlaut). Budapest had no Freud, but it did have his disciple Sándor Ferenczi, who caused a sensation among the ladies. He had a 'very poor repu-tation', but 'there was a sect there that was called the "Jewesses of Leopoldstadt" [the Jewish quarter of Vienna]. Very rich women, who had run through all the sensations.' They all went to be treated by Ferenczi (even Adele's hairdresser) and came back delighted, 'with whole novels' to relate.

Not to be outdone, Adele started to read Freud. Then she met a young woman who was undergoing analysis in Vienna. This woman was in love with a man her age, but her parents would not hear of marriage and sent her to seek treatment from a psycho-analyst in Freud's circle. 'She went there very often and the result was that she committed suicide.' Paradoxically, this fatal outcome finally convinced Adele of the power of psychoanalysis: 'And then I said to myself, somewhere there must be something about this subconscious for it to tell her so many things that led her to commit suicide, don't you think? . . . So, I was really converted to Freudianism from that point on.'

Adele's son, Arthur, also crossed paths with Freud. He visited the psychoanalyst in London in the autumn of 1938 and obtained from him 'A Word on Antisemitism' – in fact Freud was quoting an unknown author – which he published in Die Zukunft, a news-paper for German immigrants that he edited in Paris. We do not know if Koestler mentioned his mother to Freud, but it is doubt-ful. According to his biographer Michael Scammell, Koestler's relations with her were execrable and, 'under Freud's influence' and his theories, 'he blame[d] his mother for his later miseries.' However, he kept among his papers a copy of the interview she had given Kurt Eissler in London in 1953. When Michael Scammell found this text and asked Eissler for permission to quote passages from it, the latter threatened to sue him. Fortunately, Scammell ignored him.

11

ILONA WEISS

(1867–1944)

I n *Studies on Hysteria*, Freud gave her a nobiliary particle – 'Elisabeth von R.' – but her name was actually Helene (Ilona) Weiss. She came from a wealthy Jewish family in Budapest, where she spent her childhood on a large estate before moving to Vienna with her parents in 1886. Her father, Max Weiss, settled there as an investor after a long period managing the wholesale business Gersen Spitzer & Co., which he had inherited from his own father, Moritz Weiss. He had married Emma Schlesinger, a remarkable woman whom Ilona greatly admired. (Emma's sister was also the grandmother of the philosopher – and fierce critic of psychoanalysis – Karl Popper, which makes Ilona Weiss his first cousin once removed.) However, Ilona's daughter Paula Gross, in a memorandum written in 1953 for the Freud Archives, described her grandmother Emma as 'nervous', like other members of the Schlesinger family.

Freud was called to Ilona Weiss's bedside in the autumn of 1892 to examine her for leg pains that were making it difficult for her to walk. It was 'a doctor I knew' – presumably Breuer – who had asked him to come, as he suspected hysteria, 'though there was no trace of the usual indications of that neurosis'. Freud determined that there was rheumatic infiltration of the muscles, but that the pain caused was being exaggerated by the patient in a characteristically hysterical way. He therefore decided to go in search of the 'secret' hidden behind this symptom, without, however, systematically using hypnosis as he had done hitherto. Inspired by a technique he had learned from Bernheim in 1889, he asked the patient lying in front of him to tell him 'what was known to her', then insisted by pressing her on the forehead when a link in the story seemed to be missing or she 'resisted' the demand to summon up the memory. Ilona spontaneously fell into a quasi-hypnotic state when a memory affected her more particularly. This was, wrote Freud, 'the first full-length analysis [Analyse] of a hysteria undertaken by me.'

The Weiss family had endured many trials over the previous years. Since 1891 Ilona's mother had suffered from an eye condition and other probably nervous troubles that required constant attention. Her father, whom Ilona loved very much, died in January 1888 of a heart disease that had kept him bedridden for more than a year. Two years before, her older sister Vilma had married Edmund (Edmondo) Richetti von Terralba, a bright and ambitious man who showed little regard for his in-laws. Richetti worked for the insurance company Generali and in 1890 he moved with Vilma and their three children to Trieste, far from Vienna, to pursue a brilliant career as an insurer (and a less successful one as an automobile manufacturer: the Alba Fabbrica Automobile S.A. that he co-founded in 1906 with another prominent Triestine went bankrupt two years later).

Ilona's other sister, Josefine, married in 1889 a young textile industrialist much more to the liking of Ilona and her mother: Richard Schüller, with whom she had a child, Marianne, the following year. It was at this time that Ilona's pains and mobility difficulties appeared, which made her 'the invalid of the family' (Freud). Then, in June 1891, while she was undergoing treatment in Gastein with her mother, her sister Josefine died of heart disease aggravated by a second pregnancy. Arguments over money arose between the two brothers-in-law, leading Josefine's husband to distance himself from the family, taking with him the little Marianne, to whom Ilona had become particularly attached. There she was, trapped at home, lonely, an invalid with an invalid mother, without a suitor and without any prospects for the future. There were plenty of reasons for her to take refuge in disease.

Freud came every day to the Weiss home to 'extract' Ilona's traumatic memories, but he still could not find the key to her pains. One day he observed how her pains had intensified during a visit from Josefine's husband. This explained everything: Ilona was in love with her brother-in-law, and had been so right from the start. Ilona could not consciously admit this love for the husband of her dear sister and she had therefore punished herself by inflicting these pains on herself, from which she derived a hidden pleasure. When Freud communicated this deduction to Ilona, 'the recovery of this repressed idea had a shattering effect on the poor girl.' In July 1893, with the holidays approaching, Freud ended the treatment, considering the patient cured. Breuer (if he was indeed the colleague in question) confirmed this impression. 'In the spring of 1894,' concluded Freud, 'I heard that she was going to a private ball for which I was able to get an invitation, and I did not allow the opportunity to escape me of seeing my former patient whirl past in a lively dance.' In Vienna, even neuroses end in a waltz.

In July 1894 Ilona Weiss became engaged to Heinrich Gross, a partner in the paternal transport company Alois Gross in Vienna. Their marriage, which took place in early 1895, was to be very happy. Ilona and Heinrich had three daughters. According to the memorandum of the youngest, Paula Gross, they were made for each other, even if Heinrich was not as wealthy as his wife. Ilona loved her husband and was totally devoted to him. However, she was not easy-going: she was touchy, jealous, stubborn (Freud had already mentioned this trait in her case history), demanding, bad-tempered and prone to mood swings.

Waltzes or not, she still suffered from the same ailments: 'My mother was forty when I was born, and I cannot remember any time when she was not in some way "ailing". She underwent countless treatments of all sorts, took the baths at various spas, was often in severe pain, but none the less really very active and fond of walking. I am not sure exactly what her illnesses consisted of. Certainly they included rheumatism and sciatica, perhaps neuritis, etc., mainly affecting her legs, but also other parts of her body.' One of her doctors viewed her as a hypochondriac, but her daughter qualified this: 'She did use her illness to gain attention; yet she undoubtedly did suffer a great deal of pain.'

Ilona had read Freud's case study of her – closely enough to be able to quote the last sentence from memory, many years later – but she never talked to anyone about it. It was only after the death of her husband in 1935 that she laughingly told the story to her daughter. Freud, she said, was 'just a young, bearded nerve specialist they sent me to. He wanted to persuade me that I was in love with my brother-in- law, but that wasn't really so.' Richard

Schüller, the brother-in-law, had died in 1906, but Ilona remained 'on the friendliest terms' with his second wife, Olga Kuffler, and their two daughters, Anna and Eleonore, as well as with her niece Marianne.

Unlike her three daughters, Ilona Weiss did not emigrate to the United States after the Anschluss. She stayed in Vienna and somehow was spared deportation. According to her daughter Paula, she died in 1944, 'presumably of a cerebral haemorrhage', at the age of 77.

12

AURELIA KRONICH

(1875–1929)

T he story of Aurelia Kronich takes us as far as possible from
the waltzes and neuroses of Vienna: more than 1,700 metres
above sea level, in a rustic mountain refuge perched on the
Rax, one of the highest mountains in the eastern Alps. Here we
begin with Freud's account in *Studies on Hysteria* (1895).

During the holiday of 189*, having started to climb up an
alpine mountain, Freud stopped to rest in the 'well-run refuge-hut'
near the summit. (We have to imagine him there, in the Tyrolean
costume he loved, wearing the traditional feathered hat and armed
with his faithful alpenstock.) As he contemplated the magnificent
view spread out before him, he was approached by the niece of the
shelter's owner, an eighteen-year-old girl by the name of Katharina.
Sensing that this elegant mountaineer was a doctor from the big
city, she wanted to consult him about her nerves. In her disarming
local dialect, she told him that for two years she had been suffering from bouts of anxiety, accompanied by feelings of suffocation,
buzzing and dizziness, as well as the vision of a terrifying face and
the fear that someone was about to grab her from behind.

Freud immediately realized that this was a case of 'virginal anxiety', a concept he had formulated just two months earlier in a letter
to Fliess (30 May 1893): this kind of anxiety was due to 'the horror
by which a virginal mind is overcome when it is faced for the first
time with the world of sexuality.' Armed with this diagnosis, he
therefore suggested to Katharina that two years earlier she must
have seen or heard something that had bothered her. Katharina
readily confirmed as much: at that time, when she was in another
refuge run by her aunt on the mountain opposite, she had caught
her uncle in bed with her cousin, Franziska. It was here that she

had suffered her first bout of anxiety, without understanding why: 'A was only six'een.' Three days later, she had fallen prey to the same anxiety and was obliged to stay in bed. As her aunt tried to find out why, she told her what she had discovered, and the scandal was brought into the open. After some painful scenes, the aunt left with her children and Katharina and took over the management of the current refuge, leaving behind her husband and Franziska, who had meanwhile become pregnant by him.

Then Katharina spontaneously mentioned another incident that had occurred two or three years earlier than the first – in other words, when she was only thirteen or fourteen. This time, it was she herself who had suffered her uncle's advances, which she had vigorously repelled. But on this occasion, too, she had not grasped what was happening: 'It had become clear to her much later on.' For Freud, the matter was perfectly obvious: the young girl's anxiety had arisen during the second incident, which made her understand retrospectively, as she had reached puberty, the sexual significance of the first incident, thereby arousing an immediate disgust. (Here we have the first appearance of the notion of 'deferred' trauma, which soon became central to Freud when he was developing his so-called 'seduction theory'.) After having related this story, Katharina seemed transformed. Her expression was no longer sullen, 'she was lightened and exalted.' His mission accomplished, the doctor-mountaineer could therefore descend into the valley, at the end of what was undoubtedly the shortest therapy session in the history of psychoanalysis.

In 1924 Freud added a note to his charming case study in which he revealed that Katharina was not the niece, but the daughter of the innkeeper. This conveniently enabled him to re-read the case in the light of the Oedipal theory he had developed in the meantime: 'The girl fell ill, therefore, as a result of sexual temptations [Versuchungen] that originated in her own father.' In other words, the paternal advances had awakened in her desires for incest that had to be repressed. (We can recognize in passing the classic reinterpretation of the 'seduction theory' in terms of Oedipal fantasies, except that Freud here continues to maintain that the paternal attack really happened.)

Thanks to the meticulous research of Freudian sleuth Peter J. Swales, we now know that Freud's alert narrative is only half-accurate. With the help of historians Gerhard Fichtner, Albrecht Hirschmüller and Henri Ellenberger, Swales was able to identify the real Katharina and reconstruct her story in detail. Her name was Aurelia Kronich and she was born on 9 January 1875. Her parents, Julius and Gertrude Kronich, lived in Vienna, and it was not until 1884–5, when Aurelia was ten years old, that they took over the management of the Baumgartnerhaus, a hotel-refuge popular with Viennese tourists on the Schneeberg opposite the Rax mountain. So Aurelia was far from being the somewhat simple-minded mountain girl portrayed by Freud. It is also very likely that Freud already knew her, since he spent all his summer holidays in Reichenau, in the valley, and regularly climbed the two neighbouring mountains. This would also explain how Aurelia knew he was a doctor.

As for the incident that triggered Aurelia's anxieties, it did actually take place as Freud reports. The case was well known in the family and in the neighbourhood: Aurelia had caught Julius Kronich in bed with her 25-year-old cousin, Barbara Göschl; this had caused a huge scandal and the breakup of the Kronich family. Publicly humiliated, Gertrude Kronich had moved with her children and taken over the management of the brand new Erzherzog Otto-Schutzhaus (Archduke Otto refuge) on the Rax, on the other side of the valley. Julius, meanwhile, had stayed in the Schneeberg refuge-hotel and settled there with his niece, with whom he was to have four children.

It is essentially at the level of chronology that Freud's story deviates from reality. We can date with precision the moment when Freud stopped at the Archduke Otto refuge and listened to the confidences of Aurelia Kronich: it was at the beginning of August 1893. However, the scandal that had brought Aurelia to the Rax had not occurred two years earlier, as Freud writes. It was very recent – barely nine months before, according to Swales's reconstruction. It is therefore understandable that Aurelia, through whom the scandal had come about, and whom her father had threatened several times during some violent scenes, would suffer attacks of anxiety. No need in this regard to refer to an improbable virginal terror at the traumatic discovery of sexuality, since Aurelia was around eighteen years old at the time. Besides, her repression does not seem to have been particularly intense, judging by the ease

Greetings from the Archduke Otto refuge, c. 1900.

with which she entrusted the doctor with this very open secret, of which everyone in the region – quite possibly including Freud himself – was aware.

As for Julius Kronich's incestuous advances, it should be noted that Aurelia's daughter and granddaughter, interviewed in Montreal by Henri Ellenberger, had never heard of them and had great difficulty believing them. According to them, Aurelia was not inclined to secrecy and would have inevitably told such a story to her children, especially since she was barely in touch with her father and cousin any more. But even supposing that this incident had indeed taken place, as Freud recounts, 'two or three years earlier' than the other trauma, Aurelia would still have been fifteen or sixteen years old – an age when it is unlikely that she could have been unaware of the sexual significance of her father's advances. No need here to invoke a delayed traumatic effect and a deferred repression: the anxiety-provoking impact of such an incestuous attack would inevitably have been very direct.

One cannot help but think that the freedoms taken by Freud with chronology are explained above all by his desire to fit the Kronich case into the pre-established framework of his new theory on virginal anxiety and the deferred repercussions of the trauma: 'In every analysis of a case of hysteria based on sexual traumas we find that impressions from the pre-sexual period which produced no effect on the child attain traumatic power at a later date as memories, when the girl or the married woman has acquired an understanding of sexual life.' But in reality, Aurelia Kronich's anxiety attacks were nothing but a fairly normal response to upsetting events that she did not in the least repress from her consciousness and whose meaning she must have necessarily perceived right from the start.

Did Aurelia Kronich really belong in a volume on hysteria? One or two years after her alpine analysis, she fell in love with Julius Öhm, a 27-year-old Silesian who administered the forests of Count Philipp Hoyos Wenkheim on the Rax. The marriage took place in the church at Peyerbach on 26 September 1895, after which the couple moved to Hungary, near the Romanian border, where the count owned other estates. Aurelia and Julius had six children (as well as several miscarriages and stillbirths). Julius was a good father and husband, and Aurelia loved him dearly. She was happy. Family testimonies describe a person who was lively, cheerful and good-tempered. No signs of 'nervous' disorders, anxiety or asthma – at most some emotional instability during menopause.

However, she felt isolated in Hungary (she never learned to speak Hungarian) and returned every summer to spend a few weeks in the Archduke Otto refuge, which had been taken over by her brother Camillo and gradually transformed into a luxury hotel. In 1926 a funicular railway was opened between the valley and the Rax plateau, which allowed Freud to return to the place of his former sporting and psychoanalytical exploits. Gisela, one of Aurelia's daughters, remembers seeing the famous doctor walking slowly, with the aid of a cane, down the path leading from the refuge to the valley.

In 1929, during her annual stay at the family refuge, Aurelia Öhm suddenly felt ill. She had pains all over her body and her complexion turned green. Instead of immediately sending her to the hospital in the valley, her husband telephoned a doctor to come up to the refuge. When he arrived the next day, Aurelia's condition was critical. The doctor injected her with a large dose of morphine to relieve her pain, which finished her off. The death certificate indicates that she died on 3 September 1929, of a cardiac arrest. She was 54 years old. She is buried next to her mother, Gertrude, in the Reichenau cemetery.

13

EMMA ECKSTEIN

(1865–1924)

Emma Eckstein,
c. 1890–95.

E
mma Eckstein came from a prominent family in the Viennese Jewish bourgeoisie. Albert Eckstein, her father, had invented a process for making parchment and owned a successful paper factory. Like the Federn and Meyreder families, to which they were close, the Ecksteins were resolutely progressive. Albert Eckstein's circle of friends included the social reformer Josef Popper-Lynkeus, the positivist physicist Ernst Mach and the Darwinian zoologist Carl Brühl. Several of Emma's brothers, notably the Marxist journalist and theorist Gustav Eckstein, were active members of the Austrian Social Democratic Party. Her sister Therese Schlesinger-Eckstein was a member of the General Association of Austrian Women and was to be one of the very first women to enter the Austrian Parliament in 1918. Emma was friends with the son of Karl Kautsky, a socialist leader. She was also closely involved in the Austrian feminist movement led by her friends Rosa Meyreder, Auguste Fickert and Marie Lang, with whom she maintained a regular correspondence which attests to her political and social concerns. She also published several articles in their review *Dokumente der Frauen* (Women's Documents), notably an essay on 'The Maidservant as a Mother' in which she protested against the sexual exploitation of young domestic workers by the gentlemen of families.

Emma Eckstein was said to have been very pretty. She had also always been neurotic, without anyone knowing exactly what she was suffering from. It seems that she had gastric troubles and

dysmenorrhoea (painful periods). It is not surprising that she
ended up consulting Freud: the Ecksteins were linked to the Freuds,
with whom they often spent their holidays, and Friedrich (Fritz)
Eckstein, Emma's brother, was part of Sigmund's inner circle
(they met on Saturday evenings at Leopold Königstein's to play
the card game Tarok with Hermann Teleky, Oskar Rie and Ludwig
Rosenberg). Her treatment began in 1892 and continued until at
least the beginning of 1897. Freud did not ask for payment – he
considered it a favour to friends, as might be expected. He came
to see Emma in the family home, where she lived with her mother,
but of course everyone in the family knew that this was not just
a friendly visit. Her favourite niece, Ada Elias (née Hirsch),
recounts how Freud paid his coach driver to take the children out
for a ride while he himself looked after Aunt Emma (the sessions
most likely led to the irruption of noisy 'cathartic' relivings of
traumatic scenes).

Freud was later to tell Albert Hirst (Hirsch), Ada's brother,
that he considered all Ecksteins to be neurotic because their father
had suffered from neurosyphilis (he died of locomotor ataxia, the
final stage of untreated syphilis). This conviction regarding the
hereditary cause of illness, which he was also to express in his
article on 'Dora', did not prevent Freud from advancing several
other aetiologies during the treatment, depending on his theories
of the moment. He thus seems to have established a link between
Emma's dysmenorrhoea and masturbation, a practice that he
more generally saw as the cause of neurasthenia. He shared these
views with his friend Wilhelm Fliess, who had developed a theory
of 'reflex nasal neurosis' that appeared to apply eminently to
Emma's malady. Fliess, an ear, nose and throat specialist from
Berlin, postulated a special relationship between the nose and the
female genital tract, and he prided himself on making dysmenorrhoea (among other symptoms) disappear thanks to the application
of cocaine to the nasal mucosa or, in the most reluctant cases, by
resorting to an operation on the nose cones (turbinate bones).
Freud was, at the time, a fervent follower of his friend's 'nasal
therapy' and he readily prescribed cocaine to his patients, both
male and female, for all kinds of psychosomatic and neurasthenic
symptoms. In the case of Emma Eckstein he seems to have decided
that a more energetic treatment was necessary, because at the end

of 1894 he asked Fliess to come specially from Berlin to operate on his patient's turbinates (as well as his own).

The rest of the story has been known in part since Max Schur, Freud's doctor, lifted the veil of silence that had weighed on this episode in an article published in 1966. The operation took place on 20 or 21 February 1895, after which Fliess returned to Berlin. On 3 March Freud published an account of a work by the neurologist Paul Julius Moebius in which he mentioned the 'surprising therapeutic effects' obtained by the 'daring technique' of Dr Fliess from Berlin. The reality was very different. Two weeks after the operation, Emma's nose was sore and had purulent secretions that gave off a foul odour. By 2 March a piece of bone the size of a small coin had broken loose, causing massive bleeding. A second haemorrhage occurred two days later, and Freud hastily called upon his ENT friend Ignaz Rosanes. While cleaning the wound, Rosanes noticed a piece of thread in the nose and pulled it out, suddenly extracting half a metre of stinking gauze that Fliess had left there during the operation. 'A flood of blood' poured out: Freud felt ill and had to leave the room hurriedly before fainting, much to the amazement of the Eckstein family. When he returned to the room after having knocked back a glass of cognac, Emma greeted him bluntly with the words 'So this is the strong sex!'

Emma hovered for several weeks between life and death, and Freud at one stage even gave her up for 'lost'. Fliess's operation left her disfigured for life, with a recess in the spot where the nose bone had been broken. However, neither Emma nor her family seem to have borne a grudge against either Freud or Fliess, whose reputation as a miracle worker remained intact in Vienna. Breuer sent him several female patients, including his own daughter Dora. In August Freud brought his brother Alexander to Berlin so that Fliess could operate on him for neurasthenia (Freud took the opportunity to have the operation himself for the second time). As for Emma, she continued her analysis with Freud as if nothing had happened.

This was the time when Freud was starting to track down in the unconscious of his patients the sexual traumas supposedly at the origin of their hysterical and obsessional symptoms. Emma reappears in this regard in the *Project for a Scientific Psychology*, written by Freud in the autumn of 1895. She was afraid to enter shops alone, explains Freud, because she had been fondled sexually by a shopkeeper when she was eight years old. This 'scene' had no effect until she understood its meaning at puberty, during a second incident in which salesmen made fun of her in a shop, suddenly causing a pathological repression of the initial incident. Emma thus illustrated the mechanism of delayed or 'deferred' action of the trauma postulated by Freud.

Manifestly, Emma Eckstein was one of the patients on whom Freud was testing his new 'seduction theory' (*Verführungstheorie*), a theory which it would be better to call 'the statutory rape theory' (this is the meaning of the word *Verführung* in this context). In an article published in April 1896, Freud affirmed that hysteria was due to sexual abuse perpetrated on the child by an adult, 'unhappily all too often, [by] a close relative', and that he had been able to confirm this aetiology on the eighteen cases at his disposal. As we know from a letter to Fliess of 27 September 1897, Freud quickly came to the conclusion that 'in all cases', it was the father who was guilty of these perverse acts. Had he obtained from Emma 'scenes' of incestuous fondling by the respectable Albert Eckstein? (Albert Hirst, Emma's nephew and Albert's grandson, asked him one day what kind of 'trauma' his aunt suffered from, but Freud refused to answer.)

What is certain is that in January 1897 Emma remembered a satanic scene. Intrigued by the resemblance between the memories of perverse abuse related by his women patients and the confessions of sexual intercourse with the Devil obtained under torture by the Inquisitors, Freud had indeed put to Fliess the hypothesis 'of a primeval devil religion whose rite is still carried on secretly'. Emma confirmed this: 'Eckstein has a scene where the diabolus sticks needles into her fingers and then places a candy on each drop of blood. As far as blood is concerned, you are completely without blame!' A week later, another confirmation, another exoneration of Fliess: 'Imagine, I obtained a scene about the circumcision of a girl. The cutting off of a piece of the labium minor (which is even shorter today), sucking up the blood, after which the child was given a piece of the skin to eat . . . An operation you once performed was affected by a haemophilia that originated in this way.' The bleeding from which Emma had almost died two years earlier was therefore not due to Fliess's professional misconduct, but to a hysterical haemophilia caused by perverse acts within the Eckstein family.

Emma, who had always been more than just a patient, had now become a collaborator and a student. Freud sent her at least one female patient, perhaps several. Emma Eckstein was therefore the first psychoanalyst trained by Freud. In December 1897 she found in her nineteen-year-old patient scenes of 'seduction' by the father that were identical to those obtained by her analyst. As a result, Freud regained confidence in his 'paternal aetiology', which he had abandoned three months earlier (Emma had probably not been made aware of the doubts that he had confided to Fliess).

Everyone agreed that Freud's treatment of Emma had been successful. According to Hirst, 'it was important to him in his practice that he had this great success, this well-known girl, this girl of a well-known family. Now she was a very beautiful woman and after he had this great success, she for several years led a perfectly normal life.' In October 1900 Emma published a glowing review of *The Interpretation of Dreams* in the *Arbeiter-Zeitung*, Victor Adler's socialist newspaper. While wondering whether all dreams really were fulfilments of desire, as Freud claimed, she welcomed the 'ingenious arguments' of a book that 'pioneers the exploration of regions of the psychic life which until now were hidden from our eyes' and aroused hopes for 'a significant contribution to the solution of psychical problems'.

Four years later, Emma Eckstein published a small book, *The Question of the Sexual Education of Children*, in which she warned against the dangers of masturbation, an 'insidious enemy of the child' that 'can have consequences fatal for the mental develop-ment of the individual'. It is not difficult to see in these statements an echo of the diagnosis of her own case made by Freud and Fliess. Taking up ideas put forward by Freud around the same time, she also stressed the link between infantile masturbation and fanta-sizing. Freud, as we know from his correspondence with her, had advised and encouraged her throughout the writing of the book and had even written a favourable review, which had been rejected by the *Neue Freie Presse*. In 1909 Emma brought out another article on 'The Sexual Question in the Education of Children' in a col-lected volume entitled *At the Source of Life: A Home Book for Sex Education*.

It appears from a letter Freud wrote on 30 November 1905 that Emma had again been in analysis with him some time previously, because it mentions an 'interruption' of treatment due to friction between them. Emma had apparently been offended by a remark by Freud about her transference onto him (or the transference he imputed to her), which had 'inspired him again', he says, with 'respect for the elemental femaleness with which I have to constantly fight'. It is not known how Emma the feminist responded to this remark.

In his letter Freud also questioned whether Emma's 'pains' were 'organic'. This is probably an allusion to a sequence of events described by Emma's niece, the paediatrician Ada Elias, in a long interview with Kurt Eissler in 1953. At about the same time (Elias could not be any more specific), it had been determined that Emma's excessive menstruation and dysmenorrhoea were due to a benign uterine tumour or myoma (another of Eissler's informants, Ludwig Teleky, spoke of cervical cancer). Following a myomectomy performed by the gynaecologist and obstetrician Josef von Halban, Emma's symptoms had disappeared, which tended to demonstrate their organic rather than, as Freud had supposed, their hysterical character.

However, the pain had reappeared two or three years later, due to adhesions, according to Elias. Emma had insisted on Halban again performing the operation, against the advice of Freud, who considered that the pain was a return to her former hysterical symptoms. This second operation was a total fiasco. In Elias's account, Emma 'got heavy bleeding again, she was given a lot of saline IV infusions, from one she got a severe phlegmon [acute inflammation] on her thigh and was seriously ill for weeks. And from that time on she couldn't walk. As she said, she could no longer walk because of the contracture of the scar, which was on the outside of the thigh' (Emma was probably referring to muscle adhesions following the scarring-over of the phlegmon). Around 1910 Emma attempted suicide by taking an overdose of sleeping pills, and resumed treatment with Freud (if she had ever stopped). According to her nephew Albert Hirst, she had long been in love with a certain Viennese architect (perhaps Karl Meyreder, the husband of her friend Rosa Meyreder?) and she had finally realized that her love was impossible – hence her collapse. The analysis revolved

around Emma's difficulties in walking. Unlike Freud, Emma continued to maintain that they were organic in origin. Still, according to
Hirst, 'there was a conflict between him and her. She claimed that
her then troubles were physical and not neurotic, and he insisted
that they were neurotic . . . And I remember once when she told
me that I had no idea how vain Freud is, and it is just this vanity
on his part that colours his judgment and makes him think that
she is neurotic.'

One day when her friend the gynaecologist Dora Teleky came
to visit Emma, she remarked that Emma had an 'abscess' on the
aforementioned scar and decided to make an incision. As the whole
family knew, this was actually a sham operation (*Scheinoperation*, as
Ada Elias called it), that is to say, a pretend operation from which
a beneficial placebo effect was hoped for. And indeed, Emma was
able to walk better for a few days (but not much longer), which had
the effect of confirming her rejection of Freud's diagnosis.

Dora Teleky, a member of another prominent Jewish family in
Vienna and very closely involved in the feminist movement, was
no stranger to Freud. She was the daughter of Hermann Teleky, one
of his good friends and Tarok partners, and like her brother Ludwig
she was among the very first to hear him lecture at the university.
She was also married to the son of his revered master, Ernst
Wilhelm von Brücke. Freud was nonetheless furious that she had
interfered in Emma's treatment. In his unauthorized biography of
Freud, Emil Ludwig relates the remarks of Dora Teleky von Brücke:
'I made a new incision and at one stroke freed the patient of her
pains. When I later told this to the master at his home, he blew up.
With biting scorn he asked whether I actually believed that hysterical pain could be cured by the knife. Quaking, I objected that
an obvious abscess must be treated. Despite the fact that the patient
was cured of all complaints, Dr. Freud became so unfriendly to me
that I was obliged to break the discussion and leave him.'

Freud was also furious with Emma. When Hirst, who was
being analysed by Freud at the same time as his aunt, told him
the following day how the pseudo-operation had turned out, he
exploded: 'I remember how indignant Freud was about Dr Teleky
for this interference, and he immediately stopped the analysis [of
Emma Eckstein] and said: "Well, that's the end of Emma. That
dooms her from now on, nobody can cure her of her neurosis."'

Freud's curse came true. Dismissed from the psychoanalytic couch, Emma Eckstein returned to her bedroom couch, to which she remained permanently confined. She died on 30 July 1924 of a cerebral haemorrhage.

14

OLGA HÖNIG

(1877–1961)

B orn on 2 October 1877 in Vienna, Olga Hönig was the sixth child in a family of seven. Her childhood was marked by a series of tragedies. Her father died when she was very young, two of her brothers shot themselves, and her younger sister, who had suffered from infantile paralysis, attempted suicide. Two of her sisters became actresses, while a third, Marie Valerie, had a career as a pianist.

Olga Hönig arrived in Freud's consulting room in May 1897, apparently sent by Breuer. She was nineteen, and suffered, according to a letter from Freud to Fliess of 7 June, from 'almost pure obsessional ideas'. Freud considered at the time that obsessional neurosis was due to sexual abuse perpetrated on the child after the age of four – unlike hysteria, which, according to him, was caused by an earlier 'seduction', usually by the father. The Hönig case provided him with magnificent confirmation of this: 'According to my speculations, obsessional ideas go back to a later psychic age and therefore do not necessarily point to the father, who tends to be more careful with the child the older the child is, but rather point to the slightly older siblings for whom the child is yet to become a little woman. Now in this case the Almighty was kind enough to let the father die before the child was eleven months old, but two brothers, one of them three years older than the patient, shot themselves.'

In short: Olga Hönig fell prey to an obsessional neurosis because she had been sexually abused by her two brothers. When Olga told this story to her mother, the latter was horrified and flatly refused to continue paying for her daughter's analysis. According to the later testimony of the man who would become her husband, Max Graf, 'this young lady [Olga] went to Freud and said, "Professor Freud, unfortunately I can no longer continue the treatment, I no longer have the money for it," and told him the story. And Freud said to her: "So, because you are a poor girl, you cannot make up your mind to continue treatment?" She accepted that, you see – he treated her without any fee. He told me later, occasionally, that he treated one patient for free every week. That is the kind of charity he can practise and that he practises habitually.'

At the same time, Olga Hönig met a young man four years older than she was. Max Graf had just taken his doctorate in law in 1896, but he was moving towards a career as a musicologist and music critic. He was a brilliant and versatile man who was interested in politics as well as science and literature. He regularly attended meetings of the literary group *Jung-Wien* and had already published two books by the age of 25. He was quickly won over by Olga. As he later told Kurt Eissler, who interviewed him in 1952 for the Freud Archives, he found her 'very interesting, very bright, and very beautiful. No doubt, she was a hysteric, something I was not at all able as a young man to judge. In her moments of hysteria – it surely was hysteria – she was for me also attractive and interesting.'

During the walks they took together every evening, Olga told Max in detail about the progress of her analysis. Max was fascinated. Finally, he went to see Freud to ask if Olga's mental state allowed him to marry her. Freud, who also found Olga very 'pretty', strongly encouraged him: 'Just marry her, you'll have your fun!' Having received Freud's blessing, Olga and Max married on 20 December 1898, a year and a half after the start of the analysis. She was 21, he was 25.

Max Graf and Freud quickly became friends, despite their age difference. Graf was interested in psychoanalysis, which he saw as a way of explaining the creative process, and Freud appreciated the company of this young writer who was a familiar figure in Viennese intellectual and artistic circles. They often saw each other at the *Kaffeehaus* where Freud went in the evenings after work with his sister-in-law Minna Bernays. Freud invited Graf to participate in the small study group that met at his home on Wednesday evenings – the nucleus of what would later become the Vienna Psychoanalytic Society. Here, Graf met Alfred Adler,

Max Graf, c. 1920.

Wilhelm Stekel, Max Kahane and Rudolf Reitler. Freud, for his part, often came to dine informally in Max and Olga's small apartment, in the company of their musician friends. There he met, among others, the composer Eduard Schutt, whose music he very much liked.

It is not known if Olga was still being analysed by him, or until when exactly. What we do know is that the 'fun' promised by Freud was missing: 'I didn't really have fun,' Graf commented bitterly later. From the start, the marriage was unhappy. Olga was unsociable – she quarrelled with everyone – and never wanted to leave her home, which was a problem for her husband and his social ambitions. She was jealous of Max's intellectual activities, going so far as to tear up the manuscripts of some of his articles. Things were not exactly going well in bed, either, and Olga regularly made scenes or fell into a depression the next day. After a year of this ordeal, Graf went to complain to Freud: '"Herr Professor, this marriage isn't working." He was very surprised, and I made another effort. I thought, maybe children will change the situation, but that didn't happen. Still, I lasted eighteen and a half years in this marriage, until the children were old enough for me to leave with an easy conscience.'

The Professor could not be wrong. Thus was born, on 10 April 1903, little Herbert Graf, better known in psychoanalytic literature as 'Little Hans'. The Grafs had first tried for a baby immediately after Freud's intervention, but Olga had a molar pregnancy (a shapeless embryo consisting of a simple skin bag). Herbert was followed, on 4 October 1906, by a little girl named Hanna. According to Max Graf's later testimony, Olga was 'self-centred' and hardly cared for Herbert, though did not completely neglect him. In Hanna's case, however, there was a total rejection. She pushed the child away when she was presented to her at birth and, according to Max Graf, harboured feelings of jealousy towards her. Much later, when Olga was 82, Herbert Graf reported to Eissler that she had always resented Freud for encouraging the couple to have children: 'My mother still has complaints, saying that Freud was not good in her life, and advising father to have children, and so forth, etc. It more or less broke up, ultimately, the marriage.'

The couple must have thought that Freud's treatment had been incomplete, because Max Graf re-analysed his wife some time after analysing his son (1908). Shortly after, an epic theoretical conflict between Freud and Alfred Adler broke out, which led to Adler's walking out of the Vienna Psychoanalytic Society to found his own Society for Free Psychoanalytic Research. The Graf couple were friends of Adler's and, on this occasion, Olga clearly took Adler's side against Freud. Herbert Graf still remembered this in 1959: 'My mother had later a very great friendship with Alfred Adler. She didn't like Professor Freud because of what she felt was not good advice to my father. But she was a great personal friend of Alfred Adler.' Questioned the following year by Kurt Eissler, Liselotte Graf (née Austerlitz), Herbert's wife, confirmed: 'My mother [in-law] had broken with Freud, and then she went to Adler. And whenever you see her, she still talks about Freud and Adler.' Kurt Eissler: 'But against Freud?' 'Against Freud!'

Max Graf, who did not like conflicts, tried for some time to reconcile Adler and Freud, but when the latter bluntly asked him to choose sides, Graf left the Vienna Psychoanalytic Society, albeit without joining Adler. He was to explain later that he did not want to take sides in 'these scholastic disputes that reminded [him] of the council debates of early Christianity', but it is also quite possible that he could not take sides without destroying his marriage. The marriage therefore continued to struggle along until the children were old enough for a divorce to be envisaged. This was made final on 30 September 1920. Less than a month later, on 20 October, Olga remarried; her new husband was Franz-Josef Brychta.

Her personality does not seem to have changed fundamentally, however. As late as 1960, Olga's daughter-in-law was telling Kurt Eissler that 'Herbert's mother's nerves are not so good and never were.' Herbert, 'Little Hans', agreed: his mother, he said, 'is very nervous and always was a very nervous person, and I am quite sure that . . . analysis probably could have resulted in some damage'. When Kurt Eissler asked him, 'You think it has helped her?', Herbert Graf repeated firmly: 'No! It didn't help my mother at all!'

As for Olga herself, she flatly refused to allow herself to be interviewed by Eissler when he asked her in 1953. It was all too painful, she wrote to him in a slightly inconsistent letter: 'It doesn't work, the Freud thing.' She did not want to talk about it or testify in writing, lest it prevent her from sleeping. 'Freud wreaked havoc with us.' And sleep is one of the great blessings of existence, she added.

15

WILHELM VON GRIENDL
(1861–1898)

I n the opening chapter of *The Psychopathology of Everyday Life*, Freud tells us how, while holidaying in Dalmatia (today southern Croatia) in the early days of September 1898, he had undertaken a short day-trip in a hired horse and carriage to visit the town of Trebinje in neighbouring Bosnia-Herzegovina: 'I was driving in the company of a stranger from Ragusa in Dalmatia to a place in Herzegovina; our conversation turned to the subject of travel in Italy, and I asked my companion whether he had ever been to Orvieto and looked at the famous frescoes there, painted by . . .' By whom? Suddenly, Freud found himself unable to remember the name of the artist: 'Instead of the name I was looking for – *Signorelli* – the names of two other painters – *Botticelli* and *Boltraffio* – thrust themselves on me, though they were immediately and decisively rejected by my judgement as incorrect.'

Attempting to make psychoanalytic sense of this transient memory lapse, Freud then explains that the name of Signorelli had been swallowed up by the repression of thoughts regarding 'death and sexuality' that the immediately preceding conversation had evoked. This conversation concerned the customs of the Muslims living in Bosnia and Herzegovina, especially their fatalistic attitude towards death: 'Herr, what is there to be said?' was their customary reply to the doctor who gave them the bad news. At that moment, Freud being Freud, he had also thought of their diametrically opposed attitude towards the loss of sexual potency: 'Herr, you must know that if *that* comes to an end, then life is of no value.' But Freud had said nothing about this to his companion, out of a sense of propriety. Sex and death? Freud preferred not to think about this topic anyway, shaken as he still was by 'a piece of news which had reached me a few weeks before while I was making a brief stay at *Trafoï*, a mountain village in South Tyrol where he had stopped on 8 August 1898 at a coaching inn while en route with his sister-in-law Minna Bernays to the Alpine town of Bormio: 'A patient over whom I had taken a great deal of trouble had put an end to his life on account of an incurable sexual disturbance [*Störung*].'

Here then is Freud's elegant, if improbable, reconstruction of the unconscious trains of thought that had led to his forgetting: the name of Luca *Signorelli* had been wiped out of his memory because of its association with *Herr* (*Signor*) and the underlying 'repressed thoughts' about death and sexuality, only to return in a truncated fashion to consciousness in the guise of *Botticelli* and *Boltraffio* by way of *Bosnia* and *Trafoi*. 'Thus the names have been treated in this process like the pictograms in a sentence which had to be converted into a picture-puzzle (or rebus)':

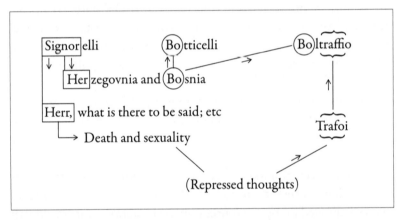

But who was the patient whose suicide Freud learned about in Trafoi? And what were these 'repressed thoughts' that had been so subtly encrypted?

The first question can now be answered thanks to some recent sleuthing done by Freud scholar Christfried Tögel. Knowing that Freud and his sister-in-law had stopped in Trafoi on 8 August 1898, Tögel had the idea of combing through Viennese newspapers to see if a suicide had been reported in the preceding days. And indeed, the *Neue Wiener Tagblatt* of 7 August 1898 featured the announcement of the 'Suicide of a Psychiatrist (Dr Wilhelm V. Griendl)', news that was taken up the next day in the *Neues Wiener*

Journal as well as in Freud's dear *Neue Freie Presse*. (Griendl's death seems to have been noteworthy enough for two German-speaking newspapers in the United States, the *Scranton Wochenblatt* and the *Indiana Tribüne*, to report on it in the following weeks.) Freud may have chanced upon this issue of the *Neue Wiener Tagblatt* at the inn in Trafoi, or he may have learned the news from some fellow-traveller.

Wilhelm Ritter von Griendl came from a prominent family in Graz that had been raised to knighthood in 1783. At the time of his demise, he was head physician and full professor (ordinarius) of psychiatry at the Niederösterreichische Landesirrenanstalt, one of Vienna's main psychiatric hospitals. He seems to have conformed to the stereotype of the mad psychiatrist: 'He suffered from extreme nervousness,' we read in the *Neue Freie Presse*. And in the *Neue Wiener Tagblatt*: 'Dr. v. Griendl had an irritable constitution; he had already been himself in treatment with a nerve doctor for some time, from which he emerged completely cured so that he could resume his medical practice.' This last piece of information clinches the matter: the patient 'over whom [Freud] had taken a great deal of trouble' can evidently be none other than Wilhelm von Griendl.

But 'completely cured' he was not. He seems to have been treating his 'nervousness' with liberal amounts of spirits – usually cognac – which did not do him much good: 'Even small quantities increased his irritation, and in such a mood the doctor caused many a conflict that left him mortified' (*Neue Wiener Tagblatt*). On 2 August 1898 he left the hospital in a hurry and was nowhere to be found for several days. Worried, his colleagues searched his room and found a note in which he declared his intention to end his life. The case in which he kept his revolver was empty. On 6 August his body was retrieved from the Danube. Standing by the river, he had apparently shot himself three times with his revolver and let himself be carried away by the stream.

Freud writes that his patient killed himself on account of an 'incurable sexual disturbance'. What did he mean by that? Homosexual leanings? Some sexual dysfunction? Neurosyphilis (which can indeed cause manic-depressive features consistent with Griendl's behaviour)? We will never know; nor will we know how Griendl's death was linked in Freud's mind to thoughts that he had wilfully

repressed, except that sexuality and the village of Trafoi were somehow implicated in this.

It may or may not be relevant in this regard to note that on
13 August 1898, just five days after Freud and Minna Bernays had
gone through Trafoi, the two registered at an inn in the Swiss town
of Maloja as '*Dr Sigm Freud u Frau* [Dr and Mrs Sigm. Freud]', and
stayed there for two nights in Room 11.

16

BARONESS MARIE VON FERSTEL
(1868–1960)

arie Charlotte Thorsch, born in Prague on 28 February 1868, came from a long line of bankers that still exists today. When her father Eduard died in 1883, the family bank M. Thorsch Söhne was, according to the *Neue Freie Presse*, 'the largest bank in Austria-Hungary'. Like Anna von Lieben and Elise Gomperz, Marie led a life of luxury and culture: music, tennis on the Thorsch family's private court, whist, horse riding, hunting and croquet parties, and social events. In 1889 she married a diplomat, Baron Erwin von Ferstel, son of the famous architect Heinrich Freiherr von Ferstel who had built in Vienna the Votivkirche, the new university and several buildings on the Ringstrasse. Her sister Melanie had married Erwin's brother, Wolfgang von Ferstel.

Marie von Ferstel was also related to the family of Freud's wife because her mother, Anna Thorsch, was the niece of Martha's grandfather. Anna, who had inherited the fortune of her husband Eduard, had financially aided Martha's brother, Eli Bernays, at the time of his bankruptcy and precipitate departure for the United States. The ties between the two families were therefore close. On 27 September 1899, while correcting the proofs of *The Interpretation of Dreams*, Freud announced to his friend Wilhelm Fliess a significant catch: 'The goldfish (Marie von Ferstel, a Thorsch by birth and as such a distant relative of my wife) has been caught, but will still enjoy half her freedom until the end of October because she is remaining in the country.'

The 'goldfish' suffered from various phobias, as well as constipation. According to her grandson the banker Heinrich Treichl, this beautiful woman was afraid of her reflection in the mirror

Marie von Ferstel with her daughter Dorothea, c. 1897–8.

and needed the help of her maid Loni to do her hair. She was also claustrophobic and could not bear to be in a room with a closed door (it had been necessary to add an anteroom to the toilet so that she could withdraw without having to lock herself in). She often made highly unpleasant scenes for her diplomat husband, as when she refused at the last moment to attend a dinner given in honour of Emperor Wilhelm II by the Austrian ambassador to Berlin.

We know practically nothing about Freud's treatment of her. In his memoirs, however, Heinrich Treichl reports that his grandmother said that she had been hypnotized by Freud, which would therefore mean that the latter continued to use this method long after his official abandonment of it in favour of the method of free associations. What is certain is that the 'goldfish' quickly became infatuated with Freud, the 'fisher of men' in the Berggasse. Marie von Ferstel offered him tickets to *Don Giovanni* in Salzburg and invited the Freuds to her home. At Christmas the Freud children would dress formally to go and collect their presents from under the Christmas tree at the von Ferstels' home. In the autumn of 1901 Marie von Ferstel formed an alliance with her friend Elise Gomperz to lay siege to the Minister of Education, Wilhelm Ritter von Hartel, urging him to accelerate Freud's appointment as Professor extraordinarius. According to the account given by

Freud to Fliess and to his biographer Ernest Jones, she obtained from von Hartel the promise 'that he would give a professorship to her doctor, who had cured her', in exchange for a painting by Böcklin, *Eine Burgruine*, which her aunt Ernestine (Tini) Thorsch owned and which Hartel coveted for a new art gallery, the Galerie Moderne. Once the donation had been made, Marie von Ferstel came to her session triumphantly brandishing a telegram from the minister announcing Freud's appointment.

In reality, Freud's appointment owed nothing to any haggling. Once von Hartel had been alerted by Elise Gomperz, and Freud's candidacy was officially relaunched, the bureaucratic process ran its course quite normally. It is true that Baroness Marie von Ferstel sent a painting to the ministry with an accompanying note, but this was a minor work by Emil Orlik (Aunt Tini had no intention of getting rid of her painting by Böcklin, 'especially not for that Dr Freud'). In addition, it appears from the record of the donation that the minister was irritated by the untimely intervention of the baroness and the appearance of a conflict of interests that it created. The cynical explanation given by Freud to explain his appointment was thus groundless.

This was not the only time that the baroness was generous with her therapist. He encouraged her to be so, as Heinrich Treichl recounts: 'One of [Freud's] recommendations for fighting her eternal digestive problems was the following: "You must learn to let go of something! You have to give more money, for example"' (the reader will recognize the famous symbolic equivalence of excrement = money, postulated by Freud). Marie von Ferstel followed this medical recommendation to the letter. According to the historian Renée Gicklhorn, who received her information from a niece of Marie's, the latter transferred to Freud's name the ownership of a villa that she owned in a holiday resort near Vienna. Freud soon sold it.

This was too much for the von Ferstel family; they had been worried for some time about her infatuation with Freud. The baroness was placed under legal guardianship, so that she could no longer pay for her analysis. At the same time, in 1904–5, Freud agreed to Marie von Ferstel's hospitalization at the Schlachtensee psychiatric clinic in Berlin, where her husband had been appointed consul general of Austria-Hungary in 1902. According to Heinrich

Treichl, she never forgave Freud's treachery: 'When the governess, after visiting the institution, established that the doors had no handles inside, they turned back. With that, my grandmother definitely broke up with Freud.' Turning against what she used to hold dear, Marie von Ferstel now told everyone about Freud, calling him a 'charlatan'. According to her grandson, she considered that 'the exclusive fixation on "the sexual" was a mistake.'

Freud had patently not cured her, contrary to what he had written to Fliess, because afterwards she went to Bern to be treated by Paul Dubois, who had developed a 'persuasive' psychotherapy very fashionable at the time. Marie von Ferstel greatly appreciated Dubois and spent a few weeks each year in Bern to continue her treatment with him. His *Self-education* was among her favourite books, along with the *Meditations* of Marcus Aurelius and the *Dietetics of the Soul* by Feuchtersleben.

Surprisingly, Marie von Ferstel got through the Second World War without a hitch. Even though she had been married to an Aryan (Erwin von Ferstel died in 1925), she was of Jewish descent and therefore in great danger of being deported by the Nazis. As she nonetheless refused to emigrate, her son resorted to subterfuge. He got the family's servants to certify that Marie was in reality the fruit of an illegitimate affair between her mother Anna Thorsch and an Aryan, and submitted a request for revision of his mother's parentage. Due to the slowness of Austrian bureaucracy, this procedure protected Marie for almost five years. In 1943 she was finally summoned to the Anthropological Institute in Vienna to have her cephalic index and her cognitive abilities measured, in order to establish whether or not she was of Jewish origin. Her grandson, who accompanied her that day, still remembers the scene: 'The monstrosity of the laws of Nuremberg and the madness of racial doctrine were reduced to a banal procedure carried out with a pair of measuring instruments. A hatter would not have taken his measurements otherwise. But the alternative, in this case, was called Auschwitz.' A few months later, Marie and her descendants were declared *deutschblütig*, a term reserved for people of both Aryan and Jewish origin.

Baroness Marie von Ferstel, née Thorsch, died on 20 February 1960. At the age of nearly 92, she still could not do her own hair.

17

MARGIT KREMZIR
(c. 1870–1900)

Margit Kremzir, née Weiss de Szurda, was the cousin of Ilona Weiss (whose father, Max Weiss, was her paternal uncle). Married to Moriz Kremzir, and the mother of two children, she came to Vienna from Budapest in 1900 to consult various specialists on acute stomach pains. One of these specialists was Sigmund Freud, to whom she had probably been sent to check whether these pains were of a hysterical nature. On 25 April 1900 Freud reported to Fliess: 'The patient whom I treated for fourteen days and then dismissed as a case of paranoia has since hanged herself in a hotel room (Frau Margit Kremzir).' A brief notice in the *Neue Freie Presse* of 20 April 1900 stated: 'This morning, in a local hotel, a lady from Hungary . . . hanged herself

Obituary of Margit Kremzir in the *Neue Freie Presse*.

out of desperation over her hopeless condition.' She was buried on 22 April at 11 a.m. in the Jewish section of the central cemetery in Vienna.

18

IDA BAUER

(1882–1945)

'Dora', the heroine of Freud's famous case history, was actually called Ida Bauer. She was born on 1 November 1882 at 32 Berggasse in Vienna, a few steps away from the building where Freud would receive her in his consulting room eighteen years later. Her father, Filipp Bauer, came from an assimilated Jewish family from Bohemia that had come to settle in Vienna at the end of the 1850s. An astute businessman, he had made a fortune in the textile industry and owned two factories in Bohemia, in what is now the Czech Republic. His wife, Katharina (Käthe) Gerber, also came from a family of textile manufacturers in Bohemia. Having learned after their marriage that Filipp had contracted syphilis in his youth, she had developed an obsession with contamination and a mania for cleaning that made family life particularly burdensome. When her niece Elsa Foges (Friedmann) asked her why she was spoiling her own life – and the lives of others – in this way, Käthe is said to have replied: 'I cannot help it!' Elsa Foges commented, 'She belonged with Freud. Much, much more than Ida!'

Barely older than Ida, her brother Otto was a precocious child who had written a play about Napoleon at the age of nine. He was to become a brilliant Austro-Marxist theorist and one of the main leaders of the Austrian Social Democratic Party during the inter-war period. (According to his friend and biographer Otto Leichter, he had been in contact with Freud, and the sage from Berggasse had advised him not to enter politics: 'Don't do it! People don't want happiness . . . and we shouldn't try to make them happy.')

In 1888, when he was 35, Filipp Bauer was diagnosed with tuberculosis. On medical advice, the Bauer family moved to Meran

(Merano), a posh health resort in the Tyrol, to seek cleaner air. The Bauers remained there until 1897, while Karl, a brother of Filipp, managed the firm Bauer & Gerber in his absence. It was there, in 1890, that Ida had her first attack of dyspnoea, a difficulty in breathing of an asthmatic character that would cause her problems until the end of her life. In 1892 Filipp Bauer temporarily lost the use of one eye, a first sign of the advance of his syphilis. Two years later, when the syphilis had reached the tertiary stage, he had an episode of confusion followed by temporary paralysis. His friend Johann 'Hans' Zellenka, the director of the local branch of the luxury textile factory Philipp Haas & Sons, accompanied him to Vienna to consult the neurologist Dr Freud. The latter prescribed an anti-syphilitic treatment that proved to be effective.

Käthe Bauer refused to care for him because of his infection, so Filipp was treated in Meran by Hans Zellenka's wife, Bella Giuseppina ('Peppina') Heumann. Peppina, the daughter of the director of the prosperous family bank Biedermann from Meran, was young, pretty and playful. Just as Filipp could hardly find satisfaction with Käthe, Peppina suffered from Hans's continual infidelities. So Peppina and Filipp consoled each other and began a quasi-official affair that was to last until Filipp's death in 1913, while Käthe Bauer shut herself up in her 'housewife's psychosis' (Freud) and Hans

The 'Kurpromenade' in Meran, *c.* 1900.

Zellenka pursued all the women in the neighbourhood. In the spring of 1896 Hans set his sights on Ida, who was thirteen and a half at the time. Having drawn her into his office (Freud, in his case history, speaks of a 'shop'), he suddenly embraced her, but Ida, disgusted, rejected his advances. However, she said nothing to her parents, and the family intrigue continued, with everyone turning a blind eye. Young Ida looked after the Zellenka children, Klara and Otto, and had even become the confidant of Peppina, who introduced her to the realities of life and made no attempt to hide her own husband's infidelities from her.

In 1897 Filipp's tuberculosis improved and the Bauers moved to Reichenberg in Bohemia, where the main factory of the family business was located. In the early summer of 1898 Ida again had an asthma attack accompanied by coughing and aphonia. Filipp took his daughter to Freud, who immediately diagnosed a neurosis and proposed 'psychic treatment'. With the asthma easing, however, things ended there and Ida's father didn't pursue the idea. Ida left with her father for Lake Garda, where she had been invited to spend some time with the Zellenkas to take care of their children. Hans Zellenka, as usual, courted the governess, while Filipp took a few days off with Peppina before going back to Bohemia. Ida was fifteen at the time (Freud, in his case history, added a year to her

Wedding of Johann (Hans) Zellenka to Bella Giuseppina Heumann in Meran on 22 September 1889.

age). One day when she was walking along the lake with Hans, he again made advances to her, resorting to the same sweet talk as with the governess. Revolted, Ida slapped him and ran away. The next day, no longer feeling safe with the Zellenkas, she abruptly decided to leave with her father.

When she returned home, she told her mother what had happened. Filipp Bauer had no choice but to ask Hans Zellenka for an explanation. Hans denied everything, accusing Ida of getting titillated by erotic books and of having totally invented the scene by the lake. Rather than disrupting the delicate balance of their ménage à trois, Filipp accepted Hans's explanations. Hans thereupon renewed his advances to Ida at the end-of-year celebrations. Angry at being sacrificed on the altar of family tranquillity, Ida loudly demanded that her father sever all relations with the Zellenkas. Nothing happened.

In spring 1899 Ida returned to Vienna after the death of her favourite aunt, Malvine Friedmann (an acquaintance of Freud's, who from a distance would diagnose in her 'a severe form of psychoneurosis'). In Vienna she had an attack of appendicitis that left her with a lifelong tendency to drag her right foot. (This seems to indicate that this was a pelvic appendicitis, which often causes this kind of after-effects in the right leg.) In 1900 the Bauers returned to settle in Vienna, where they were soon joined by the Zellenkas as Hans had been promoted to director of the flagship store of the Philip Haas company in the capital. Having quarrelled with her father, and feeling exasperated by her mother, Ida had no one to turn to. She was depressed and no longer ate properly. She wrote a note, found by her parents, in which she spoke of suicide. Then, during a heated argument with her father over the Zellenkas, she lost consciousness. Filipp Bauer brought her forcibly to Freud. She was seventeen, the age of teenage revolt.

The treatment began around the middle of October 1900. Filipp Bauer clearly wanted Freud to cure his daughter of her 'illness' and rid her mind of all those annoying 'fictions' about Herr and Frau Zellenka. Freud, to his credit, recognized the merits of Ida's accusations. However, he did not question the diagnosis of mental disturbance made by Hans Zellenka and Filipp Bauer. He was in any case convinced, as he repeats twice in his case history, that 'the offspring of luetics [persons with syphilis] were very specially predisposed to severe neuropsychoses.' Thus the aversion felt by Ida when Hans Zellenka embraced her was clearly hysterical, because a girl of this age (thirteen and a half) should normally have felt pleasure in feeling 'the pressure of his erect member against her body': Ida had *repressed* her love for Hans Zellenka and converted the excitement she had felt in her clitoris into oral disgust. Likewise, her periods of aphonia corresponded to the absences of Hans Zellenka and expressed regret at not being able to speak to the loved one. Ida's cough expressed the desire to feel in her throat the organ of her father, the original love object for which Hans Zellenka served as a substitute. Asthmatic dyspnoea mimicked her father's panting as he had intercourse with her mother.

However, none of these assertions met with Ida's approval. Two and a half months into the treatment, Freud informed the girl that the 'alleged appendicitis' from which she had suffered in the spring of 1899, nine months after the scene by the lake, was the fulfilment of a childbirth fantasy. As for the leg that had been dragging ever since, it symbolized the 'faux pas' she had ardently wanted to commit: 'So you see that your love for Herr K. [the pseudonym given by Freud to Zellenka] did not come to an end with the [lake] scene, but that (as I maintained) it has persisted down to the present day – though it is true that you are unconscious of it.' The next day, 31 December 1900, Ida politely announced to Freud that this session was to be the last. She had heard enough. According to her cousin Elsa Foges, daughter of Malvina Friedmann, whom the historian Anthony Stadlen interviewed in 1979 at the age of 97, Ida had told her at the time about her treatment with Freud: 'He asks me lots of questions and I want to make an end to it.' It was, writes Freud, 'an unmistakable act of vengeance on her part. Her purpose of self-injury also profited by this action.'

Filipp Bauer did not oppose his daughter's decision because he had realized that Freud was not ready to be an accomplice in his affair with Peppina Zellenka. The situation hardly changed, so Ida went through a few difficult months until the opportunity arose for her to settle the problem that Freud had failed to resolve. Klara, the Zellenka daughter to whom Ida had devoted a great deal of care, died in May 1901 of congenital heart disease. Ida, a true family therapist, took advantage of a condolence visit to obtain confessions from Hans and Peppina Zellenka: the former for the scene at the lake, the latter for her affair with Filipp Bauer. Now that the truth had come to light, Ida was doing well again. In October, however, there was a new asthmatic episode, apparently following the fear she had felt one day when she had seen Hans Zellenka being hit by a car after they had met by chance in the street.

The following year, in April 1902, she consulted Freud for a very painful facial neuralgia. Freud was pleased to note that this 'alleged facial neuralgia', as he called it, had started a fortnight earlier, shortly after Ida had read in a newspaper the announcement of his appointment to the post of Professor extraordinarius. Evidently, Ida was punishing herself ('slapping' herself) for having left him – he himself serving as a transferential substitute for Hans Zellenka whom she had so brutally slapped by the lake. 'She was not in earnest over her request,' but Freud 'promised to forgive her for having deprived [him] of the satisfaction of affording her a far more radical cure for her troubles'. We can deduce from this remark that Freud thought Ida was still sick, but that he was not keen on helping her given the way she had rejected him.

Ida, who was very pretty, had no suitors and was still living with her parents. She had confessed to her cousin Elsa that she was in love with someone but had not wanted to tell her who it was (which had led Elsa to suspect that it was her own fiancé, Hans Foges). In the summer of 1903, while on holiday in Reichenau, a popular holiday destination for the Viennese bourgeoisie, Ida met Ernst Adler on a tennis court. Adler was a nephew of the famous Jewish actor Adolf von Sonnenthal and heir to a fine fortune. He apparently had an engineering background, but does not seem to have ever exercised this profession. Elsa Foges and Julius Bauer, another cousin of Ida's, both described him to Kurt Eissler as a 'playboy', a 'viveur', a charming but superficial 'snob' who moved in aristocratic circles. He was also an amateur musician.

Ida was dazzled; she was in a hurry to escape the suffocating atmosphere of her family and to launch herself out into society. On 6 December 1903, after a rapid engagement, Ida Bauer married Ernst Adler. She was 21 years old. Filipp Bauer took his son-in-law into the family business. On 2 April 1905 Ida gave birth to a son, Kurt Herbert, who would become a renowned conductor and opera director (in the interwar period he worked with, among others, Max Reinhardt, Toscanini, Solti and Herbert Graf, Freud's 'Little Hans').

Ida Bauer showed no signs of neurosis or mental instability in her adult life. Kurt Eissler, who had interviewed Elsa Foges and others close to Ida Bauer at length in the early 1950s, confirmed this in a letter to Anna Freud: 'Apparently the information I got from Dora's cousin two years ago is correct and she never developed serious neurotic or psychotic symptoms after her treatment by Freud' (20 August 1952). According to people who knew her, Ida was a good mother, loved going to the theatre and was interested in music and things of the mind. She was lively, even 'intense' (Otto Leichter), and endowed with a critical mind that spared few people, especially her husband. 'She was far from being a silly goose [sie war keine dumme Gans]' was the verdict of Otto Zelenka, the son of Peppina and Hans. She was also an excellent bridge player, and she chain-smoked, which was of course not good for her asthma.

Suffering briefly from Ménière's disease in 1922, she was referred to Felix Deutsch, who also happened to be Freud's personal physician and the husband of psychoanalyst Helene Deutsch. On this occasion, Deutsch wrote to his wife that he had met the Professor's Dora and that 'she has nothing good to say about analysis' – which he took care not to repeat in the highly unreliable article he wrote on her in 1957, where he suggested, on the contrary, that she had 'display[ed] great pride in having been written up as a famous case in psychiatric literature'.

Ida's marriage to Ernst Adler was not a happy one. It soon became clear that Adler was not made for business. Neglecting his wife and son, he spent his time at the Automobile Club playing bridge for money, and he regularly built up debts that had to be paid off. Already in Filipp Bauer's lifetime, the family business had started to collapse and Ernst's comfortable legacy had gone. The situation only grew worse with the fall of the Austro-Hungarian Empire and the ensuing economic crisis. Factories in Bohemia were nationalized by the new country of Czechoslovakia, ruining the Bauer family and increasing tensions between Ida and Ernst. Divorce was often discussed, but they stayed together for Kurt, who it turned out was a child musical prodigy and had started studying music seriously.

Ernst embarked on interior decoration, an activity which was not enough to support the family. Ida, on the other hand, had caught the gambling bug and had created a bridge circle whose members came to play for money, paying a subscription for the privilege. She was helped by Peppina Zellenka, who had become a widow in 1928 and with whom she had kept good relations. She herself twice lost large sums at the casino in Baden-Baden, which her brother Otto paid off just as he had done for her other debts. A wealthy friend, Steffi Strauss, also helped. On 28 December 1932, Ernst Adler collapsed, the victim of a thrombosis. Ida was with her bridge circle; when she was told what had happened, she replied that it was nothing serious and phlegmatically completed her game. By the time she returned home, Ernst had died.

Otto Bauer took care of his sister, but in 1934, when the Social Democrats were repressed by the Dollfuss dictatorship, he had to take refuge in Czechoslovakia and then in Paris. He died there of a cardiac arrest in July 1938 and was entitled to an official funeral organized by the Popular Front government. Ida, who had stayed in Vienna, was actively sought by the Nazis after the Anschluss because of her brother. She hid for a time with her friend Peppina before succeeding in obtaining a travel pass for Paris in 1939, thanks to the help of the anti-fascist resistance network of Joseph Buttinger, a comrade of Otto Bauer. (The ex-wife of her son Kurt, who was the daughter of a high Nazi dignitary, had also offered help.) Fleeing the approach of the German army in June 1940, Ida took refuge in the 'free zone' in the south of France, and from there went on to Casablanca, Morocco, before sailing to New York in September 1941. Here she joined Kurt and other relatives who had also escaped the Holocaust: Elsa Foges (who reconciled with her after a long period of alienation), her cousin Julius Bauer and Otto Zellenka, the son of her friend and quasi-mother-in-law Peppina. The latter was deported to Theresienstadt (Terezín) in 1942 before being liberated by the Red Army in May 1945. Ludwig Bauer, Ida's paternal uncle, was not so lucky: he died in Theresienstadt in August 1942. Hans Foges, Elsa's husband, who had ruined himself in Ida's gaming circle, died in the Nazi ghetto of Łódź in May 1942.

Ida Bauer died of cancer in New York on 21 December 1945, barely three months after the end of a war that had engulfed her world.

Continuing the pathologization for which she had paid the price in her youth, psychoanalysts and their historians did as much as possible to describe the life of Ida Bauer as a long and unpleasant symptom. Freud himself, on the basis of what Felix Deutsch had reported to him, added a footnote to his case story relating that Dora 'had recently fallen ill again' and that it was no fault of the analysis if her brief three-month treatment 'was unable to give her protection against subsequent illnesses'. In the early 1950s all kinds of rumours circulated in the psychoanalytic milieu of New York about the alleged schizophrenia from which Dora suffered and her supposed internment at the Bellevue Sanatorium of Ludwig Binswanger (who firmly denied this when Eissler asked him for confirmation). Ernest Jones, in the second volume of his biography of Freud, painted a portrait of 'a disagreeable creature who consistently put revenge before love; it was the same motive that led her to break off the treatment prematurely, and to retain various hysterical symptoms, both bodily and mental.' Felix Deutsch, on the other hand, in 1957 quoted an anonymous witness who said that the death of Ida Bauer 'seemed a blessing to those who were close to her. She had been, as my informant phrased it, "one of the most repulsive hysterics" he had ever met.'

The historian Anthony Stadlen, who interviewed this witness's wife, was able to establish that he was hardly any more reliable than Hans Zellenka, to whose family network he belonged. Yet the rumour, launched in 1898, is still circulating.

19

ANNA VON VEST
(1861–1935)

Anna Katharina von Vest, born on 25 November 1861, belonged to a prominent family from Klagenfurt, Carinthia. Her grandfather, Lorenz Edler von Vest, had been the private doctor of one of the daughters of Empress Marie-Thérèse, the Grand Duchess Marianne. Her father, Johann Edler von Vest, had amassed a considerable fortune as a notary. In 1857 he married Natalia Werzer, with whom he had six children. The marriage was hardly happy. Very musical and a poetry lover, Natalia was sixteen years younger than her husband and relations always remained distant with the person she ceremoniously called 'Herrn Doktor'. She consoled herself with religion.

The education of the children was strict. Like her four sisters, Anna was sent to boarding school in a religious establishment run by the Salesian Sisters. She was a conscientious student; she learned French and English, which she spoke to perfection. She was also a good pianist and was skilled at drawing. Then, towards the end of her adolescence, she became anti-religious and unruly. She had a difficult character and quarrelled constantly with her younger sister Cornelia ('Nelly'), with whom she maintained a life-long relationship of rivalry, first for the attention of their mother, then, later, for a man. At twenty she fell over while skating and suffered a disappointment in love that permanently affected her. In 1885 she underwent a removal of the ovaries that after the fact proved unnecessary. The result was a hirsutism (undue hairiness) that bothered her considerably, which she tackled with cosmetic interventions that disfigured her face.

The unfortunate oophorectomy also caused difficulty in walking, which eventually took the form of complete paralysis of the legs. Questioned by historian Stefan Goldmann, one family member summed up the sequence of events as follows: 'Following an unhappy romantic experience, she went to bed and remained paralysed.' Anna could only move about in a wheelchair and had to be carried up the stairs by the servants. She went from spa towns to seaside resorts for treatment (in particular the hydrotherapy offered by the famous pastor Sebastian Kneipp), but nothing helped, and her 'nervous pains' obstinately resisted.

In May 1903 she decided to go to Vienna to consult Freud. She was 41 years old and had been disabled for almost two decades. She had to be carried from the train to her hotel, where Freud came to see her. A week later, she could already walk to his office. The following week, she started going to the theatre. During the day, she would be on Freud's couch, at a rate of fifty Austrian crowns an hour (an extremely high fee for the time). She also took drama lessons with actor Ferdinand Gregori of the Burgtheater, who told her to eat a carrot a day for her voice. In the evening she roamed the salons, where she was appreciated as a pianist and accompanist of *Lieder*. Miss Anna von Vest was a snob, and these social occasions were to her liking. It is said that the walls of her room were covered with photos and portraits of all the famous people she met.

In a memorandum written for Kurt Eissler, her niece recounts how Aunt Anna described her analysis to her on the excursions they took together: 'Cause [of symptoms]: fathered without joy! She laid everything at her parents' door, 60% of the conversations [were] of a sexual nature, jealousy toward a sister, etc.'

The treatment was interrupted in mid-July by Freud's sacrosanct holidays, when he left to seek fresh air by the Königsee lake, near Berchtesgaden. Anna returned to Klagenfurt, where she was again paralysed. Her family members began openly to question the authenticity of her illness. How was it that she was disabled in Klagenfurt and healthy in Vienna? It also seems, according to the testimonies collected by Goldmann, that the family wondered about the appropriateness and the length of Freud's treatment: 'Freud, the Jewish doctor in Vienna, wanted to earn a lot of money.'

Anna was most upset, and laid siege to Freud to have him agree to see her in Königsee. She knew that Marie von Ferstel had been granted this preferential treatment and she was jealous of the baroness, whose social status and fortune were superior to her own. Freud politely declined to interrupt his holiday, arguing that Anna's relapse was of little consequence: 'I consider you to be completely healthy. No matter what events you have to go through, never forget that' (20 July 1903). As Anna insisted, Freud did a bit of epistolary psychoanalysis: 'In your project, did the model of MF [Marie von Ferstel] not play a certain role? Yes, she habitually comes for a week or so, but I hope you don't model yourself on her in other directions. And what would you say if you knew that I have just now a second woman patient, a real and constant object of concern? Would you apply your two fantasies to her – that of wealth and that of social position?' (29 July 1903).

Treatment resumed when Freud came back to Vienna, and it lasted until July 1904, when Freud left again for his annual holiday. Freud had decided to end the analysis, but Anna tried to oppose his decision by developing symptoms as soon as she returned to Klagenfurt. Again, she asked Freud to receive her at Königsee. Again, Freud declined: 'Trust me on two points 1) that it has never happened that someone fell back permanently into their old illness after such well-being and such hard-deserved health, 2) that this is merely nostalgia and it would be very stupid to give in and come to Königsee' (17 August 1904). Upon Anna successfully persuading her family to let her settle in Vienna after the summer, Freud congratulated her, and was looking forward, he says, to seeing her again not as patient but as 'a noble, saved portion of humanity' (2 August 1904).

However, there were relapses in the years that followed – a lot of relapses. In December 1906 there was a new crisis. Freud tried to dissuade Anna from embarking on a new round of analysis by presenting her with the New Year wish 'to seek your salvation neither in sickness nor in treatment' (20 December 1906). 'Finally, whenever I tackled your [unanalysed] remnant, it was always clear that you would still hold something back, just so that you wouldn't have to stop the process' (10 January 1907). Anna tried to force his hand by sending him money, which he initially refused. However, he finally gave in and kept Anna in analysis until 25 April of the same year.

We know that there was another round of analysis in June 1908. The correspondence between Freud and Anna von Vest was interrupted at that time, but the calendar on which Freud noted his patients day by day mentions two other analyses with 'Vest' from 1910. Then, in 1912, Anna von Vest went to stay in England. In 1914 she was back in Klagenfurt, where Martin, Freud's son, went to see her. That year the First World War began, which brought its share of miseries. Anna's brother-in-law, who was in charge of family affairs, died in 1915, leaving behind a delicate financial situation. In 1916–17 Anna went to work as a nurse in a military hospital in Olmütz, Moravia. On her return, the von Vest fortune having evaporated, she settled with her mother and sister Cornelia in the countryside, near Klagenfurt, in a mill and a small adjoining farm, the produce of which supported them.

We know from the correspondence between Freud and Anna that there were new relapses and appeals for help in 1920, 1925 and 1926. The second time, Freud agreed to take Anna back for analysis, free of charge: 'Dear Miss Anna, Bad news! You are still sick and without money, and I am so much reduced in the time and energy I can devote to work. What shall we do then? I can see only one way out. We must say it was a bad treatment that paved the way for such a relapse, and we must correct that. It must no longer be a question of money this time.' One of his patients, his daughter Anna, agreed to give Anna von Vest her time slot: 'I am replacing one Anna with another' (26 March 1925).

This further round of analysis began on Monday 4 April 1925, at 6.30 p.m. We do not know how long it lasted. The following year, Freud was really sorry 'to hear that you are unwell again' (11 April 1926). In a last letter to Anna von Vest on 14 November 1926, he explained to her why she still had not recovered after all these years: 'I always regret that I did not manage, during your last attempt at treatment, to persuade you about your death wishes towards your father. But it is also very difficult for other girls full of tenderness' (a reference perhaps to the other Anna, his own daughter?).

In his article of 1937, 'Analysis Terminable and Interminable', Freud refers under the seal of anonymity to two cases where 'obstacles' came in the way of 'a cure by analysis'. One is the case of his ex-friend and disciple Sándor Ferenczi, the other most certainly that of Anna von Vest (rather than Emma Eckstein, as suggested by Freud historians Lisa Appignanesi and John Forrester). This patient, recounts Freud, had been cured by a nine-month analysis of a paralysis of the legs that occurred after puberty, and she remained healthy afterwards despite the financial setbacks that forced her to support her family: 'I cannot remember whether it was twelve or fourteen years after the end of her analysis that, owing to profuse haemorrhages, she was obliged to undergo a gynaeco-logical examination. A myoma was found, which made a complete hysterectomy advisable. From the time of this operation, the woman became ill once more. She fell in love with her surgeon, wallowed in masochistic phantasies about the fearful changes in her inside – phantasies with which she concealed her romance – and proved inaccessible to a further attempt at analysis.'

There is no mention of this hysterectomy in Freud's letters to Anna von Vest, but the whole passage leaves little doubt as to the identity of the patient in question, despite the vagueness main-tained by Freud regarding the chronology of the events. Freud added to the story of his patient's relapse that no conclusions could be drawn from it about the first analysis, which in any case went back to 'the earliest years of my work as an analyst'. Without 'the new trauma' of hysterectomy, which had awakened the same repressed emotions as before, neurosis would in fact not have re-appeared. Now, we remember that Anna von Vest's paralysis was triggered by her oophorectomy. Thirty years later, Freud therefore attributed to an external 'obstacle' what he described as Anna von Vest's sole relapse into neurosis.

Four years earlier, Anna von Vest had developed what her niece described as an 'ulcer' in the stomach, but was more likely a cancerous tumour. She died the following year, on Sunday 20 January 1935, in Ebenthal near Klagenfurt. (On 23 January Freud noted in his diary: '†Anna von Vest'.) According to the testimony of her relatives as noted by Stefan Goldmann, Anna attributed her pain to her sister Cornelia: 'I'm not dying from a stomach ulcer, but because of Nelly.' She also said that she owed Professor Freud for having enjoyed another thirty years in good health.

20

BRUNO WALTER

(1876–1962)

Bruno Schlesinger, better known as Bruno Walter, was one of the great conductors of the twentieth century, along with Toscanini, Böhm, Klemperer and Karajan. He was also, in 1906, one of Freud's most unexpected patients. At the time he was conductor at the Opera of the Imperial and Royal Court in Vienna, where he worked under the direction of his friend and mentor Gustav Mahler. This was, as he recounts in his memoirs, a particularly fortunate period of his life. He was a happy husband and father, and professionally recognized; he was leading a bourgeois existence – too bourgeois, it seemed to him. So his body then undertook to recall him to a more 'Faustian' anxiety: shortly after the birth of his first daughter, he developed a painful 'professional cramp' in his left arm that prevented him from conducting and playing the piano.

This was most likely a contracture or a cervico-brachial neuralgia (sciatica of the arm), but either way the pain would not go away. Walter consulted all kinds of specialists; he tried mud baths and magnetism: nothing helped. Finally, as a psychological element was suspected, Walter decided to consult Freud, probably on the advice of his friend Max Graf. He expected to undergo months of psychological exploration to find some sexual trauma in his childhood, but Freud was content to examine his arm (Freud, let us not forget, was a neurologist by training). When Walter asked him if, in his opinion, the cramp could have come from having been wronged some time before, Freud interrupted him: 'Have you ever been to Sicily?' When Walter answered no, Freud explained that Sicily was a magnificent island, more Greek than Greece: 'In short, I was to leave that very evening, forget

Bruno Walter, 1912.

all about my arm and the Opera, and do nothing for a few weeks but use my eyes.'

Walter complied. He took a train to Genoa and from there a boat to Naples and then Sicily, where he marvelled at the landscape and the Greek temples. But the cramp persisted: 'In the end, my soul and mind had greatly benefited by the additional knowledge I had gained, but not my arm.' Walter therefore left for Vienna and went to complain to Freud. The latter imperturbably told him to ignore his pain and start conducting again. Walter hesitated; could he take the responsibility for ruining a concert? Freud replied: 'I'll take the responsibility.' So Walter began to conduct again, very gradually, and at times managed to forget the pain. During their sessions, Freud insisted on this forgetfulness, a bit like a hypnotist enjoining a subject to stop thinking about his or her pain. Yet the cramp did not disappear: 'I tried once more to conduct, but with the same discouraging result.'

At this point, Walter discovered a book by the Romantic poet-physician Ernst von Feuchtersleben, *The Dietetics of the Soul* (1938). In this short book, the considerable impact of which lasted throughout the nineteenth century, Feuchtersleben insisted on the role of the mind in medicine and proposed what might be called recipes for mental hygiene to influence the course of the disease. Walter delved into Feuchtersleben's book: 'I read and studied, trying assiduously to find my way into the lines of thought expressed in the brilliant book, in which a physician, who was at the same time a poet, wisely tried to point out to suffering humanity a way that has since been made practicable.' Little by little, adapting his conducting to his physical handicap,

Bruno Walter ended up regaining full use of his arm. He never had a problem again.

After the publication of his memoirs, Bruno Walter was interviewed by the American psychoanalyst Richard Sterba about this 'masterpiece of brief psychotherapy' accomplished by Freud. In the article based on this interview, Sterba stated that Walter, after all these years, 'was still deeply impressed by Freud's personality'. Certainly, Sterba recognized that there was not enough clinical material to shed light on 'the psychodynamics of Bruno Walter's short-term spell of professional neurosis.' But, he concluded, 'the success and the katamnesis [clinical history] of forty-two years proves the therapeutic result.'

21
HERBERT GRAF
(1903–1973)

erbert Graf was born on 10 April 1903, in the circumstances
that we have already described in Olga Hönig's vignette.
His childhood was placed under the double sign of music
and psychoanalysis. His father, Max Graf, was a renowned musicologist and music critic who had studied with Hans Richter,
Eduard Hanslick and Anton Bruckner. One of his maternal
aunts, Marie Valerie Hönig, was a concert pianist. His godfather
happened to be Gustav Mahler, and at home he met his father's
many artist and musician friends: Arnold Schoenberg, Richard
Strauss, Bruno Walter, Adolf Loos, Oskar Kokoschka and many
more. From an early age, Herbert showed musical dispositions.
At two years old, he was already singing Viennese melodies, and
he and his little sister Hanna built a miniature opera set for fun.
Opera was to become the great love of his life.

Then there was the psychoanalytic side. Both Herbert's
mother and father were psychoanalysis aficionados, the former as
a patient, the latter as a disciple and follower. After the publication
of the *Three Essays on the Theory of Sexuality*, Freud had asked the
members of the small 'Wednesday society' that met at his home to
gather data likely to corroborate his theories on infantile sexuality,
and so Max Graf informed him conscientiously about the slightest signs of erotic activity in Herbert. In his 1907 article on 'The
Sexual Enlightenment of Children', Freud mentioned 'a delight-
ful little boy, now four years old', whose understanding parents
did not repress (and no doubt actively promoted) the expression
of his sexuality. Now this 'little Herbert', who 'has certainly not
been exposed to anything in the nature of seduction by a nurse'
(an allusion to the 'seduction theory' that Freud had repudiated

in the meantime), had been showing ever since the age of three a keen interest in his 'widdler'. Little Herbert, added Freud, was not a pathological exception: 'The fact is simply, I think, that, not having been intimidated or oppressed with a sense of guilt, he gives expression quite ingenuously to what he thinks.'

We now know that the family atmosphere, however Freudian and permissive it may have been, was far from idyllic. Herbert's parents did not get along and his mother had constant emotional outbursts and fell into depressions. She cared little for him, while, according to Max, behaving 'seductively' towards him. And yet, in the view of his father, Herbert was a very cheerful, carefree child: 'In fact, there was nothing special, up until the phobia.' One day when Max and Herbert were in the public park, Herbert had been scared by a horse carriage standing at the entrance, and he had not wanted to go out. He was only four years old. Then, at the beginning of 1908, he did not want to leave the house any more because he was afraid of meeting horses. This is what Freud and his father called his 'phobia', which they undertook to submit to a proper analysis.

This was the first child psychoanalysis in history. Max would ask his son questions following Freud's directives, and Freud would rewrite the notes provided by Max, complementing them with theoretical comments of his own. Apart from a visit to Freud at the

end of March 1908, Herbert was therefore analysed mainly by his father. According to the Oedipal interpretation proposed in the article 'Analysis of a Phobia in a Five-year-old Boy' co-written by Freud and Graf, the anxiety of 'Little Hans' (the pseudonym given to little Herbert) was linked to his jealousy of his little sister, to hostile desires towards his father, whose place vis-à-vis his mother he sought to take over, and to his fear of being punished with castration for these illicit desires. Herbert, for his part, more prosaically attributed his fear of horses and large animals to an omnibus accident he had witnessed in which a horse had fallen backwards, making a great din

Herbert Graf in the early 1930s.

with its whinnying and the noise of hooves striking on the pavement. A few months later, in early May, his animal anxieties disappeared as quickly as they had arrived, a development that Freud attributed to the analysis. To celebrate the event, he came in person to the Grafs' home to bring Herbert a beautiful rocking horse. 'You will see,' he predicted, 'the boy will want to serve in the cavalry one day.'

Herbert grew up without any particular problems. He had forgotten his fear of horses. He was completely unaware that he had been analysed by his father under Freud's direction and that he had been immortalized by the latter under the name 'Little Hans'. He was even unaware that his mother had been analysed by Freud, as evidenced by his exclamation during his interview with Kurt Eissler in 1959: 'I wasn't aware that my mother underwent any treatment. I never thought so! . . . She did not *ever* speak to me about it.' It was not until the age of seventeen, when his parents divorced in 1920, that Herbert discovered the family secret. While helping his father to pack his books before he moved out, he opened Freud's piece on 'Little Hans' and ended up recognizing himself because of certain biographical elements that Freud had not taken the trouble to conceal. Nearly forty years later, Herbert Graf was still shaken by this discovery. When Eissler tried to get him to say he was proud to have been the first child ever to have been able to confess his parricidal wishes to his own father, Herbert Graf replied that he was 'a bit shocked' by this revelation and that he 'didn't want to give everybody the opportunity to know it'.

In 1922, when Herbert had started his studies, his father urged him to go and visit Freud so that he could see what had become of 'Little Hans'. Freud was delighted: before him was living proof of the harmlessness and effectiveness of child psychoanalysis. He hastened to add a postscript to his case history to record the visit he had received from this 'strapping youth of nineteen' who 'suffered from no troubles or inhibitions'.

Encouraged by the warm welcome Freud had given his son, Max Graf made an appointment with him to try to re-establish the bond between them. He had just divorced from Olga Hönig and therefore had no reason to be concerned any longer by the conflict between Freud and Alfred Adler that was previously described in Olga Hönig's vignette: 'When I arrived, he received me in a very withdrawn and unfriendly manner. I could not get him to chat amicably as before, and so I asked him: "Tell me frankly, Professor, why have you so greatly changed your tone, your attitude towards me?" He replied: "Well, you have resigned from the Psychoanalytic Society, you haven't paid the subscription you owe either, and you have not played any part in it" . . . This was possible, true enough. But I saw that the conversation would not take place on the terms of our former friendship, and I took my leave. I met Freud only from time to time on the street. Naturally, I greeted him very politely, because my opinion about him had not changed. But he always turned away, with that wary look in his eyes.'

Herbert, meanwhile, was pursuing studies in musicology, scenography, composition and singing. During the war, he had seen Max Reinhardt's shows in Berlin, where he had spent some time with one of his aunts, and he had decided to do for musical theatre what Reinhardt had done for spoken theatre: he would become an opera director. After completing a doctoral thesis in musicology on 'Wagner as Director' in 1925, he took up a position as a singer and opera director at the municipal theatre of Münster, in Westphalia. He was happy to leave Vienna and all that this city meant to him, as he explained to Kurt Eissler: 'I look back at these years in Vienna with a feeling that I have left a very decadent place, you see . . . And this was personal misery because of the divorce of the parents, a certain amount of poverty . . . And all these pictures of Hofmannsthal and Schoenberg and Freud, and all this, somehow we young people left Vienna in an opposition and went to Germany for that reason. And as far away from Vienna as possible! . . . So we had sort of an aversion against the whole world. – Kurt Eissler: Psychoanalysis was included? – And that was included, practically symbolized [it].'

Far from Vienna, Herbert Graf began a brilliant international career as an opera director. This eventually brought him to the United States, where he emigrated in 1934 to flee Nazism. He worked in Philadelphia, then at the Metropolitan Opera in New York and elsewhere, with the greatest figures: Toscanini, Bruno Walter (an old friend of Max Graf), Oskar Kokoschka (another friend of Max's), Furtwängler, Solti, Tito Gobbi, Gottlob Frick, Maria Callas, Elisabeth Schwarzkopf, Irmgard Seefried

Herbert Graf
directing singers
in Verdi's *Othello*,
Stadttheater Zürich,
September 1960.

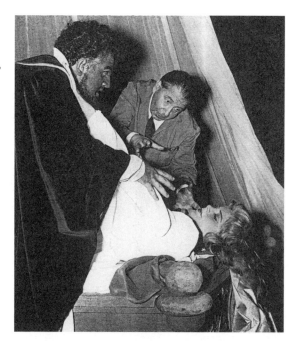

and many others. He took American nationality in 1943 and for a time directed the musical activities of the NBC television network. In 1946 he even went to Hollywood to direct opera scenes in an MGM film.

His father and sister Hanna, whom he loved very much, had also emigrated to the United States. Beautiful and intelligent, Hanna had always been rejected by her mother. In mourning for her husband Paul Sujeff, who had been deported to Dachau, she committed suicide in 1942, succumbing in turn to the curse of the Hönigs.

Herbert married in 1927 and had a son, Werner, in 1933. Liselotte Austerlitz, his wife, seems to have been an alcoholic (testimony of Harold P. Blum, director of the Freud Archives, but not confirmed by Colin Graf, grandson of Herbert and Liselotte). No doubt it was these 'difficulties' that Herbert Graf alluded to when he confided to Eissler: 'We had one or two years of a more difficult period and then I went myself to a psychoanalyst to help me in this situation. But I didn't like it at all! . . . I had always the feeling that this is the most wonderful thing on earth, as a thought, as a science and everything, but it is too easily an . . . I mean the hands of people who handle it are often not worthy of handling it.'

Liselotte Graf died in 1967, apparently as a result of her alcoholism. Herbert Graf, who had returned to settle in Europe in the late 1950s, remarried in 1966; with his new wife, Margrit Thuering, he had a daughter, Ann-Kathryn. This second marriage seems to have been much happier than the previous one. Herbert Graf ended his career in Switzerland, and he died of cancer in Geneva on 5 April 1973. He never entered the cavalry.

22

ALOIS JEITTELES
(1867–1907)

Alois Jeitteles was born on 7 September 1867. He belonged to the same prominent Jewish dynasty from Bohemia as Adele Jeiteles, although members of his side of the family preferred to write their surname with two 't's. Alois was named after his paternal grandfather, Alois Isidor Jeitteles, a noted physician, journalist, dramatist and poet who was friends with Ludwig Tieck, Franz Grillparzer and Ludwig van Beethoven (the latter set to music his song-cycle 'An die ferne Geliebte'). Alois's father, Richard Jeitteles, was general director of the Kaiser Ferdinands-Nordbahn, Austria's steam railway company financed by Salomon Rothschild, and he himself sat on the board of the Credit-Anstalt für Handel und Gewerbe, the powerful Rothschild bank in Austria-Hungary.

Through his sister Marie, Alois Jeitteles also happened to be on the periphery of Freud's inner circle, for she had married Alfred Fürth, whose brother Adolf Fürth and his wife Helene were very close to the Freuds (their children called Freud 'Uncle Sigi'). Helene Fürth's cousin Sophie Schwab married Joseph Paneth, another close friend (and benefactor) of Freud, and became Sophie Freud's godmother. One of Alfred and Marie Fürth's daughters, also named Marie, would later marry Sophie and Joseph Paneth's son Otto. During the Second World War Marie Paneth developed a method of art therapy for children in conjunction with her friend Anna Freud, thus further strengthening the ties between the Fürth family and the Freud constellation (Marie Paneth also had a great love affair with the psychoanalyst Hermann Nunberg, the son-in-law of yet another of Freud's close friends, Oskar Rie).

When Alfred Fürth died prematurely in 1899, leaving his wife with scant resources and four young children, Alois Jeitteles moved in with his sister and became the legal guardian of his nieces and nephews. In a memorandum written for the Sigmund Freud Archives, Marie Paneth remembered her uncle Alois fondly, an exuberant bear of a man who would jump on a table and re-enact for the children a play or an opera he had been to the previous evening, or hide sweets under their pillows when he came in their room to say goodnight: 'We all loved him very much.'

In the spring of 1906 his mood changed abruptly after returning from a trip during which he had broken his foot. He was gloomy, barely spoke any longer, looked unkempt and quarrelled with his sister, which distressed her very much and frightened the children. He made several stays in sanatoria from which he came back unchanged. Trying to cheer him up, his sister had him join her when she read Fritz Reuter's funny tales to the children before they went to bed, but he would simply sit there stony-faced, without showing any emotion. Then, one day as the children were laughing at a particularly comical episode in Reuter's *Ut mine Stromtid* (During my Apprenticeship), Alois joined in as he used to do in the old days. Marie Paneth remembers that she went to bed that evening with the wonderful feeling that 'Now everything is fine again.' The date was 13 October 1907. The next day, when Marie returned from school for lunch, she learned that Uncle Alois was dead. During the night, leaving nothing to chance, he had turned on the gas tap, taken sleeping pills and shot himself. His sister had heard the shot but had thought nothing of it. The maid found him in the morning.

Marie Paneth learned other details: 'I also remember that "the doctor who wanted to test (*probieren*) a method on him" had told my mother shortly beforehand that a crisis was imminent that could either save him or make him even sicker.' It was only much later, as she was conversing with Anna Freud in the mid-1950s, that Marie Paneth came to know who this bold experimenter was. They were chatting about recent events in Marie's family and Anna, ever the child therapist, volunteered that 'The worst for kids is a depressive mother,' to which Marie replied that she should know as her own mother had long mourned her husband: 'I also knew what it means to have "a suicidal person [in English]" at home, for her brother, my uncle, was for a year in this state with us at home and then killed himself.' 'But you are a Fürth, aren't you?' Anna objected (Anna knew of course that there had been no suicide in the Fürth family.) 'Yes,' Marie continued, 'but they weren't Fürths. My mother and her brother were Jeitteles.' After a pause, Anna said: 'There was a Jeitteles among my father's early cases. I remember notes about it.'

None of these notes have surfaced, so we will probably never know what 'method' Freud tried on Alois Jeitteles with such dire results.

23

ERNST LANZER
(1878–1914)

This patient of Freud's has been given all kinds of pseudonyms in the psychoanalytic literature – the 'Rat Man', 'Dr
Lorenz', 'Dr Langer' – but his real name was Ernst Lanzer.
Born on 22 January 1878 in Vienna, he belonged to the solid Jewish
bourgeoisie of the city. His mother, Rosa Herlinger, had been
adopted by her distant Saborsky cousins and had thus entered one
of the great industrialist families of Vienna. His father, Heinrich
Lanzer, was nineteen years older than his wife. Coming from a
modest background in Silesia, he had clearly climbed a rung on
the social ladder by marrying Rosa and obtaining a position of
responsibility in the Saborsky company.

Ernst was the fourth child in a family of seven. The Lanzer family
atmosphere was warm, and they were not particularly observant.
Ernst got along very well with his father, a generous and unpreten-
tious man who was perhaps a little boorish. As a teenager he began
to have obsessional thoughts that connected his first erotic stir-
rings, especially masturbation, with the fear that his father would
die. For a while he became intensely religious and scrupulously
performed all the rites prescribed by the Torah.

In 1897 Ernst began studying law at the University of Vienna.
The following year, a Saborsky employee committed suicide after
she had asked him if he liked her and he had answered evasively.
Lanzer saw this as confirmation of the agonizing idea that thoughts
can kill. At the same time, he fell in love with Gisela Adler, a poor
and sickly cousin who, alas, did not meet with his father's approval.
Lanzer, not at all irrationally, found himself thinking that when
his father died he would have enough money to marry Gisela
anyway. His father died six months later, on 20 July 1899, suddenly

causing intense guilt in his son. Lanzer inherited 59,000 crowns from his father but did not marry Gisela.

From 1901 Lanzer's anxieties became more and more pressing, forcing him to adopt all kinds of rituals – not religious ones this time – to forestall the realization of the horrible thoughts that crossed his mind. Thus, every evening between midnight and one o'clock in the morning, he absolutely had to open the door of his apartment to let in his father's ghost, after which he would gaze at his erect penis in a mirror. Or again, during one particularly hot summer, he forced himself to go running in the oppressive heat of the sun, while beset with thoughts of suicide (cutting his throat with a knife, throwing himself from a precipice). He also prayed compulsively while pronouncing propitiatory formulas like '*Gigellsamen*', which combined 'Gisela' and 'amen' (or *Samen*, 'sperm', according to Freud's interpretation). Although he had encountered no problems in his studies until then, he could now no longer pass his exams. Gisela, no doubt exasperated by his end-less procrastination, rejected him several times, arousing intense jealousy on his part. In 1906 he underwent hydrotherapy treatment in Munich, which did him some good, mainly because it was the occasion for him to have an affair with a young girl of the estab-lishment. He also consulted the psychiatrist Julius Wagner von Jauregg, who was of little help.

In July 1907 Lanzer finally obtained his doctorate in law, after ten years of study. In August of the same year, while participating as a reserve officer in military manoeuvres in Galicia, he fell prey to a veritable delirium revolving around the fear that a torture involving rats would be inflicted, through his fault, on his father (even though the latter was deceased) and on his beloved cousin (he had read the description of this horrible torture in the famous erotic work by Octave Mirbeau, *Le Jardin des supplices* (The Garden of Torments). Driven half-crazy by obsessional and bizarre 'oaths' that he could not respect, he returned to Vienna where he ended up consulting Freud, whose *Psychopathology of Everyday Life* he had read.

The treatment began on Tuesday, 1 October 1907 and lasted a little less than four and a half months, with a few isolated sessions later. Freud, who intended to give a presentation three weeks later on 'The Beginning of a Patient's Case History' to members of his

'Wednesday society', took very detailed notes from the first seven sessions. These notes survived, as did the less systematic ones that Freud took for the next four months, so we can get a fairly accurate idea of the course of Lanzer's analysis. Now we need simply to compare these notes with the case study that Freud published a year later to find in the latter all kinds of extremely disturbing distortions, noted by many historians of psychoanalysis. On several occasions, Freud puts into the mouth of Lanzer interpretations that the latter had explicitly rejected, such as the idea that his father had married his mother for money, or even that he went running in hot sunshine so as not to be fat (*dick* in German) and thus kill 'Dick', an English cousin allegedly named Richard (actually an uncle with the perfectly Germanic name of Conried) of whom he was jealous. Elsewhere, Freud presents his own interpretations as proven facts or else simply modifies the data of the analysis to make them coincide with his hypotheses, as when he invents from scratch a certain postwoman in the small town near which the manoeuvres had taken place.

The treatment itself, however, does seem to have helped Lanzer. According to the testimony of a niece and two nephews of his, collected by the historian Anthony Stadlen in the 1980s, the consensus in the family was that his analysis had enabled him to find a job and to get married. In early April 1908 Lanzer began working in the law firm Schick. In October 1909, after ten years of procrastination, he finally became engaged to Gisela Adler. The marriage took place on 8 November 1910 in the great Moorish synagogue on the Tempelgasse in Vienna.

A year after the end of the treatment, however, Freud wrote to Carl Gustav Jung to say that he had met his ex-patient: 'The one point that still gives him trouble (father-complex and transference) has shown up clearly in my conversation with this intelligent and grateful man' (17 October 1909), which seems to indicate that Lanzer was not completely rid of his symptoms. One sign of Lanzer's instability was that he changed jobs four more times before passing the bar in 1913 and entering the Heller law firm as a partner. We will never know what the future had in store for him. Called up to the front as a reserve officer in August 1914, Ernst Lanzer was captured by the Russian army on 21 November and died four days later, presumably executed.

24

ELFRIEDE HIRSCHFELD

(1873–1938)

Freud called her his 'great patient' and his 'chief tormentor'. She figures anonymously in at least six of his articles and appears under various pseudonyms in his published correspondence – 'Frau A.' in letters to Karl Abraham, 'Frau H.' in letters to Pastor Pfister, 'Frau C.' in letters to Jung, and 'Frau Gi' in letters to Ludwig Binswanger. These all refer, however, to the same person, and her name, as historian Ernst Falzeder has revealed, was Elfriede Hirschfeld, née Cohen. Her treatment spanned almost seven years and took around 1,600 hours, making it one of Freud's longest.

Elfriede Hirschfeld was born in 1873 and grew up in Frankfurt. She was the oldest of five daughters. Her father, Levi Ludwig Cohen, whom she loved very much, had no head for business and the family often struggled to make ends meet. As an older child, Elfriede felt responsible for her family and developed a keen sense of duty. At the age of nineteen, she had already turned down several suitors when William Hirschfeld, a much older cousin on the maternal side who had made his fortune in business in Russia, came on the scene. She agreed to marry him so as to preserve her family from need and converted to Catholicism after the marriage in order to follow him to Moscow (she would reconvert to Judaism later). Elfriede learned to love her husband and the marriage was initially harmonious (Freud specifies that she was 'sexually satisfied'). However, the couple had no children. Convinced that she was responsible for this state of affairs, Elfriede was preparing to undergo a gynaecological operation to remedy it when her husband admitted that he had been made sterile by an epididymitis (infection of the genital tract) contracted in his youth.

Shocked by this revelation, Elfriede Hirschfeld began to develop obsessional symptoms that Freud would later attribute to her frustrated desire to have a child from her father. Conscious of being responsible for his wife's condition, the husband became impotent for a while, which did not help matters. Elfriede was now obsessed with housekeeping and personal hygiene. She put in place all kinds of rituals intended to prevent herself from giving in to immoral or sexual temptations. In particular, she attached the bed-cover to the sheets each night with safety pins.

There then began a long medical quest, which conveniently kept her away from her husband. For years, writes Freud, she was 'the leading figure' at the clinic of Dr Eugen Poensgen, an 'Institute of electrotherapy, physiotherapy, pine-needle baths and cold water baths' in Bad Nassau, in the Palatinate. Over a ten-year period, she was treated by Arthur Muthmann, Pierre Janet, Ludwig Binswanger, Robert Thomsen, Eugen Bleuler, Pastor Oskar Pfister and Carl Gustav Jung, among others. The latter finally sent her to Freud, who initially hesitated to take on this 'most difficult case of obsessional neurosis' for treatment. As he would say in 1921 to the members of his 'Secret Committee' (the inner circle of his disciples): 'Later, I was sufficiently curious, ignorant, and interested in earning money to start an analysis free of compulsion [without institutionalization] with her nevertheless.'

The analysis began in October 1908. We do not have the calendar in which Freud noted his analytical sessions for the years 1908–10, but we know that from October 1910 onwards, Elfriede Hirschfeld would lie on the analyst's couch nine to twelve times a week. In concrete terms, this means that she spent most of her time at 19 Berggasse, and the bill for this marathon analysis would have been huge. Two and a half years after the start of treatment, in May 1911, Freud informed Jung of the progress of Elfriede Hirschfeld's analysis: 'Her symptoms have grown much worse. Of course this is part of the process, but there is no certainty that I can get her any farther. I have come very close to her central conflict, as her reaction shows' (12 May 1911).

Two weeks later, Freud asked Pfister to treat Elfriede Hirschfeld in Zurich during Freud's summer holiday. This was duly done. Then Freud let Pfister know that he wanted to 'hand over this burden permanently (i.e., for a couple of years)'. Pfister should under no circumstances encourage the patient to come back to see Freud. However, this was exactly what Elfriede did: Elfriede Hirschfeld disappeared from Zurich without leaving any information in early December 1911, and reappeared in Vienna shortly before Christmas. Freud resumed treatment, which seems to have offended Pfister and caused a quarrel with Jung.

Elfriede Hirschfeld liked to ingratiate herself with Freud and get involved in the little intrigues of the psychoanalytic movement (Freud described this to Ludwig Binswanger as 'a need for association, friendship with people whom she knows to be with me'). She told Freud that she had gone to see Jung when she was in Zurich, apparently to complain about the lack of 'sympathy' that Freud had shown her and to ask Jung if she should return to Vienna. Jung had been reckless enough to tell her that she was indeed entitled to her therapist's full sympathy and that he would give her his – in short, he had advised her to stay in Zurich and continue her treatment with either Pfister or himself. Freud took this as an affront and dryly put Jung in his place by warning him against the temptations of 'sympathy' and 'countertransference': 'One should rather remain unapproachable, and insist upon receiving.' This marked the beginning of the historical conflict between the two men, which therefore owes its origins to Hirschfeld's indiscretion.

However, Freud's prognosis for the Hirschfeld case had not changed. On 2 January 1912 he wrote to Pfister: 'She has no chance of getting cured . . . at least psychoanalysis should learn from her case and profit by her.' A little earlier, he had stated to Jung: 'It is still her duty to sacrifice herself to science' (17 December 1911). So the treatment continued. Hirschfeld insisted on being watched around the clock by nurses so that she could not commit the immoral acts she kept thinking about. In June 1912 Freud brought Pfister to Vienna for a week to help him 'detoxify' her from this habit.

The treatment ended in January 1914 . . . and resumed in June of the same year, though we do not know why. In July there was talk of the patient going to see Karl Abraham in Berlin, which she did. Then the war broke out and Hirschfeld decided to settle in Zurich, on neutral ground (her husband was apparently English). The following year, she assailed Ludwig Binswanger with phone calls demanding that he treat her, either in Zurich or in his clinic in Kreuzlingen: 'She does not want analysis,' Binswanger told

Freud (19 April 1915). Freud replied: 'She is a case of obsessional neurosis of the severest kind who was nearly analysed to the end, has proved incurable and has resisted all efforts because of particularly impropitious circumstances and is supposedly still dependent on me. However, she has in fact been running away from me ever since I let her into the real secret of her illness. Analytically useless to anyone' (24 April 1915). Hirschfeld was interned (forcibly, it seems) in Binswanger's Bellevue Sanatorium some time later. From some remarks made by Binswanger to Freud in their subsequent correspondence (8 November 1921) we can deduce that she had been treated by 'constraint' to force her out of the habit of her obsessional rituals (the methods used at the Binswanger clinic were not always as gentle as the legend of the founder of existential psychoanalysis would have it).

Her medical records at Kreuzlingen for 14 April 1916 give an idea of what Binswanger called her 'compulsion to wash': 'She has breakfast at 8.30 a.m. Then she goes to the toilet, then we come to the ceremonial of cleaning with toilet paper, then she washes for about one hour, seated on the bidet, then she washes for about one hour in the bath, then she washes her face, seated at the washstand. While she is washing, one of the chambermaids is constantly watching her, otherwise she cannot complete the task. She has lunch in the bathroom. It is 4 p.m. She lies down and gets up again for dinner. She washes for just twenty minutes in her room. She goes to bed around 10.30 p.m.'

In bed, Elfriede insisted on being tied down (the ritual of the pins) and continuously monitored: 'She must continually be controlled, either by being tied down or monitored, so that if the idea were to come to her, she could be certain that there was no possibility of her having committed a murder . . . It is impossible to influence her . . . [She] is starting to say again that she would commit suicide if she did not have to keep living for her husband's sake. She is very concerned about the release of stools, and always wants there to be nothing left. She insists on her qualities and in particular her love of the truth, which has not suffered from her illness.'

Elfriede Hirschfeld tried to see Freud again twice, in 1921 and 1922, but each time he refused and recommended institutionalization at Binswanger's sanatorium. The situation had changed. Due to runaway inflation in Austria, Freud was only taking patients who could pay in foreign currency. As he wrote to Anna von Vest, 'I hardly treat patients any more, but I analyse doctors from England, America, Switzerland, etc., who want to train in analysis. In this way we have all managed to escape the misery of the crown [Austrian currency]' (3 July 1922). The Hirschfelds, for their part, had lost a large part of their fortune in Russia as a result of the war and the Bolshevik revolution. Elfriede Hirschfeld moved with her husband to the Bellevue Sanatorium in November 1921; she lived in one of the villas in the park, in which she could cross paths with the dancer Nijinsky and the art historian Aby Warburg. Her husband, 'under the pressure of financial circumstances' (Binswanger), wanted her to be weaned from some of her overly costly symptoms (probably her army of nurses). Elfriede Hirschfeld refused to be subjected to 'constraint' again, but Freud, consulted by Binswanger, nevertheless recommended the use of force: 'Regarding Frau Hirschfeld, my opinion is that in her case it is probable that nothing will be accomplished except by a combination of analysis and prohibition (counter-compulsion). I regret very much that, at the time, I could only avail myself of the first; the second can only be imposed in an institution' (27 April 1922).

In 1923 Elfriede Hirschfeld was still at the Bellevue Sanatorium and things had not changed much: 'I hardly believe that since she has left you she has elaborated and grasped essentially new aspects of herself. Mostly she seems to be ruminating about the analysis she had with you and everything still resolves around her husband' (Binswanger to Freud, 31 January 1923). It seems that the patient then returned to Pastor Pfister in 1924. In June 1927 she visited Freud and conveyed to him a message from Pfister, who wanted him to destroy previous correspondence relating to an extra-marital affair.

In September of the same year Binswanger went to visit Freud in the Semmering, where Freud was spending the summer. In his journal, Binswanger reports that Freud 'related his views . . . about the Hirschfeld case and the reasons the treatment failed' (nothing more is known about these reasons, unfortunately). On 8 May 1936, when he had again come to see Freud, this time in Vienna, Binswanger noted: 'Visited Frau Hirschfeld, same old patient who had just been rescued from an unfortunate suicide attempt, creepy case.'

Elfriede Hirschfeld died on 8 April 1938 in Montreux, Switzerland, where she had retired to a luxury hotel with one nurse, Lina Block. According to the letter Block sent to Binswanger to inform him, Elfriede Hirschfeld died of an intestinal obstruction after stubbornly refusing treatment for liver and gallbladder problems (24 April 1938). She was 64 years old.

In his interview with Kurt Eissler in 1953, Pastor Pfister still remembered poor Elfriede Hirschfeld and expressed his pity for her: 'Our common patient really was a sorrowful person! And one day I said to Freud: I would rather lose a leg than endure such an obsessional neurosis. To which he said: One?! One!! [Laughs] Better lose four legs!!'

25

KURT RIE

(1875–1908)

We probably would not know anything about Kurt Rie were it not for an interview with Margarete Krafft that Kurt Eissler conducted in 1954 for the Sigmund Freud Archives. Margarete 'Grete' Krafft, née Rosenberg, was born into Freudian royalty. Her father was the pediatrician Ludwig Rosenberg, one of Freud's oldest friends. Her mother, Judith 'Ditha' Rie, was the sister of Oskar Rie, another close friend of Freud and the paediatrician who looked after the Freud children (he was also married to Melanie Bondy, the sister of Wilhelm Fliess's wife Ida). Margarete's younger sister, Anna ('Anny') Katan, was to become a child psychoanalyst closely associated with their common childhood friend Anna Freud, and the same holds for Margarete's cousin, Marianne Rie Kris. As for Oskar Rie's other daughter, Margarethe Rie, she married the psychoanalyst Hermann Nunberg and went on to translate into English the minutes of the Vienna Psychoanalytic Society for publication. Blood will out: Anny Katan, Marianne Kris and Margarethe Nunberg all had children who became psychoanalysts themselves.

The lifelong friendship between Freud, Rie and Rosenberg dated back to when Freud returned from his stay at Charcot's Salpêtrière in Paris and took the post of neurologist at the Vienna paediatric clinic directed by Max Kassowitz. Rie and Rosenberg worked there under Freud as *Sekundarärzte* (assistant physicians) and so it was that the three of them started playing Tarok together when they were on duty (at the time it was the preferred card game in Viennese coffeehouses). These Tarok parties soon became a weekly ritual that took place on Saturdays, sometimes at Freud's place or in Rosenberg's consultation room, sometimes at the home of another colleague, the ophthalmologist Leopold Königstein. Over the years, the players would be joined by Alfred Rie, one of Oskar's three brothers, Emma Eckstein's brother Fritz and the internist Hermann Teleky.

Margarete Kraft remembered how she would play with the Freud children at the Professor's place: 'We often spent Sunday afternoons at the Berggasse. The Professor would go through the room and look at us playing. I remember . . . when I was 14 or 15 years old. I was very shy at the time. The Professor again went through the room and observed me being silent, without saying a word.' The next Saturday, during their Tarok party, Freud told the pediatrician Rosenberg: 'There is something wrong with your girl; something must be done.' Freud meant, of course, that Grete should undergo an analysis, which is something he was wont to recommend when it came to the children of his inner circle: 'I was often told at home that the Professor was very prejudiced regarding his friends' children, in terms of diagnoses and treatments.'

But Grete was not sent to the couch, for her father, like Rie, had doubts regarding the efficacy of Freud's new psychical treatment (something we can also glean from Freud's *Interpretation of Dreams*, where the two friends make a cameo appearance in the famous 'Irma dream' as the sceptical doctors 'Otto' and 'Leopold'): 'I often heard my father say when Freud was mentioned: "I am first and foremost his friend, but absolutely not his follower."'. However, Rosenberg and Rie would occasionally refer some of their difficult cases to Freud. Margarete Krafft recalled how her father brought a young boy who suffered from fainting fits to Freud and how Freud bombarded him with sexual questions, which angered Rosenberg: 'The distraught boy reportedly didn't know what was expected of him . . . The pediatrician [Rosenberg] concluded that the boy didn't suffer from a pseudo-epilepsy, but had a real one.' Rie also referred an anorectic girl to Freud: 'The child – well into pre-adolescence – couldn't eat and died despite treatment.'

Then there was the case of Uncle Kurt. Kurt Rie was Oskar and Ditha's youngest brother. In a family photo he looks stern, unhappy. Around the turn of the century he had gone to America, probably to join his older brother Paul who had established himself as a merchant in New York, but once there he fell into a deep depression. The depression was so bad that he had to be shipped

The Rie siblings, 1894.

back to Vienna, accompanied by a nurse. Three years later, having recovered, he married the future journalist and novelist Therese 'Risa' Herz (pen name L. Andro), with whom he had a child, Robert Maximillian, in 1904. In 1907 the depression came back. A family council was convened with all the Rie brothers, Rosenberg and Freud, and it was decided to place Kurt in Freud's care: 'Freud then had Uncle Kurt in treatment. And here I have the following memory.' As Grete, who was by then thirteen years old, was getting ready to go to school, she distinctly overheard her father speaking to Oskar Rie on the telephone. The date was 31 January 1908: 'And I have word for word in memory that my father with the strongest energy and emphasis told Uncle Oskar: "Listen, I will point out to you that I am his [Kurt's] physician and I will not assume responsibility any longer. This is *not* a psychoneurosis. He belongs now to a closed institution! I tell you! I am *not* going to allow any experiments any longer." At five minutes to 3 p.m. came the phone call: Kurt had shot himself.'

Families have ways of burying their dead. Margarethe Krafft is the only one who ever talked about this episode. Neither Kurt's son Robert, nor Bella Rie, Kurt's sister-in-law, mentioned it when Eissler interviewed them in the early 1950s. Eissler did not ask, either.

26

ALBERT HIRST

(1887–1974)

Born in Vienna on 16 January 1887, his real name was Adalbert Joseph Hirsch and it was only later, when he emigrated to the United States, that he anglicized his name to Hirst. He had known Freud since his early childhood because his mother, Käthe Hirsch, was none other than the older sister of Emma Eckstein, who lived in the house next door with their mother. Before the Hirsch family moved from Vienna to Prague in 1895, Albert and his older sister Ada would often visit the Eckstein household and would bump into Freud when he came to treat Aunt Emma. Albert's father, Emil Hirsch, was a savvy businessman who had taken over the Eckstein paper mill after Emma's brother Fritz Eckstein had brought it to the edge of bankruptcy. Like Albert Eckstein, his father-in-law, Emil Hirsch was a progressive who paid high wages to his employees. He was also a member of B'nai B'rith, where he regularly ran into Freud while the Hirsch family was still in Vienna.

Albert went through a fairly classic teenage crisis. He lacked confidence, panicked before exams, wrote poems in secret and was obsessed by intractable moral problems. He also masturbated, which worried him and made him fear for his mental and physical health (it was just at this time that his aunt Emma warned in her writings against this dangerous practice). He fell madly in love with a certain Emmy Becker, who gave him the cold shoulder. Finally, he made an 'unquestionably very insincere' attempt at suicide in 1903. He was sixteen, an age when we do not know who we are going to be.

His parents were alarmed and sent him to spend the Easter holidays in Vienna with Aunt Emma and his grandmother, so that he could consult with their friend Freud. The latter was considered in the family circle to be a genius and Albert was well aware of being in the presence of a great man. Freud did not put him on the couch. He made him sit on a chair and 'ordered me to assume in that chair the position in which I masturbated'. Then he told him that masturbation was not harmful – an astonishing assertion, since he publicly stated the opposite, as we still see in his 'Discussion on Masturbation' in 1912. (We also know that he regularly prohibited other patients from masturbating during a course of psychoanalysis, as with Mark Brunswick and Carl Liebmann.) For young Albert, it was a great relief to learn from the mouth of the main authority on the matter that his solitary pleasure did not condemn him to neurosis. Freud gave him some additional commonsensical advice, but it was already the end of the holidays and so Albert returned to Prague. Later, Hirst would conclude that this therapy had been too brief and that it 'did me no good'.

Hirst had ambitions to become a lawyer and to enter politics on the socialist side, like his Eckstein uncles and aunts, but he did not work hard enough and soon had to abandon his law studies. He continued to have low self-esteem, harboured an inferiority complex compared to the brilliant Eckstein family members and his older sister Ada, and thought he would never amount to anything. Various sexual problems also undermined his morale. He continued to masturbate – far too often, he thought – and unlike all his friends he was awkward with women. Above all, he was afflicted with a 'peculiar, rare form of impotency': he could not ejaculate inside a woman (anorgasmia). Besides, he was still in love with Emmy and had accepted a well-paid position in the family business merely in the hope of being able to marry her. When Emmy and her family rejected him, his world fell apart. He had renounced his ambitions and his ideals for nothing: 'I had lost the prize for which I had sold my soul.' He started thinking about suicide again. Finally, he asked his parents to send him once more to see Freud.

So, in the autumn of 1909, he found himself again in Vienna with Aunt Emma. He succeeded Ada, who the previous year had also been sent to Freud for treatment by their parents (Freud had ended her analysis when he realized that she had not come to see him of her own free will). Hirst had already started his analysis when Emma attempted suicide and resumed (or continued?) her treatment with Freud. The latter, a veritable family therapist, did not hesitate to share with Hirst the details of the analyses of his aunt and sister. However, he refused to answer when Hirst asked if Emma had suffered a sexual trauma during childhood. The Ecksteins were all neurotic, he said, because of Albert's maternal grandfather's syphilis.

Hirst saw Freud six times a week, at nine in the morning, Monday to Saturday. Freud demanded forty Austrian crowns per hour, a rate 'which at the time was very high' and quite shocked Hirst's parents. According to Hirst, Freud was very 'money-minded' and spoke about it as frankly as he did about sexuality: 'Certainly he wasn't going to die the poor doctor.' One day, when Hirst informed him that he was going to have to miss two sessions because he had been recalled by the army for administrative formalities in Moravia, Freud had wondered what to do about the fees. Hirst replied that

it seemed proper for Freud to bill the two sessions as usual, since the cancellation was not his fault; Freud complimented him for his business acumen and urged him to commit to a commercial career, rather than law or politics. Payment for missed sessions has since become the rule in psychoanalysis.

Hirst had prepared for his analysis by mugging up on *The Interpretation of Dreams* and *Jokes and Their Relation to the Unconscious*. He therefore expected Freud to dissect his Oedipus complex and exhume some forgotten trauma. The treatment, however, took a very different turn, closer in fact to the 'persuasive' psychotherapy of Paul Dubois, Freud's rival in Bern, than to psychoanalysis. Freud seems to have tried to restore

Freud's prescription for a vaginal suppository for birth control.

Hirst's self-confidence by paying him all kinds of compliments: Hirst should not blame himself for being critical of his aunt Emma, because Freud was critical of her too; he was much smarter than his sister Ada; he had a good business sense; he wrote very good poems; the interpretations he gave of his own dreams were brilliant, and so on. The analyst even treated his young patient as an equal, taking him as a witness that, in the last sentence of his article 'On Coca', he had anticipated the discovery by his colleague and rival Carl Koller of the local anaesthetic properties of cocaine. He also confided in him his loathing of the United States and told him how he had struggled to find public toilets in New York. Hirst was flattered. One day when Freud praised him particularly highly, he left his session 'in a daze, walking on air'.

Freud also gave him 'instructions'. When Hirst was once again unable to ejaculate with a young woman he had met, Freud, like a modern sex therapist, told him not to be discouraged and to keep on trying. Shortly after, Hirst finally managed to have complete intercourse and Freud celebrated the event by writing him a prescription for a vaginal contraceptive suppository, which he said was more pleasant than the traditional English condom (the prescription is now in the Sigmund Freud Collection at the Library of Congress in Washington). Suddenly, Hirst was fornicating up to ten times every Sunday afternoon that he spent at the hotel with the young lady. Freud also urged him to try his luck with another young woman, despite Hirst finding her less amiable, but this time the 'instruction' was less effective and Hirst was unable to ejaculate.

In the late spring of 1910 Hirst's father came to Vienna to see Freud and ask him to end the treatment. (Had he been alerted by the Ecksteins to the split between Emma and Freud over the gynecologist Dora Teleky's operation?) Hirst returned to Prague and continued working for his father. At the end of 1911 he emigrated to the United States to take up a position in the New York branch of the family business. (Freud, to whom he had gone to say goodbye, strongly advised him not to go to the United States, suggesting that he go to South America instead.) In 1913 Hirst married Helene Marie Kohn, a long-time friend, with whom he had a son two years later, despite a temporary return of his ejaculatory difficulties. His father died soon after the war ended. The family business had not survived the collapse of trade with Central Europe and in the early 1920s Hirst found himself in a difficult financial situation. He began to think of himself as a failure, unable to earn a decent living unlike all the other men his age. Then one day, as he was coming down the stairs in his apartment block, he suddenly realized that he was repeating the old pattern of thought that had inhibited him so much in the past in sexual matters.

He subsequently decided to resume his law studies by taking evening classes at the New York Law School, and this time he persevered. He came top of his class in 1925 and drafted a law for New York State that protected the heirs of life insurance underwriters against creditors, which was then adopted by the majority of American states. Having become a renowned lawyer, he was elected president of the American League for the Abolition of the Death Penalty and actively participated in the American Civil Liberties Union, thus fulfilling his old dream of combining law and politics. He published a book, *Business Life Insurance and Other Topics* (1949), as well as several hundred articles in law journals.

Hirst felt that he had not really overcome his neurosis until ten years after his analysis with Freud, when he finally became aware of his defeatist patterns of thought (of his cognitive distortion, as we would say today) and decided to put an end to them. However, he was grateful to Freud for showing him the way by restoring his self-confidence. Mere contact with the great man had been beneficial. Hirst's admiration for Freud's person did not, however, extend to psychoanalysis as therapy: when his son Eric Albert seemed eager to undergo analysis, he resolutely opposed the idea.

In 1938 Hirst returned to Vienna, which was then under Nazi occupation, to help his family and friends to emigrate to the United States. He tried to see Freud on this occasion to return a packet of letters which Freud had written over the years to Emma Eckstein, but Anna Freud told him that her father was too ill to receive him.

Ada, Hirst's sister, came to live in New York in 1941 and the two habitually lunched together once a week to talk about old times. In his autobiography, written in 1972, Hirst concluded that he had had a good life, for which he was grateful to God, to America and to Freud. He died in New York on 13 March 1974.

27

BARON VICTOR VON DIRSZTAY
(1884–1935)

The expressionist writer Victor Adolf von Dirsztay was a familiar figure in Viennese literary and artistic circles. An aesthete and bohemian, he was known for his eccentricities. Some considered him a clown, but the author and dramatist Arthur Schnitzler, in his journal, described him rather as a 'funny figure': 'He makes a comic impression, literati-like, slightly self-ironic, not entirely unsympathetic.'

He was also very wealthy. His grandfather, Guttman Fisch (or Fischl), came from a prominent Jewish family in Hungary and had made a fortune in the grain trade and horse breeding for the Austro-Hungarian army, before being ennobled Fisch/Fischl von Dirsztay in 1885. Victor's father, Ladislaus (Laszlo) Fischl von Dirsztay, had been created a baron by the Austrian emperor Franz Joseph in 1905 and then shortened his name to 'von Dirsztay'. As the Imperial Consul General of Turkey, he had an imposing three-storey palace built in the diplomatic district of Vienna to go with his title. Theodor Herzl had been forced to deal with him in negotiations with the Turkish administration and found him 'grotesque', 'absolutely comical'. In his autobiography, the painter Oskar Kokoschka, who was very close to Victor and who at the start of his career had drawn on the generosity of the Dirsztay family, similarly describes the Dirsztay parents as 'nouveaux riches' who understood nothing of their son's literary and artistic aspirations. Also according to Kokoschka, Victor von Dirsztay was ashamed of his family. He suffered from a very bothersome skin condition and 'Freud himself, whom he consulted for years, could not heal him, for his disease came from his contempt of his family.'

Victor von Dirsztay, 1917, postcard to Alfred Loos.

The treatment probably started at the end of 1909 or even before, since Freud mentions in a letter to Sándor Ferenczi of 3 December 1909 that 'Dirsztay's parents were with me and proved themselves quite friendly to the treatment.' We can deduce that it was Victor's parents who paid for the treatment, or that it was at their instigation that he went to consult Freud. This first phase of analysis – there were two others – lasted until July 1911. Dirsztay lay on the couch up to twelve times a week, making his analysis one of Freud's most intensive.

At the same time, in 1909 Dirsztay had published a collection of aphorisms and commentaries, *Streichquartett* (String Quartet). He had also made unsuccessful attempts to publish pieces in the satirical newspaper *Die Fackel* and had contacted its editor Karl Kraus, for whom he felt an admiration close to idolatry. Kraus, a sharp and caustic spirit, was not unknown to Freud. In 1906 Freud had asked Kraus to support him against his ex-friend Wilhelm Fliess, who was publicly accusing him of having been an accomplice in the plagiarism of Fliess's ideas by Otto Weininger, author of the best-selling *Sex and Character* (1903). Initially rather favourable to psychoanalysis, Kraus had defended Weininger and Freud in the controversy. By 1907, however, Kraus had become increasingly critical and mocking of psychoanalysis, and Freud had taken umbrage. In January 1910 Fritz Wittels, a disciple of Freud who had previously been a friend of Kraus and shared with him the favours of the young actress Irma Karczewska, made a presentation to the 'Wednesday society' in which he presented *Die Fackel* as a symptom of Kraus's neurosis, to Freud's enthusiastic approval. War between the two camps was openly declared when Kraus sued Wittels in order to block the publication of a vengeful *roman à clef* in which Wittels exposed Kraus's private life. Worried that this new scandal would harm the image of psychoanalysis, Freud had asked Wittels to bury his book, whereupon the latter, furious at being disowned, left the Vienna Psychoanalytic Society.

One can imagine the impact of this controversy on Dirsztay, inevitably torn between his analyst and his huge admiration for Kraus. On 15 July 1911, barely a week after the (provisional) end of his analysis with Freud, he wrote a sombre and exalted letter to Kraus, who had just gone on holiday to Ostend: '*I am eager*, today on the first evening of your absence whose *crippling effect has already begun* to make itself felt and the intense feeling of *abandonment* by all good spirits – more than that: *by the best spirit*, leads me – *to show my gratitude* for every thought you ever had and for every sentence you have ever written down.'

In September and October of the same year Dirsztay published aphorisms and a satire in *Der Sturm*, a Berlin art review edited by a friend of Kraus and Kokoschka, Herwarth Walden. Dirsztay financially supported the magazine at Kokoschka's instigation, in return for which Walden published some of his texts. In October Kraus let Walden know that he was deeply 'shocked' that he had let himself be bribed and that he had agreed to publish 'such swill': Dirsztay was a 'totally original and droll person', but he could not write. The

Drawing of Karl Kraus by Lajos Tihanyi, 1925.

matter was serious enough in Kraus's eyes for him to tell Walden that he was cutting all ties with him and his magazine. Dirsztay could not fail to pick up the news of this devastating judgement on the part of his literary idol, as well as its consequences. Whether or not there is a causal relationship here, he seems to have had a breakdown that same October and to have stayed in a psychiatric hospital. Presumably, on this occasion, he had been placed under financial guardianship and no longer had free access to his money. However, none of this lessened his devotion to Kraus in the least.

In 1912 Dirsztay divorced his first wife, Ilona de Losada (a distant cousin by marriage). In May of the following year he began a second phase of analysis with Freud, which was to last until 31 December 1915. The day after his last session with Freud, he sent a telegram to Kraus: 'Am in a terrible state . . . phoned you in vain last night.' There followed a long letter in which Dirsztay explained why he had not been able to tell him in person how good he thought the last issue of *Die Fackel* had been, or to attend one of his public readings: '[It] took place a week before the end of my five-year-long treatment and this time was so critical that, except at great risk, I could not seek any distraction . . . From the beginning of this year my treatment is ended for good, without my having until now any clear sense of its result . . . I once more belong to life, having seen a higher form of existence during the hour I was writing to you.' Evidently, Dirsztay felt guilty for seeming to have neglected Kraus for Freud and was trying to get back into his good graces now that the analysis was (provisionally) finished. But an invisible impediment prevented him from speaking to Kraus directly. Had Freud forbidden it? Did he forbid himself to do so? Whatever the answer, it is clear that Dirsztay was uncomfortably wavering between two allegiances.

In the summer or autumn of 1916 Dirsztay suffered another mental breakdown and had to take a rest cure. In December of the same year, when he left Vienna for the post of literary director at the Kammerspiele theatre in Munich, he sent another long letter to Kraus in which he once again alluded to the obscure reasons that prevented him from going to see him: 'Many times I have sought the way to you in order to bid you farewell and to be able to *speak to you once more before my parting*. After a hard battle, however, I had to *give that up for, believe me, the parting would have become too difficult for me* . . . However difficult it is, I do not intend coming to Vienna for a long time and at any rate *I intend to take precautions against it* lest I weaken and fall prey to temptation. With great longing and admiration.'

A year later, we find Dirsztay in Dr Teuscher's sanatorium in Weisser Hirsch, near Dresden. Teuscher was a pacifist and his sanatorium served as a refuge for artists and writers who were simulating mental disorders to escape the trenches. Dirsztay found his friend Kokoschka there, who was writing plays during his stay, as well as the expressionist poet Walter Hasenclever. He offered the latter his book *Lob des hohen Verstandes* (In Praise of High Intellect), which had just appeared in the spring with illustrations by Kokoschka, as well as a copy of Freud's *Psychopathology of Everyday Life*, dedicated: 'To my dear Walter Hasenclever at a moment of great need when under torture I decided, as a shipwrecked man, once again to spend a period of intense work with the Master of this book, in melancholy farewell mood and in the clear knowledge that I am still stumbling in darkness and far from myself, your poor, faithful sanatorium room neighbour, hoping you will think of him now and again! VD 27.10.17'

Dirsztay resumed his treatment with Freud on 3 December 1917. This third analysis lasted two and a quarter years, until 3 March 1920. It was interrupted for two weeks by Dirsztay's stay in the Cottage Sanatorium run by Rudolf Urbantschitsch, a fellow-traveller of psychoanalysis. All the while, Dirsztay continued to refrain from seeing Kraus. In 1918 he wrote to him that his condition was 'unbearable' and that he had to be alone with his misery: 'You can imagine, my dear Mr Kraus, how much of a struggle it costs me to have to stay away from your readings – the days on which you read are the darkest for me!'

According to calculations by the psychoanalyst Ulrike May, who has carefully reconstructed Dirsztay's biography and treatment, his analysis in three distinct periods was one of the longest Freud undertook: 1,400 hours at least. Nothing is known of its content, except that in a letter addressed in June 1920 to his 'Dear Baron', Freud alludes to 'the conquest so far achieved of your masochism'. As we now know, thanks to the declassification of the interview granted by Theodor Reik to Kurt Eissler in 1954, the masochism that Dirsztay had apparently abandoned while in treatment with Freud was of a sexual nature: he enjoyed being whipped by his female partners, without having sex with them.

This 'conquest' of his masochistic practices does not seem to have enabled Dirsztay to make much of an advance, however. Again according to Reik, he was now impotent and had traded his sexual masochism for a 'social' masochism (or a 'moral' masochism, as Freud would conceptualize it in 1924 in his article on 'The Economic Problem of Masochism', over which hung Dirsztay's shadow). He humiliated himself in public in many ways, such as making jokes at his own expense. In a 1939 article on masochism where Dirsztay is mentioned anonymously, Reik writes that he 'produced a constant stream of witticisms – killing ones moreover more than not [sic] – which made unmerciful fun of his own stupidity, tactlessness or egotism . . . The self-depreciation had become a social mask.' Reik reported to Eissler that Dirsztay, once so elegant, 'neglected himself, didn't wash'. To punish himself, he forced himself to have no fixed abode and never to stay in the same hotel for more than one night. Or he adopted risky behaviour with the intention of getting caught. Obsessed with fantasies of being a serial killer, he haunted the red-light district of Kärtnerstrasse and hit prostitutes on their backsides in passing, which necessarily placed him in delicate situations. In 1920 Freud and Reik had to attend a legal hearing to testify in his favour in an obscure case linked to his nocturnal expeditions (he escaped without being convicted).

In June 1920, four months after the end of his treatment with Freud, we again find Dirsztay in a private clinic for nervous disorders, the Sanatorium Mariagrün, near Graz (this stay seems to have coincided with his legal problems). From there, he asked Freud to resume analysis with him. Freud was about to set off for his long summer holiday and he seems to have referred him to Theodor Reik, no doubt because the latter was interested in masochism. In any case, Reik already knew Dirsztay because, as he told Eissler, he moved in the same literary milieu: 'I socialized with Schnitzler . . . there was this circle, Hofmannsthal, Salten, Beer-Hofmann, and then there was Dirsztay.' Besides, Reik and Dirsztay shared a love of Mahler.

The analysis with Reik lasted for approximately three years, from 1920 to 1923 or 1924 (the chronology is not very clear). Dirsztay

Nude drawing of Ea von Allesch by Gustav Klimt, 1904.

was a difficult patient. Having previously been with the Master, he knew everything better than Reik, who at the time was only starting his career as a psychoanalyst. However, if we are to believe Reik himself, the analysis was 'successful, as it were'. Among other things, Dirsztay was no longer impotent. In 1924 he married Klára Unreich, a 35-year-old ex-dancer whom he divorced six years later 'only for reasons of civil law'. Previously, he had had an affair with the famous journalist and muse of the Viennese avant-garde Ea von Allesch, which had provoked the jealousy of her lover, Hermann Broch.

Again thanks to analysis, according to Reik, Dirsztay managed to free himself from his writer's block and write *Der Unentrinnbare* (The Inescapable), a novel that was published in 1923 with seven drawings by Kokoschka. Dedicated 'To Dr Theodor Reik in gratitude', the book was a classic tale of doubles, visibly inspired by Freud's article on 'The Uncanny' and Otto Rank's *Der Doppelgänger* (it was under this title that Reik remembered the novel of which he was the dedicatee): the hero undergoes depersonalization and finds his 'self' in the form of another character, the Inescapable, until the latter commits suicide and drags the hero down to death with him. Schnitzler, who writes in his journal that Dirsztay was trying to 'liberate himself' from a 'twenty-year-long "double self"', said the novel was 'snobby' and 'weakish'.

The book was not reviewed and went completely unnoticed. Successful analysis or not, Dirsztay was at the end of his tether. He had no money, since the end of the Austro-Hungarian Empire had led to the ruin of his family. The man whom his companion in psychoanalysis Sergius Pankejeff called the 'Jewish baron' was only a shadow of his former self: 'He was very fat when I saw him during [Freud's] office hours, elegantly dressed, and normal looking. But then, after the war, he looked terrible and was in the company of an altogether impossible woman. One could tell that he had come down in the world, that somehow he had not become well' (Pankejeff, interviews with Karin Obholzer).

In 1925 Dirsztay wrote a long letter to Kraus in which he confided that every evening he walked back and forth in front of his house, because he had a 'terrible secret' to reveal to him: 'What I have to say and report is, however, so monstrous, so different from anything which has ever taken place, that it is infinitely difficult for me to bring it to light . . . For many years I have been totally lost, dead, without the slightest sign of life for *anyone* – relations or friends. Nobody knows – not a soul guesses – *what has happened here* and I had to remain silent – *more dead than the dead in the grave.*' What kept him alive was the desire 'to bring the incomprehensible that happened here to people's knowledge and *to summon them to atone for the crime* that for year after year has been committed against me in public daily and hourly. And now I have pronounced the word: it is a matter *of a crime* – an infamous soul murder which has been allowed to be practised upon me in full view of everyone unhindered for year upon year. – I was so bewitched, so entangled and blinded was my soul that it was *only one year ago that the fearful enlightenment came to me* and it has been only such a short while that I have understood what happened here! . . . Now it seems that my strength is at an end – *I can* no longer remain silent – *do not want to remain buried* – I cannot determine when the day will come that I speak to you as to the First Man – *but I feel that it is no longer distant!*'

However, it would take another six years for Dirsztay to finally reveal the exact nature of the 'soul murder' of which he had been the victim (*Seelenmord* was a term from the delirium of President Schreber, which Dirsztay definitely knew about thanks to the article that Freud had devoted to it). In 1931 Dirsztay wrote a letter to Karl

Kraus's lawyer, Dr Oskar Samek, to justify selling the manuscripts Kraus had given him (he had also sold a manuscript by Richard Strauss and a letter from Freud, which led Kraus to write a mocking note in which he congratulated Dirsztay, without naming him, for having protected himself from psychoanalysis by selling Freud's 'prescription'). Dirsztay explained his gesture by the fact that he was ill, living in misery and also had to 'take care of a second person'. Now all that was left was for him to vegetate 'until I am released from this life, in which case – as you should know – I have prepared for *Karl Kraus* himself (in the form of a bequest) the *exact explanation* of my tragedy (*destroyed by analysis*) together with the declaration of my *wonder and love* (for about the last 15 years) – an *admiration* which I have described in *this very* document as the only gain of this life of mine that has been eliminated by a quack. (My case is clearly described in this document.)'

The document in question has not survived, so that we are reduced to speculate as to the identity of the 'quack' responsible for the unspeakable 'soul murder' suffered by Dirsztay. Was it Theodor Reik, who had indeed been accused of being a charlatan in 1924 and who had been prohibited from practising in February 1925, two months before the letter to Kraus in which Dirsztay mentioned his recent 'enlightenment'? Or Freud himself? Or both? The fact that Dirsztay speaks of 'analysis' and of a crime committed 'year after year' and 'daily and hourly' seems rather to indicate that he incriminated the analytical process as such, which had cut him off from the rest of the world, including Kraus.

On 6 December 1935 Baron Victor von Dirstay decided to end it all. His ex-wife, with whom he was still living and who had spent several periods in institutions over the years, had just returned from the Steinhof psychiatric hospital. They turned on the gas stove. A note left on the kitchen table said, 'By consent'. The newspapers widely reported the death of this quintessential Viennese character, a lover of music and psychoanalysis. The *Reichspost* ran the headline: 'Tragic End of a Freud Disciple'. Kraus was silent, for once.

28
SERGIUS PANKEJEFF
(1887–1979)

Freud nicknamed him the 'Wolf Man' because of the contents of one of his dreams, but his name was actually Sergius (Sergei) Konstantinovich Pankejeff. Born on 6 January 1887 near Kherson, Ukraine, he belonged to a family of large landowners. His paternal grandfather was said to be one of the wealthiest men in southern Russia. His father, Konstantin Pankejeff, owned a palatial house in Odessa, as well as a property in southern Russia and another 130,000 hectares in an area of wilderness in present-day Belarus, where the family spent most of the summers. Konstantin Pankejeff organized big wolf hunts there and in the evening people danced round the bodies of the dead wolves (the Library of Congress holds several photos of the young Sergius standing with his mother and sister in front of a heap of slaughtered animals).

Konstantin Pankejeff, who was a magistrate, had been elevated to the rank of 'noble', *dvorjanin*. He was an intelligent and cultivated man with excellent taste (he owned two Kandinskys from the artist's pre-abstract period). He edited a liberal magazine, the *Southern Mail*, and financially supported the Democratic Constitutional Party, a movement to the left of the Octobrists. He also suffered from bouts of deep depression, which he fought by indulging in alcoholic binges that left him dead drunk (the Russian psychiatrist and psychoanalyst Moshe Wulff, who had treated him in a clinic, discreetly described him as a 'dipsomaniac'). He spent several periods in the Munich clinic of the great psychiatrist (and Freud's opponent) Emil Kraepelin, who diagnosed him with manic-depressive psychosis.

Other members of Pankejeff's family also suffered from mental illness. Sergius's paternal grandfather died of alcoholism. His wife

Irina Petrovna had sunk into depression after the death of her only daughter and appears to have committed suicide by taking an overdose. Peter, one of Sergius's paternal uncles, developed a paranoid delirium and had to be interned, before ending his life as a hermit on land he owned in the Crimea (Sergius inherited his fortune on his death). Two maternal cousins who lived in the palace with the Pankejeffs were treated for schizophrenia by Moshe Wulff. Anna, Sergius's older sister, committed suicide in 1906 at the site of the duel in which the poet Mikhail Lermontov had died. After his daughter's suicide, Konstantin Pankejeff decided to honour her memory by founding a hospital for nervous disorders bearing her name. His wife withdrew into a state of permanent mourning. Then, in 1908, Konstantin Pankejeff ended his life by taking an overdose of Veronal.

Shortly after the death of his sister, Sergius Pankejeff too began to suffer from depression, accompanied in his case by obsessional ruminations that made him incapable of making decisions. In St Petersburg, where he was studying law, he went to see the neurologist Vladimir Bechterev, who diagnosed 'neurasthenia' and tried in vain to 'de-suggest' it under hypnosis (he also took the opportunity to suggest in passing that Pankejeff's father subsidize a research institute he wished to set up). Pankejeff interrupted his studies and then began to live the life of a 'gilded neurotic', travelling from specialist to specialist in an attempt to escape his melancholy. He spent two periods in Kraepelin's clinic, in March and then in the autumn of 1908. Kraepelin, who knew Pankejeff's family history, diagnosed an inherited manic-depressive state. Pankejeff was subsequently treated in the clinics of two further opponents of Freud's, Adolf Friedländer in Frankfurt (winter 1908–9) and Theodor Ziehen in Berlin. Then he returned home to Odessa.

During his first stay at the Kraepelin clinic, Pankejeff fell in love with an older divorcée, Teresa Keller. Teresa was a beautiful woman, but she came from a modest background and was barely educated. Pankejeff's mother, his family and his doctors were all strongly opposed to the affair. Pankejeff was paralysed by indecision: should he break up with Teresa or join her in Munich? He decided not to decide anything before he had consulted the famous psychotherapist (and Freud's rival) Paul Dubois in Bern. His personal physician Leonid Drosnès, who accompanied him, had heard of Freud from Moshe Wulff and proposed they stop off in Vienna for a consultation. Freud, no doubt delighted to see arriving in his consulting room a patient whom several of his opponents had failed to cure, convinced him to stay with him, promising that he could join Teresa after the treatment (this is what he called the 'breakthrough towards the woman', an expression which struck Pankejeff deeply).

The treatment began in February 1910. The psychoanalyst Ruth Mack Brunswick and Ernest Jones, Freud's biographer, were later to claim that Pankejeff was in a state of total mental collapse when he arrived in Vienna, to the point of needing to be helped to dress by his servant. This had the effect of irritating Pankejeff in his old age: 'Good God, what idiocy!' he declared to the Viennese journalist Karin Obholzer when she questioned him about it in the 1970s. In an 'evaluation' of his analysis written in 1970 at the request of the psychoanalyst Muriel Gardiner, he wrote: 'My emotional state was already much improved under the influence of Dr D[rosnès], the journey from Odessa to Vienna, etc. Actually Professor Freud never saw me in a state of really deep depression.' If he were being treated by Freud, this was only so as to obtain medical authorization to marry Teresa. Freud would no doubt have agreed, because in his case history he rejected the diagnosis of 'manic-depressive insanity' supported by 'the most authoritative quarters' (Kraepelin). For him, Pankejeff suffered from an obsessional neurosis, the consequence of an earlier 'infantile neurosis'.

Freud's first decision was to send Pankejeff to the Cottage Sanatorium for nervous disorders run by his disciple Rudolf Urbantschitsch, where he came to visit him over a period of six weeks. His second decision was to forbid him to see Teresa or marry her until he gave him express permission. (We know from the letters written by a grateful Teresa that he allowed Pankejeff to visit her in 1911 and 1912.) Pankejeff was not to have children: when Teresa unexpectedly became pregnant, Freud demanded that she have an abortion, and the operation caused an infection that left her sterile. Pankejeff was also not allowed to leave Vienna during the analysis: 'But I remember, I once wanted to go to Budapest, for one or two days, but Freud did not let me go . . . "There are many beautiful women in Budapest; you might fall in love with one of them there!" . . . – Eissler: Why didn't the Professor want you to fall in love? – Pankejeff: Well, I think he thought that the treatment would no longer progress' (interview with Kurt Eissler, 30 July 1952).

Pankejeff saw Freud six times a week (sometimes more), at the rate of forty crowns an hour. To give an idea of what this amount represented at the time, Pankejeff explained to Karin Obholzer that forty crowns corresponded to three and a half times the price of a day in a first-class sanatorium, treatment and doctor included (between 1,100 and 1,400 present-day u.s. dollars, if based on prices at an equivalent private institution in Europe or North America): 'Very expensive . . . The drawback of psychoanalysis is surely that only the rich can afford it.' But money did not matter to Pankejeff and thanks to this 'fortunate concatenation' (Freud), the analysis could take place 'timelessly', without being limited by a 'short-sighted therapeutic ambition' (Freud again).

On the strength of Freud's promises, Pankejeff had believed that everything would be settled quickly, but in fact the analysis lasted much longer than expected – four years and five months to be exact. Pankejeff therefore took quarters in Vienna with Drosnès and a servant. There was also a student whom Drosnès had brought back from Russia to administer enemas. Indeed, Pankejeff had suffered from chronic constipation ever since Drosnès had pre-scribed him an excessive dose of calomel in order to settle a problem with diarrhoea. (Very quickly, Freud ordered they stop the enemas because of their 'homosexual' character, and the student found himself with nothing to do.) They spent the time as best they could. Pankejeff was studying law, so as to take his exams when he returned to Russia. He also took fencing lessons with an Italian fencing master. In the evenings he went to the Jewish theatre (with Teresa, when she came to join him in Vienna towards the end of the analysis), or else played cards until late at night with Drosnès and the student. Drosnès, for his part, attended the sessions of the Vienna Psychoanalytic Society (he would set up as a psychoana-lyst on his return to Russia). It was a good time: 'When I was in treatment with Freud I was doing very well. I felt good. We used to go to cafes, to the Prater. It was a good life' (interviews with Karin Obholzer).

From Freud's point of view, on the other hand, the analysis had stalled: 'The patient . . . remained for a long time unassailably entrenched behind an attitude of "obliging apathy". He listened, understood, and remained unapproachable.' To Moshe Wulff, who asked him in 1912 how Pankejeff's analysis was going, Freud replied: 'Badly – and do you know why? I and the boy get on so well.' In October 1913, wishing to produce a model case study capable of countering the heretical theses of Adler and Jung, Freud nevertheless ended up rushing things forward and imposed a deadline for treatment. He obtained in record time, he tells us, 'all the material which made it possible to clear up his inhibitions and remove his symptoms', notably the famous 'primal scene' during which the little Wolf Man, at one and a half years old, was supposed to have been able to observe the lovemaking of his parents from his cradle.

Pankejeff, meanwhile, had not noticed any particular change. Nor was he convinced of the reality of the 'primal scene' postulated by Freud, of which he had no memory. Later, in 1930, Ruth Mack Brunswick wrote in a draft note that Pankejeff had 'tried to convince me that the reality forced upon him by his analysis

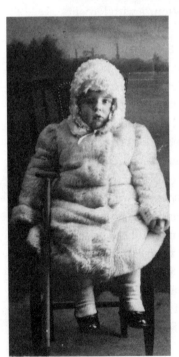

was wrong' (2 February 1930). But Freud considered that the analysis was finished and that Pankejeff could now marry Teresa. The last session took place on 10 July 1914, before Freud left for his holiday. Freud had suggested to his patient that he give him a gift 'so that the feeling of gratitude did not become too strong' (interviews with Karin Obholzer). Pankejeff therefore offered him an Egyptian statuette representing a princess, a real museum piece. Pankejeff had planned to travel with Teresa afterwards, but war broke out on 29 July and he had to return to Odessa. Teresa joined him from Munich and they married soon after.

The Tsarist empire collapsed in February 1917. Pankejeff took the opportunity to become a member of the Constitutional Democratic Party, like his father. During the troubled period following the October Revolution, Odessa successively came under

Sergius Pankejeff
at age one and a half.

Sergius Pankejeff
practising fencing in
Vienna while in
treatment with Freud.

the control of the People's Republic of Ukraine (allied with the
Central Powers against the Red Army), the French Army, the White
Army and the Soviet Republic of Odessa. In March 1918 Odessa
was taken over by the Central Powers as a result of the Treaty of
Brest-Litovsk concluded with the Bolsheviks. Pankejeff decided to
join Teresa in Freiburg, where she had gone to care for her dying
daughter Else, who was suffering from tuberculosis.

On the way, he stopped in Vienna at the end of April 1919 to
pay Freud a visit. The Austro-Hungarian Empire was falling apart.
Communists were marching through the streets of Vienna; there
was no money; famine reigned. According to his own testimony,
Pankejeff was at the time 'so thoroughly satisfied with my mental
and emotional condition that I never thought of the possibility
of needing more psychoanalytic treatment'. But Freud, who was
in a precarious financial situation at the end of the war, decided
that Pankejeff's chronic constipation constituted an unanalysed
'remnant of transference' (*Übertragungsrest*) and recommended a

second analysis. Pankejeff could not resist the Professor. So he went to Munich to bury Else with Teresa and returned to Vienna in November instead of returning to take care of his family and business in Odessa, which was now under English control due to the rout of the Central Powers. This was what he later called 'the catastrophe': while he and Freud were trying to work out the reasons for his constipation, the Red Army entered Odessa on 8 February 1920 and the Bolsheviks seized all of his property. 'Reason told me: "Go there right now and settle your affairs." And I said to him [Freud], "I would like to go because of my financial affairs." And he answered, "No, stay here. There is this and that to be resolved." And so I stayed. And that's why it became too late. When I went to the British, I was told: "We don't issue visas any longer, the Red Army is already in Odessa"' (interviews with Obholzer).

The analysis ended on 17 March 1920, five weeks after the fall of Odessa. Pankejeff had run out of money and could no longer pay. He was still constipated, even if Freud affirmed in a note added in 1923 to his case history that this 'remnant of transference' had been 'successfully dealt with after a few months' work'. Freud, who was now taking only those patients able to pay in foreign currency, occasionally gave him a few dollars or pounds to support him. Pankejeff, however, refuted the 'fable' (his term) according to which Freud organized an annual collection among analysts to help him meet his needs. Moreover, thanks to Freud's son Martin, he had quickly found a jurist job in an insurance company, one that he would keep until his retirement. He became a specialist in civil liability and insurance law, on which he published an article in 1939. On the side, he cultivated himself and painted some decent works in an impressionist style.

In early 1924 Pankejeff, who was very concerned with his appearance, began to harbour hypochondriac concerns about blackheads and small bumps on his nose. He kept going to see a dermatologist recommended by Freud, Dr Ehrmann, who practised several interventions. None of these satisfied Pankejeff. In June 1926 he received a letter from Freud asking him to certify in writing that he had indeed had his famous 'wolf dream' when he was a child. Otto Rank had just published *The Trauma of Birth*, in which he claimed that the five to seven wolves in Pankejeff's dream actually reproduced the photos of the seven disciples of Freud hanging on the wall of his cabinet. Pankejeff confirmed by return that Rank was mistaken and that his dream did indeed date from childhood, which allowed Sándor Ferenczi to torpedo the heretical thesis of his ex-friend and collaborator Rank in a scathing review. In the days following Freud's letter, Pankejeff suffered an acute attack of hypochondria. Convinced that the electrolysis performed by Dr Ehrmann would leave him permanently disfigured, he compulsively observed his nose in a small pocket mirror to follow the development of the scars. (Much later, in a letter addressed to Muriel Gardiner on 11 June 1957, Pankejeff would ask himself if the outbreak of this crisis 'had any connection with the request of Prof. Freud?!').

Freud, whom he went to consult, refused to take him back into analysis and sent him to his disciple Ruth Mack Brunswick. The treatment lasted four months and Mack Brunswick diagnosed paranoia. Pankejeff, who feared ending up like his uncle Peter, rejected the diagnosis and decided to get a grip on himself: 'While there, I gathered all my strength so as to not look at myself in the mirror; I somehow overcame my fixed ideas. This took several days. After a few days, it was over . . . I think I achieved such great success with Mrs Mack because I stood up against psychoanalysts, and took my own decision' (interviews with Obholzer).

However, Pankejeff had not yet finished with psychoanalysts. In 1930 he returned to Mack Brunswick to help him decide (like Freud at the time) whether or not he should leave his wife for a younger woman who was making advances to him. There were yet more periods of analysis with Mack Brunswick during the 1930s, probably caused by the depressions into which Pankejeff regularly fell. In 1938, at the time of the Anschluss, Pankejeff went through a major crisis caused by the suicide of his wife. The latter, who had been depressed for a long time, seems to have been caught up in the wave of suicides among Viennese Jews who wanted to escape from the Nazis. (Pankejeff also wondered whether she had Jewish origins that she concealed from him.)

Mack Brunswick was no longer in Vienna, and Pankejeff, in a state of extreme agitation, went to ring at the door of Muriel Gardiner, an American millionaire who had undergone a training analysis with Mack Brunswick and to whom he had in the past given Russian lessons. Married to the socialist-revolutionary leader Joseph Buttinger, Gardiner was, under the code name 'Mary', part of an underground network that helped anti-fascist militants escape from Austria. She managed to get Pankejeff a visa for Paris, where he went to join Mack Brunswick in early August for daily sessions of analysis at the home of Princess Marie Bonaparte. From there he followed Mack Brunswick to London, where Freud had just moved with his family. According to the testimony of Paula Fichtl, Freud's faithful maid, Pankejeff came to visit his ex-analyst three times: 'They took tea together and they had a long talk. After that the Professor was always terribly weary.' Then Pankejeff returned to Vienna at the end of August, relatively calm. Now that Teresa was no longer there, he brought his mother from Prague to live with him. The Second World War broke out a year later, on 3 September 1939.

In 1946 Gardiner and Pankejeff resumed contact through a mutual friend, Albin Unterweger. Ruth Mack Brunswick, who was a morphine addict, had just died in New York of an opioid overdose and Gardiner now became Pankejeff's main psychoanalytic contact, with whom he maintained a voluminous correspondence until his death. She sent him clothes and food from the United States (the famous CARE packages) and Pankejeff thanked her punctually, in his large careful handwriting, keeping her informed of the smallest details of his state of health.

He was less hypochondriacal than before the war, but still just as constipated and still subject to bouts of depression and obsessional rumination. The depressions became almost chronic after his retirement in May 1950 and the death of his mother in 1953. Pankejeff felt old and useless. In 1951 there was another, more acute crisis. Pankejeff, who had gone into the environs of Vienna to paint a landscape, mistakenly entered the Soviet zone and was arrested by Russian soldiers. He was released after four days of interrogation, but the episode left him in a state of panic about being arrested again. Shortly afterwards, when Kurt Eissler came to Vienna to interview him, he found him in an indescribable state, trembling with his whole body and shaking with sobs. Eissler told him he had nothing to fear since he was in the Allied zone, whereupon Pankejeff instantly calmed down, just as at the time of his analysis with Mack Brunswick.

Eissler got into the habit of seeing him daily during his summer holiday in Vienna for 'analytical conversations', which he recorded for a while for the Freud Archives. Eissler denied acting as a psychoanalyst on this occasion, but Pankejeff himself considered these meetings as sessions of analysis. Eissler also had Pankejeff examined by a specialist in the Rorschach test, the psychoanalyst Frederick Weil, who diagnosed a cyclothymic disorder – in other words, a manic-depressive state, as Kraepelin had clearly already noted. Gardiner, for her part, regularly sent Pankejeff 'wonder pills' (Dexamyl) that helped him overcome his depressions: 'My only consolation, dear Frau Doktor, currently lies in your pills, which are the only thing able to improve my mood' (Pankejeff to Gardiner, 27 October 1960).

In 1955, as Pankejeff's state had worsened again, Eissler sent him to the president of the Vienna Psychoanalytic Society, Alfred von Winterstein; then, when the latter retired in 1957, to his successor Wilhelm Solms-Rödelheim, who kept him in treatment practically until the end. Winterstein and Solms saw Pankejeff on a weekly basis and were paid directly by the Freud Archives – in reality by Muriel Gardiner, who helped Pankejeff financially through Eissler.

Gardiner also paid Pankejeff's taxes and Eissler sent him a monthly annuity (5,000 Austrian schillings), which essentially served to meet the increasingly pressing financial demands of Franziska (Franzi) Bednar, a woman with whom Pankejeff had maintained a fraught relationship since the early 1950s. In 1954 Bednar had threatened to leave Pankejeff if he did not marry her, and Pankejeff, out of weakness and indecision, had temporarily surrendered to her ultimatum. After coming to his senses, he broke his promise to marry her a few days later but felt compelled to compensate Bednar financially, and as a result handed over a third of his income to her. No rational argument could convince him to break with Bednar, who constantly threatened to cause a public scandal if he stopped paying, so Gardiner and Eissler ended up footing the bill. It was imperative to protect the Wolf Man, as well as his anonymity.

The cordon sanitaire established around Pankejeff did not, however, extend to psychoanalysts. Richard Sterba, Alfred Lubin and Leo Rangell travelled long distances to meet the Wolf Man in the flesh. Others, like Alexander Grinstein, commissioned him through Gardiner to paint pictures representing his 'wolf dream', which he executed in series using tracing paper. Soon, all the members of the International Psychoanalytic Association wanted to have a *Wolfsbild* on the wall of their living room (Pankejeff also tried to sell them his landscape paintings, but these were less successful).

Pankejeff was flattered by all this attention. In any case, he considered himself more as a colleague of these people than as a 'case'. In 1970 Albin Unterweger reported to Gardiner that Pankejeff, when Eissler had recorded their interviews, 'was some-what irked by the attitude of Dr E[issler]. I had the impression then, that he, our friend, felt like being considered only as a onetime patient, and not also as a person who could, as he thought, con-tribute something constructive to the field' (October 1970). Indeed, ever since the war, Pankejeff had been writing articles of psycho-analytic inspiration on subjects as diverse as human freedom, Marxism and psychoanalysis ('A Parallel'), art, Aubrey Beardsley and 'Poe, Baudelaire and Hölderlin'. One of these articles, 'Art in the Light of Freud's Depth Psychology', appeared in 1950 and 1951 in two issues of the Viennese review *Kunst ins Volk*, under the pseud-onym 'Paul Segrin'. Gardiner tried to place another, 'Psychoanalysis and Free Will', in the journal *Psychoanalytic Quarterly*, but the edi-tors declined, despite – or perhaps because of – the author's identity. Disappointed by the lack of interest shown by psychoanalysts in his theoretical essays, Pankejeff began to write autobiographical texts that Gardiner collected in 1972 in a volume entitled *The Wolf-man by the Wolf-man*, with a preface by Anna Freud.

The book was a great success, which made it possible for Gardiner to send Pankejeff regular and substantial 'advances' against royalties that inevitably ended up in the hands of Franzi Bednar. Intrigued by the book, journalist Karin Obholzer decided to find the person who was hiding behind the Wolf Man. This was not difficult, and Pankejeff seems to have been delighted to have been 'discovered' by a person outside the International Psycho-analytic Association. Having gained his trust, Obholzer managed to convince him to grant her a series of interviews, despite the pres-sure exerted on him by Eissler, Solms-Rödelheim and Gardiner not to do so. (In order to convince him, Solms-Rödelheim described Obholzer to him as a 'psychopath' whose mother had 'schizophrenic flare-ups'.) In these interviews published after his death, Pankejeff finally revealed publicly that he had never believed in the famous 'primal scene' postulated by Freud: 'But that primal scene is no more than a construct . . . But I have never been able to remember anything of that sort . . . He [Freud] maintains that I saw it, but who will guarantee that it is so? That it is not a fantasy of his?'

Pankejeff also claimed that he recognized himself neither in Freud's case history, nor in his book of memoirs edited by Gardiner: 'Instead of doing me some good, psychoanalysts did me harm . . . That was the theory, that Freud had cured me 100 percent . . . That's why [Gardiner] recommended that I write my Memoirs. To show the world how Freud had cured a seriously ill person . . . It's all false.' In fact, despite almost constant psychoanalytic monitoring over sixty years, Pankejeff was still subject to the same symptoms: 'In reality the whole thing looks like a disaster. I am in the same state as when I first came to Freud, and Freud is no more.' For Pankejeff, Freud had been completely mistaken. As he had already told Eissler in 1954, it was Kraepelin and not Freud who had been right about his case: 'Ah, Kraepelin, he's the only one who understood anything!' (30 July 1954).

Sergius Pankejeff, preparatory sketch for the *Wolfsbild*, 1964.

In July 1977, a year after the end of the interviews with Obholzer, Pankejeff suffered a heart attack followed by pneumonia. Solms-Rödelheim arranged for him to be transferred to the Steinhof psychiatric hospital in Vienna, where he was head of department, and they found him a single room where he could stay after recovering. Gardiner paid for a private nurse, Sister Anni, to whom he became very attached. Franzi Bednar dropped out of sight. Pankejeff complained bitterly, however, about being interned in a psychiatric hospital instead of being housed in a retirement home. He felt abandoned by Gardiner. He died on 7 May 1979 in the arms of Sister Anni, at the age of 92. Franzi Bednar, whom he had made his universal legatee, outlived him by ten years.

29

BRUNO VENEZIANI

(1890–1952)

Trieste: the fourth largest city of the Austro-Hungarian Empire. It is the autumn of 1914; war rages elsewhere. The city and life are in parentheses, before the dismantling of the empire. A middle-aged, wealthy idler named Zeno Cosini goes to see Dr. S., the city's only psychoanalyst, with vague psychosomatic symptoms. He is married, has a mistress and is so incompetent in business that his father, before he died, put him under the guardianship of his old company manager, Olivi. So, having nothing to do, Zeno spends his time worrying about his health: 'Illness is a conviction (*convinzione*) and I was born with that conviction.' Especially, he is unable to quit smoking. Zeno suffers from 'abulia', an utter lack of will: whenever he decides to smoke the last cigarette – *l'ultima sigaretta*, abbreviated as 'u.s.' – he cannot refrain from smoking another last one, and then another, and then another. Quitting, for him, *is* smoking.

Alongside the treatment, Dr S. asks him to write his autobiography in order to better prepare for the sessions. Zeno duly complies and describes himself at great length, halfway between self-indulgence and hilarious lucidity. Then, exasperated by the Oedipal interpretations of this 'idiot' of a doctor, he decides to stop the analysis on 3 May 1915: 'I'm done with psycho-analysis. After six full months of diligent practice, I feel worse than before.' Soon thereafter, Zeno cures himself of his improbable illness by 'persuading' himself that he is healthy and engaging in successful business ventures. Peeved, Dr S. then takes revenge by publishing his patient's autobiographical notes, which appear in 1923 under the title *La coscienza di Zeno* (more or less felicitously translated into English as *Confessions of Zeno* and *Zeno's Conscience*).

Livia Veneziani and Italo Svevo, 1896.

La coscienza di Zeno is one of the great modernist masterpieces of the twentieth century and Zeno Cosini is of course only a fictional character, but he resembles nothing so much as his creator, the Austro-Italian novelist Italo Svevo. Svevo, whose real name was Ettore Aronne Schmitz, was also a member of the good bourgeoisie of Trieste. Like Zeno, Svevo had married one of the four daughters of a successful businessman, his beautiful second cousin Livia Veneziani. Their common ancestors were Jewish, but the Veneziani branch of the family had converted to Catholicism and so did Svevo in order to please his wife. (James Joyce, who befriended him during his stay in Trieste before the war, is said to have drawn inspiration from him for the secular Jew Leopold Bloom in *Ulysses*, who likewise converted to Catholicism to marry Molly.)

Like Zeno, his other literary double, Svevo was happily married but also subject to violent fits of unfounded jealousy. He lived with his wife's family in the vast Villa Veneziani. The Venezianis owned a prosperous marine paint factory that had branches in Venice, London, Cologne and Marseille. Svevo worked in the family business and gradually took over from his father-in-law at the head of the company, all the while on the side writing novels that received absolutely no recognition until Joyce actively promoted *La coscienza di Zeno* on the European scene. Just like Zeno, Svevo considered himself up till then a failure, if not as a businessman then at least as a writer.

One last similarity with Zeno: Svevo was a guilt-laden heavy smoker who spent his time puffing on *l'ultima sigaretta*. Fulvio Anzellotti, Livia Veneziani's grand-nephew, recounts in his memoir *La villa di Zeno* that it was strictly forbidden to smoke in the paint factory that was next to the Villa Veneziani because of the danger of explosion. We may well suppose that smoking represented for Svevo the muffled resistance of the Jewish writer towards the world of work and bourgeois-Catholic respectability, just as it constituted for Zeno the major 'resistance' to his psychoanalytic healing and normalization.

Yet Svevo never went on the couch. From where did he draw, then, his very precise and somewhat caustic knowledge of psychoanalysis? In 1908 Svevo had been introduced to Freud's books by a friend, the Triestine Edoardo Weiss (Weiss's younger brother, Ottocaro, would later marry Ortensia 'Tenci' Schmitz, Svevo's niece).

Weiss, who was by then nineteen, was already a fervent Freudian and was about to go to Vienna to study medicine with a view to being trained in psychoanalysis. He was to become one of Freud's most faithful followers and the founder of the Italian Psychoanalytical Society in 1932. Thanks to him, Svevo the 'Swabian', who was fluent in German, was able to acquaint himself early on with Freud's publications. It is highly likely that it was through Svevo that Joyce was introduced in turn to psychoanalysis during his Trieste period, though Svevo himself denied this in a lecture that he delivered in 1927 on his Irish friend.

In 1911, during a stay at the Austrian spa resort of Bad Ischl, Svevo befriended Wilhelm Stekel, one of Freud's earliest followers in Vienna and at that time the co-editor, with Alfred Adler, of the principal psychoanalytic journal *Zentralblatt für Psychoanalyse*. Stekel was a colourful and expansive character, and according to Fulvio Anzellotti his remarks on Freud and psychoanalysis truly 'fascinated' Svevo. This was one year before Stekel had an epic falling-out with Freud and left the psychoanalytic group, fed up with Freud's dogmatism and authoritarianism.

It is most likely that Svevo also heard of Georgina Weiss's analysis with Freud. Georgina was Edoardo Weiss's younger sister. She studied music and was nineteen years old when she went to Vienna to undergo analysis with Freud, from 2 January to 26 June 1918. Weiss later told Kurt Eissler that Georgina suffered from 'hysterical symptoms and emotional difficulties' and that the analysis had been unsuccessful. Apparently, Freud did not like her and he referred her to his pupil Helene Deutsch, who took Georgina with her to Berlin, where she herself was undergoing analysis with Karl Abraham, another close associate of Freud's.

Georgina later developed schizophrenia and spent some twenty years in a mental hospital in Australia, where she had emigrated with her husband, Erwin Frohlich. She had the delusion that Nazis were controlling her after having taken away parts of her brain. 'They treat my brain as if it belonged to them,' she wrote to Weiss. 'It is useless to talk about this to my doctors in the hospital because they think that I have delusions.'

Svevo may also have got wind of Weiss's older sister's analysis with Freud. Amalia Weiss Goetzl suffered from obsessional neurosis and went to see Freud for six months in 1921 and then again in

Advertisement
for the Veneziani
marine paint.

1922, just as Svevo was finishing *La coscienza di Zeno*. Weiss reported
to Eissler that Freud was very fond of her: 'He helped her very,
very much. But she was not quite cured.' She and her husband
Alberto were rounded up by the Nazis in 1943 and sent to their
deaths in Auschwitz.

However, Svevo's most direct source of information on psychoanalysis was his wife's younger brother, Bruno Veneziani. Veneziani
and Edoardo Weiss had been at school together and were close
friends. Highly intelligent, cultured and a semi-professional pianist,
Veneziani seemed destined for a bright future. He had studied
chemistry (like Zeno in his brother-in-law's novel) and his doctoral
thesis was so brilliant that his supervisor had it published on the
spot. The only son of the family, he was the favourite of his mother,
Olga. Gioachino, his father, hoped he would put his talents as a
chemist in the service of the family business.

It did not happen. Despite his many gifts, Veneziani was unable
to carry anything out, for lack of will. He was idle and abulic, like
Zeno. Why work when you can count on your father's fortune

Bruno Veneziani, undated.

and your mother's unconditional love, relayed by that of your four sisters? Bruno Veneziani had it all and was good for nothing.

Svevo liked his brother-in-law and cousin very much and dedicated to him his short story 'The Cat's Death'. No doubt he obscurely empathized with Veneziani's passive resistance towards work and reality. Veneziani was also a kindred smoker. In 1910 the two men vowed to quit smoking, leaving it to the first who would relapse to pay the other 130 Austrian crowns, a very large sum at that time. (Zeno and Olivi lay exactly the same bet in Svevo's novel.) Svevo lost the bet, whereupon they both resumed smoking. Smoking was not Veneziani's only addiction. He also abused codeine, and later morphine and a variety of other opiates. Besides this, he was openly and exclusively gay, much to the consternation of his family and notably his mother.

On Weiss's advice, the Venezianis sent him in 1910 to the Viennese psychoanalyst Isidor Sadger to cure his vices. Sadger specialized in the treatment of the homosexual 'inversion' and claimed to be able to cure his patients of it. Veneziani, however, was not ready to relinquish his love of young men. The treatment with Sadger having failed, Veneziani was therefore directed to Sigmund Freud himself.

Freud took Veneziani in analysis from 4 October 1912 to 31 May 1913, for six hours a week. According to Weiss, who presumably got his information from Freud himself, the analysis went badly. Veneziani is supposed to have made antisemitic remarks, which Freud resented. (This seems odd as Veneziani was himself of Jewish origin and most of his family and friends – including Weiss himself – were Jews. However, one cannot rule out some provocation on Veneziani's part, which Freud then took literally.) Freud reproached Veneziani for being 'narcissistic' and resisting his influence. In short, the transference had not set in as expected.

Freud diagnosed a paranoia and decided to terminate the analysis, stating that Veneziani was incurable. According to Svevo's daughter, Letizia Fonda Savio, Freud told Veneziani: 'I can heal those who seek healing, not those who refuse it.'

Svevo, who watched these developments from Trieste, was deeply shocked. In a letter to Valerio Jahier, a young French-Italian journalist and writer who had initiated a correspondence with him about the merits of analytic therapy, Svevo later reminisced in December 1927: 'A great man, our Freud, but more for novelists than for patients. One of my close relatives came out completely destroyed from a treatment that lasted several years. It was through him that I learned about Freud's work about fifteen years ago.'

Jahier, who at the time was himself in treatment in Paris with the psychoanalyst Charles Odier, was incredulous. Svevo therefore insisted: 'It is a fact: I cannot lie and I must confirm to you that in a case treated by Freud in person, no result was obtained. For the sake of accuracy, I must add that Freud himself, after years of treatment involving great expenses, dismissed his patient, declaring him incurable. As a matter of fact I admire Freud, but this verdict after so much life wasted left me with a feeling of disgust.'

A month later, Svevo hammered it home: 'Just to be clear, I want to tell my experience regarding the results of the psychoanalytic treatment. After years of treatment and expenses, the doctor said that the subject was incurable because suffering from mild paranoia . . . Anyway, this was a diagnosis that was too expensive.'

(Based on statements made to Karin Obholzer by Sergius Pankejeff, we can estimate the cost of a fifty-minute session with Freud at that time at about 1,100–1,400 present-day u.s. dollars. Veneziani, who had 187 sessions with Freud, had thus spent some $205,000–$267,000 for nothing.)

Veneziani, however, had added psychoanalysis to his many addictions. After Freud, he went to see Viktor Tausk, a follower of Freud and a good friend of Weiss. Tausk was not so negative about Veneziani as Freud, but Veneziani left him after a while to see Rudolf Reitler, another veteran of psychoanalysis in Vienna. The Venezianis, meanwhile, began to worry about their offspring's interminable analysis. In May 1914, while on a business trip to Cologne, Olga Veneziani sent her husband a frantic telegram about Bruno. We do not know what information it contained, but Olga was so shaken that she was unable to even talk about it when her husband joined her in all haste in Cologne.

In response, Gioachino Veneziani penned a long letter to his son: 'My very dear Bruno . . . I gladly adhered to your first cure with Dr. Freud. It seemed beneficial at first, but this was not the case since you started another cure, with another doctor, and then yet another with the current doctor, and with what result? What is the good of these cures in which one does not see clearly and that don't have any advantageous results? For such a long time, and without even seeing the end approaching! You assert that such cures can only be understood by scientists. Therefore, since I'm not a scientist, I can't understand it scientifically. But I understand it well for the practice of daily life, and I notice that instead of a healing such a cure generated in you a regression! This is all I need to understand. [Gioachino then ordered his son to come back home:] Don't tell me no, because it would be the first time that I would reply to you: "I want it!" If you have relinquished your will, I must have it for you. Therefore, I beg you, allow yourself to be directed and come; come to your parents whose hearts beat, beat for you, and who would like to see in you a man!'

Bruno did not obey the paternal injunction. He remained in Vienna while his mother was worried sick about him. In the autumn of 1914, while the war was already raging, he decided to go to Berlin to be analysed by Karl Abraham. Having learned about this, Freud warned Abraham: 'Venez.[iani] is a bad case; you are his fifth doctor: Sadger, myself, Reitler, Tausk. He is an enigma, probably a *mauvais sujet*, up to now nothing could be done with him.' Abraham was certainly not going to disagree with Freud. Veneziani, he replied, 'will very soon leave treatment; there is no getting at his narcissism'.

Eventually, Veneziani went back to Trieste. Like Zeno Cosini in his brother-in-law's novel, he was worse off than before the analysis. In his essay *Soggiorno londinese*, Svevo writes: 'The warning given to me was the only positive effect of his [Veneziani's] cure. He had himself psychoanalysed for two years [sic] and returned from the cure destroyed; as abulic as before, but with his abulia aggravated by the conviction (*convinzione*) that, being as he was, he could not behave otherwise. It was he who gave me the conviction that it is dangerous to explain to a man how he is made and every time

I see him I love him because of our old friendship, but also with this new gratitude.'

In 1919 Edoardo Weiss moved back to Trieste to set up shop as a psychoanalyst and proposed to Veneziani that he collaborate with him on the Italian translation of Freud's *Introductory Lectures on Psychoanalysis*. Olga Veneziani had asked him to find something to do for her son, hoping that work would cure him. But as Weiss recounts in his book, *Sigmund Freud as a Consultant*, there was no curing Bruno of his idleness: 'I soon realized that Dr. A. [Weiss's disguise for Veneziani] was too disturbed to be of any help in this work. He suffered from some addictions and led a very disturbed life. With his permission I complied with his mother's wish and wrote to Freud asking if he would be willing to take him back into treatment.'

(We know that Veneziani was in Vienna at the time because the minutes of the Vienna Psychoanalytic Society mention his presence at the meeting of 7 April 1920, which was led by Freud. Apparently, he wanted to join the Society. He was asked to submit a paper in support of his application, but as usual he took no action.)

Freud replied at length to Weiss on 3 October 1920: 'Dear Doctor: I was indeed surprised when you announced Dr. Veneziani as your co-worker for the translation, considering all I knew about him. Since you are asking me today for a professional report on him, I shall not hesitate to give my opinion. I believe it is a bad case, one particularly not suitable for free analysis [that is, without institutionalization]. Two things are missing in him: first, a certain conflict of suffering between his ego and what his drives demand, for he is essentially very well satisfied with himself and suffers only from the antagonism of external conditions. Second, a halfway normal character of the ego that could cooperate with the analyst. On the contrary, he will always strive to mislead the analyst, to trick him and push him aside. Both defects amount actually to one and the same, namely, the development of an immensely narcissistic, self-satisfied ego that is inaccessible to any influence and which unfortunately can always claim his talents and personal gifts. It is also my opinion that nothing would be gained by having him come into treatment with me or anybody else. His future may be to go to pieces in his debauchery . . . I also understand that his mother will not give him up without further efforts. The mechanism is after all a neurotic one even in this case, but the dynamics are unfavourable for a change. I therefore recommend that he be sent to an overwhelming, therapeutically effective person in an institution. I know such a man in the person of Dr. Groddeck in Baden-Baden (Sanatorium) . . . If he does not want to take him, then Marcinowski in Heilbrunn near Tölz (Bavaria) comes to mind, but he probably will reject him outright. In the most unfavourable cases one ships such people, as Dr. Veneziani, across the ocean, with some money, let's say to South America, and lets them there seek and find their fate.'

When asked in the early 1950s by Kurt Eissler what Freud meant by 'find their fate', Weiss answered: 'Either in jail, in suicide, or so forth. This was his attitude towards such patients.' Freud ended his 1920 letter to Weiss by presenting the bill: 'If Mrs. V. [Olga Veneziani] intends to pay for this expert opinion, let her send 100 *lire* to Miss Minna Bernays in Meran . . . (my sister-in-law).' One month later, he acknowledged receipt of the payment and commended Weiss for having broken up with Veneziani: 'The man really is good for nothing.'

After a stay at Johann Jaroslaw Marcinowski's Haus Sielbeck sanatorium, Veneziani was sent to Georg Groddeck's clinic in Baden-Baden. He checked in on 26 May 1921, accompanied by his mother and Svevo. Svevo left shortly thereafter, but Olga stayed in Baden-Baden until August, when she had to return hastily to Trieste to bury her husband, who had been felled by a heart attack. Veneziani, meanwhile, remained at the clinic until 20 December. He took this opportunity to find himself a lover there, with Groddeck's blessing and to the despair of his mother. He later went back twice to Groddeck's clinic, from 5 March to 2 September 1922 and 19 May to 17 June 1923. (Zeno, in Svevo's novel, also has himself locked up in a clinic in order to quit smoking.)

When Veneziani arrived at the clinic, Groddeck had just released *The Soul Searcher*, a wonderful psychoanalytic novel full of humour and irreverence in which Svevo certainly could find all sorts of suggestions for his own novel in progress. Groddeck was a true writer and a larger-than-life character, too large in fact to be simply a follower of Freud. Often regarded as the founder of psychoanalytically inspired psychosomatics, he belonged rather to the earlier tradition of Romantic medicine, with its emphasis on the Unconscious and the unity of body and mind within the great totality of the Goethean *Gott-Natur*. Freud, who borrowed from him the Romantic-Nietzschean concept of 'It' (or 'Id', as it is incomprehensibly Latinized in English), thought highly of him and did not hesitate to enlist him more or less against his will in the 'wild army' of psychoanalysts.

As he later wrote to Freud with characteristic candour, Groddeck thought of himself as a much better therapist than Freud and his associates: 'I felt proud and I thought to myself: "What stupid people analysts are" . . . And I made no exception of Freud. This was also connected with the treatment of Veneziani.' Veneziani's arrival at the clinic provided him with a wonderful opportunity to outdo Freud where the latter had failed. On 2 July 1921 he wrote to Freud: 'Currently one of your patients is with me, a certain Dr. Veneziani from Trieste. I am curious to see what will come out of it.'

Veneziani makes a cameo appearance at the beginning of *The Book of the It*, a series of 'psychoanalytic letters to a female friend' that Groddeck started writing that very year, 1921, under the alias Patrick Troll. Groddeck would send the letters to Freud as he went, incorporating some of Freud's reactions in the following letters as being those of the friend. In the second letter, Patrick Troll explains to his lady friend that we are all both man and woman and that in some people who were wet-nursed as infants the It remains stuck between the two sexual orientations, giving rise on occasion to all kinds of psychosomatic symptoms. In support of his argument he adduces the alleged 'imaginary pregnancy' of the little Bruno Veneziani, whom Olga had not breastfed herself: 'I must also speak to you of a fifth child fed the milk of a nurse, a man full of talent, but who, being endowed with two mothers, feels divided in everything and tries to overcome this dissociation by the use of pantopon [an injectable form of opium, as potent as morphine]. It is by superstition, claims the mother, that she did not breastfeed him herself; she had lost two sons and did not want to breastfeed the third. But he doesn't know if he is a man or a woman, his It doesn't know. The woman awoke in him during his early childhood and he suffered from a pericarditis, an imaginary pregnancy of the heart. [Bruno had indeed nearly died from pericarditis at the age of seven.] And later it happened again in the form of a pleurisy and an irresistible homosexual drive.'

Groddeck, however, quickly became disillusioned. Veneziani remained stubbornly apathetic, a drug addict and a homosexual. Fulvio Anzellotti, in *Il segreto di Svevo*, mentions that Groddeck took the opportunity of the visit the following year of his friend and patient Sándor Ferenczi, Freud's confidant, to ask him to analyse Veneziani. Nothing helped. According to Weiss, Veneziani even attempted suicide at some point: 'When he tried to kill himself with Veronal . . . Dr. Groddeck told him that he was in doubt whether he should save him or not . . . Then in the end, he saved him.' On 31 May 1923, during Veneziani's third stay at the clinic, Groddeck finally confessed to Freud: 'I had been proud of [Veneziani's treatment] in those days, though it became apparent later on that it was a mistake.'

Svevo, meanwhile, had tasked himself in 1918 with the project (never completed) to translate Freud's book *On Dreams* into Italian. This was the time just after the war when psychoanalysis was spreading like wildfire in European intellectual and artistic circles. As the socialist intellectual Giorgio Voghera recounts in his memoir 'The Years of Psychoanalysis', Freudian theories were then the subject of a veritable craze in Trieste, especially in Jewish circles: 'More than a current, it was a cyclone. As a child, I lived in the eye of this cyclone . . . All the adults who lived around me were literally washed away.' This year was also the one in which Georgina Weiss underwent her unsuccessful analysis with Freud.

It is in this particular context that Svevo began the drafting of *La coscienza di Zeno* in February 1919, all the while engaging in a kind of self-analysis. To Valerio Jahier, he confided in December 1927: 'I will only say that after having read [Freud's] works, I made the treatment alone, without a doctor. It is from this experience that the novel was born in which, if there is a character I have created without having had a model for it, it is definitely that of Dr. S.' In other words, Svevo's self-analysis and the drafting of *Zeno* were one and the same: a writing cure, rather than a talking cure.

Knowing how the novel ends, we can easily deduce what Svevo thought of analytic therapy, whether it be Zeno's analysis with Dr S. or those of Georgina and Bruno, which were failing so evidently at the same time in real life. As Svevo told Jahier, psychoanalysis is good material for the novelist, not a good way to heal: '*From a literary standpoint* [Svevo's emphasis], Freud is certainly much more interesting. I wish I had had a treatment with him. My novel would surely have benefited from it, it would have been more complete.'

From the letters to Jahier, it is clear that Svevo felt that he had 'cured' himself by writing the story of Zeno, the man for whom 'disease is a conviction'. Zeno, at the end of the book (made up, let us not forget, of self-analytical notes), realizes that 'my health cannot be anything other than my conviction of being healthy, and it was a silliness worthy of a hypnagogic dreamer to want to cure me instead of persuading me . . . Pain and love, life in short, cannot be considered a disease because we suffer from it.' This is exactly what Svevo was to repeat in his own name to Jahier, who asked him whether psychoanalysis would allow him to cure his *mal de vivre*: 'And anyway, why wish to heal? Do we really need to wrench from mankind what is best in it? I firmly believe that the true success that brought me peace resides in this conviction.'

Sickness is the conviction of being sick, and psychoanalysis only reinforces this conviction by unearthing in all of us this disease that, in Zeno's words, 'had once been diagnosed by the late Sophocles in the poor Oedipus . . . I laugh at it wholeheartedly. The best proof that I never had this disease is that I never got cured of it.' The more we convince ourselves that we need therapy, the less likely we are to heal. When Svevo and Jahier met for the first time in Paris and the latter confessed that he had already sixty analytic sessions under his belt, Svevo replied with a big laugh: 'And you're alive?' The retort was unintentionally cruel: twelve years later and after countless sessions of analysis with Princess Marie Bonaparte and the entire roster of the Paris Psychoanalytic Society, Valerio Jahier ended up committing suicide.

Svevo, in his letters, had done his best to discourage Jahier from getting analysed: 'Why don't you try a treatment by auto-suggestion with a doctor of the Nancy school? You probably know this school only for having laughed at it. As for me, I don't laugh at it . . . Don't scoff at it because it is so simple. The healing that you should obtain is simple, too. They are not going to change your intimate "I".'

The 'Nancy school' meant at the time the 'New Nancy school' of the pharmacist and psychologist Émile Coué, the promoter of the famous 'Coué method', which was indeed often derided because of its apparent simplism. To get better, Coué advised, one should simply repeat twenty times twice a day: 'Every day, in every way, I'm getting better and better.' But Coué was far from naive or unsophisticated. His method of self-mastery by conscious autosuggestion (also the title of his book published in 1921) self-consciously extended the work of the theorist of hypnosis and founder of the first 'Nancy school' Hippolyte Bernheim. The basic principle of the Coué method can still be found today in a variety of psychotherapeutic techniques, from Eriksonian hypnosis to cognitive behavioural therapy to positive psychology. There is no point in trying to solve a problem or in trying to heal, claimed Coué, because this is the best way to generate negative thoughts. Every idea tends to turn into action (this was the principle of 'suggestion' according to Bernheim), so the negative idea will always trump the will. It is better to pretend that the problem is already solved by consciously creating positive ideas that will act on the unconscious mind's machinery, effortlessly. Repeat day and night that you are happy and healthy, and you will eventually convince yourself that you are. In fact, you already are.

This is precisely Zeno's paradoxical conclusion at the end of this book, which is not titled Zeno's Consciousness (coscienza, in Italian, means both 'consciousness' and 'conscience') by chance. Rather than try to track down the unconscious reasons for his illness, Zeno decides to consciously 'persuade' himself that he is healthy. And it works: 'I am cured! . . . I am healthy, absolutely healthy.' Autosuggestion rather than self-analysis, self-persuasion rather than insight: Zeno says 'yes' to himself, warts and all, and that is paradoxically what enables him to change. Svevo's book is not in fact the 'first psychoanalytic novel', as critics so often claim (forgetting, incidentally, Groddeck's earlier novel The Soul Searcher). It is an ironic and profound critique of psychoanalytic therapy, inspired both by Coué's ideas and by Bruno Veneziani's disastrous experience on the couch.

Freud and Weiss, to whom Svevo had sent his book, did not fail to get the message. Freud (who read Italian) did not even bother to reply. As for Weiss, he flatly refused to review the book at Svevo's request, despite their old friendship. Zeno's story, he reportedly told Svevo, had 'nothing to do' with psychoanalysis and as the only psychoanalyst practising in Trieste he resented being portrayed as Dr S. Yet Weiss was better placed than anyone to know that it was not him who was the real target of Svevo's *roman à clef*. It was Freud.

For who, ultimately, is Zeno Cosini? To use a Freudian notion, he is a composite character. Insofar as he is sick, a hypochondriac, abulic, neurotic, he is obviously none other than *cousin* Bruno (*Cosini* reads easily as an Italianization of the English or French 'cousin'), whom Dr S.[igmund] had so casually declared 'incurable'. But insofar as he recovers at the end of the book, Zeno is also Italo Svevo himself – that is, someone who, unlike his cousin and brother-in-law, had *not* been on the couch, had *not* let himself be convinced that he was sick, and thus had healed himself. *La coscienza di Zeno* is the story of Svevo's dawning conviction of the futility of Freudian psychoanalysis. At the beginning of the book's last chapter, enti-tled 'Psychoanalysis', Zeno exclaims: 'Now that I have seen through it and know that it is nothing more than a foolish illusion, a trick fit for exciting some old hysterical woman, how can I endure the company of that ridiculous man, with his eye that would be pen-etrating and the presumption that allows him to group all the phenomena of this world around his grand new theory?'

Letizia Fonda Savio, Svevo's daughter, told Svevo scholar Giovanni Palmieri that at some point her father had gone to Nancy to consult Coué for 'personal reasons', and that he had stayed in his clinic for a few days. She also stated that Bruno Veneziani went there in turn at a later date. Presumably it was Svevo who prompted him to do so in the hope of bringing him to the same realization as Zeno and himself. But Veneziani stayed only a day. He could not let go of his illness. He was addicted to therapy.

In Trieste he continued to be followed on and off in 'supportive therapy' by Edoardo Weiss, who cared enough about his friend not to abide by Freud's analytic condemnation. In 1929, on his advice, Veneziani voluntarily committed himself to the psychiatric hospital of San Giovanni in Trieste. In the medical report accom-panying his request for admission, Weiss wrote that Veneziani suffered from 'a severe mental depression' and from 'general dis-interest, pessimism, taedium vitae, agitations with convulsive crying, insomnia with heavy use of sleeping pills'. Stressing that the patient did not present any psychic dissociation or hallucina-tions, Weiss stated that he had however done so a few years earlier, following a massive intake of drugs. Veneziani was so shaken by the episode that he had made yet another suicide attempt.

In 1938, two years after his mother's death, Veneziani was admitted to the Bellevue Sanatorium, headed by Ludwig Binswanger. Underwritten by Veneziani's four sisters, the expensive stay at the Bellevue turned out to be no more effective than those at Groddeck's clinic or at other institutions where Bruno had been placed in the meantime. In a joint letter sent after yet another mischief perpetrated by their brother, the sisters made the bitter observation: 'We note with sorrow ... that everything was in vain.'

In the year 1938 the Fascist racial laws were promulgated in Italy. Edoardo Weiss, who by then was working in Rome, decided to emigrate to the U.S. in order to escape antisemitic persecution. Protected by his status as a 'half-Jew', Veneziani stayed in Rome, where he had followed Weiss. Always looking for a therapist, he ended up with a colleague and friend of Weiss, the Jungian Ernst Bernhard. Bernhard, who was Jewish too, lived hidden in a room overlooking the Piazza di Spagna where he received clients and practised meditation under the protection of a bronze Buddha. From a Freudian, Veneziani became a Jungian. He became interested in Buddhism, Taoism, Hinduism, yoga. He learned Chinese, which allowed him to collaborate on the translation into Italian of the *I Ching*, the Book of Changes, which came out with a preface by Carl Gustav Jung. He also translated Jung's *Psychology and Religion*.

He lived with a young sailor. He was still taking drugs, however, and his body began to give. Sensing that the end was near, Veneziani decided to squander the money on which he lived. His last purchase was a beautiful antique harpsichord. Fulvio Anzellotti recounts: 'As soon as the harpsichord arrived, he started playing Chopin, whom he adored. His companion recognized the adagio of the Sonata in B-flat minor, the Funeral March. This was his last concert.' In 1952 Edoardo Weiss learned in a letter from Bernhard that his old friend Bruno had died of a heart attack 'caused by various excesses and the way of life he led'. Bruno Veneziani had tried for forty-two years to be cured of these 'excesses', as vainly as Zeno Cosini had tried to quit smoking on Dr S.'s couch.

There is no cure for life, wrote Zeno: 'Unlike other diseases, life is always fatal. It admits of no cure. To cure life would amount to plug the holes in our body, considering them as wounds. As soon as healed, we would choke.' Ettore Schmitz/Italo Svevo/Zeno Cosini died on 13 September 1928 from the wounds suffered in a car accident. On his deathbed, he asked in vain for a cigarette: 'That,' he said, 'would really have been the last cigarette.'

30
ELMA PÁLOS
(1887–1970)

Elma Pálos, born on 28 December 1887, was the eldest daughter of Géza Pálos and Gizella Altschul Pálos, the mistress of Sándor Ferenczi, Freud's disciple and friend. The Altschul (Alcsuti) and Ferenczi (Fraenkel) families both came from Miskolcz, a small town northeast of Budapest, and were very close. Lajos, Sándor Ferenczi's youngest brother, married Gizella's youngest daughter, Magda, in 1909, and Ferenczi himself had been having an affair with Gizella since 1904, despite the fact that she was married and eight years older. He also had an affair with Sarolta, one of Gizella's three sisters. In a letter from Ferenczi to Freud, it is clear that the link with Gizella was coupled with an analytical relationship, in which bed and couch were mixed: 'I believe that ψa [psychoanalytic] honesty can be effected, not only among friends but also among life's companions of various genders. The analytic association with Frau G.[izella] is making decided progress, after at times overcoming very great resistances . . . Her love is stronger than the unpleasure that the analysis arouses in her, and she will pass the test of endurance' (9 July 1910).

Little is known about Elma's childhood. Unlike her sister Magda, whom Ferenczi described as a self-centred 'socialite', Elma was introverted, altruistic, complicated. On 3 January 1911, planning a visit to Vienna with Gizella and Elma, Ferenczi asked Freud if they could 'also make use of our presence to ask your advice in a rather difficult matter (marriage and love affair of the same daughter)'. Apparently, Elma found it difficult to decide between two suitors, which was 'causing poor Frau G. a lot of worry'. Freud received the mother and daughter the following month. He was not favourably impressed by Elma and on the spot diagnosed her as a case of dementia praecox (schizophrenia), which had, Ferenczi admitted, 'a rather depressing effect' (Ferenczi to Freud, 7 February 1911). Elma's 'schizophrenic' hesitation between her two suitors continued and Ferenczi resolved to take her into analysis (we do not know if it was at her request): 'Just think, I decided to take her daughter [Elma] into psychoanalytic treatment; the situation, you see, was becoming unbearable. For the moment, the thing is working, and the effect is favourable' (Ferenczi to Freud, 14 July 1911).

Elma Pálos, undated.

In October there was a dramatic turn of events: one of Elma's two suitors, a Frenchman, 'shot himself on her account a week ago . . . it is very questionable how the matter will go now' (Ferenczi to Freud, 18 October 1911). Shortly thereafter, on 14 November, Ferenczi admitted that a 'detachment of libido' from Gizella had occurred in him and that he 'had fantasies about marrying Elma. (Recurrence of a similar condition in the spring).' This latest admission seems to indicate that he had been in love with Elma even before taking her on for treatment. Aware of having abandoned 'the cool detachment of the analyst', Ferenczi invoked the circumstances: 'Elma became especially dangerous to me at the moment when – after the young man's suicide – she badly needed someone to support her and to *help* her in her need. I did that only too well' (3 December 1911).

Many years later, Elma was to give her own version of the episode to Michael Bálint, Ferenczi's disciple and literary executor: 'All in all after a few sessions Sándor got up from his chair behind me, sat on the sofa next to me and, considerably moved, kissed me all over and passionately told me how much he loved me and asked if I could love him too. Whether or not it was true I cannot tell, but I answered "yes" and – I hope – I believed so. We were cruel when telling it to Mum, who was astonished, but with her presence of mind she said that if the two people whom she loved most in the world were going to get married she could only be happy about

Sándor Ferenczi, 1910.

it. She was glad that Sándor would have children after all ... How we told this to my poor father I cannot recall, but he, who was aware of and suffered from the liaison of Mum and Sándor, must have been astounded. Probably he clapped his hands in amazement and gave a shy laugh – the way he would always do – surrender to his fate and retreated. That's what he did all his life. He was a hapless, deaf and weak man' (7 May 1966).

Gizella was in the grip of an authentically Cornelian dilemma. As a woman, she suffered from being betrayed by her lover and abandoned for her younger daughter. As a mother, she was ready to step aside to make her daughter happy. Ferenczi asked Freud to write to Gizella and persuade her to accept her fate. Freud went along with it, despite being against the idea of a marriage with Elma. 'The hard truth', he wrote Gizella, 'is that love is only for youth and that one must renounce; as a woman, one must be prepared to see one's sacrifices repaid with ingratitude. No reproach for the individual, a natural fate, as in the story of Oedipus. In addition, it is the case with *him* that his homosexuality imperiously demands a child and that he carries within him revenge against his mother from the strongest impressions in childhood' (Freud to Gizella Pálos, 17 December 1911). Simultaneously and contradictorily, Freud expressed doubts about the viability of a marriage the project of which, according to him, came from the Oedipal fantasies of the two interested parties (taking the mother's place with the father, in the case of Elma; substituting the sister for the mother in Sándor's case). More analysis was needed before making a decision.

The message thus sent by Freud was not likely to solve Gizella's problem and it locked Ferenczi in an equally insoluble conflict. Should he follow his heart and marry Elma? Or obey the harsh Freudian law and first verify by analysis if their love was genuine? On 18 December, the day he received Freud's letter, Ferenczi seemed determined to override Freud's reservations. But two weeks later, after Elma had briefly vacillated because of 'a few hesitant objections' to their engagement expressed by her father, he decided instead to send her to Vienna for further analysis by Freud: 'The family has been advised of the fee' (Ferenczi to Freud, 1 January 1912). Freud was reluctant, but Ferenczi insisted: analysis (meaning Freud) had to decide for him and for Elma. Two days later, Ferenczi added in a postscript: 'E[lma] does not suspect that you were opposed to our marriage.'

The treatment began on 8 January 1912 and lasted until 5 April, at the rate of one session per day. Elma was full of goodwill. She wanted to please Sándor and also Freud, so that she could pass this love test on which her happiness depended. Freud kept Ferenczi informed of the analysis and Ferenczi in turn quoted from the letters that Elma sent to Budapest, either to him or to her mother (one sometimes has the impression of reading a psychoanalytic version of *Dangerous Liaisons*). Elma to Gizella: 'Let Sándor know that I am almost always thinking about him. I wish so much to see him happy and myself with him. I certainly hope very, very much that everything will turn out well – but today I am anxious about the future. My character is so unbalanced, such a terrible chaos is reigning in me that it would be a risk for anyone to take me as a wife. Even if the analysis clarifies the situation, I will still be the same old way and the bad things can begin again at any occasion.' Then: 'Dear Mama, you never write about yourself. If you have reached an agreement with Sándor that you cannot live without each other, then write to me that honestly. As long as you feel yourself so deeply affected by the loss of Sándor, Sándor will neither tear himself away inwardly from you, nor will I be able to accept his love without misgivings' (quoted in Ferenczi's letter to Freud of 18 January 1912).

Out of sight, out of mind: in the absence of Elma, Ferenczi tried to renew the affair with Gizella, without success at first. However, he did not renounce the plan to marry Elma: 'I am exerting myself over a difficult possibility: to ensure for myself Frau G.'s love also in the event of my marrying Elma' (to Freud, 18 January 1912). At the same time, as a good student, he said he hoped that 'along with you . . . she will overcome a portion of her infantilisms – among them also the fantasy of becoming my wife' (20 January 1912).

Predictably, Elma's analysis confirmed Freud's initial opinion: 'With Elma, something is, in fact, happening. We are getting further

... I do not have a high opinion of her love for you up to now; I don't know whether it will stand up to analysis' (Freud to Ferenczi, 1 February 1912). Two weeks later: 'So, with Elma I am moving decidedly forward ... Just now she emphasizes her love for you, but I maintain that everything must first pass through the crucible of the treatment, and she is agreeable to that' (13 February 1912). Another month and Freud was already ready to send Elma back to Budapest for Easter: 'When she comes back, I think it makes sense for the both of you to resolve anew to consider everything that happened before to be extinguished' (13 March 1912).

It does not seem that Freud informed the patient of the conclusion that the analysis had reached. No doubt she imagined that she had successfully passed her analytical exam. But on her return, Ferenczi stuck to the course of action indicated by Freud and was 'friendly and kind but reserved. Elma evidently was hoping to be received differently and reacted with a rather strong bad temper ... Yesterday she admitted to me that this situation is disagreeable to her. She was already impatient to enjoy life finally and can adapt herself only with difficulty to waiting until I make up my mind' (Ferenczi to Freud, 17 April 1912). Gizella, for her part, self-abnegatingly encouraged him to marry Elma. And so Ferenczi's 'libidinal motions' found their way back towards Elma, after having been temporarily diverted towards Gizella: 'The pendulum-swings in my inclination between Frau G. and Elma, between mother and sister, spirit and matter, are continuing' (Ferenczi to Freud, 23 April 1912).

Ferenczi was spending all his evenings with Gizella and Elma: 'I am attempting to live together experimentally, in a threesome, as it were' (ibid.). The experiment was inconclusive: Gizella was 'suffering unspeakably' and Elma fell into a depression. Unable to make a decision one way or the other, Ferenczi therefore turned to analysis once more. He resumed Elma's treatment, setting out the terms of the contract: 'I told her emphatically that there can be no talk of engagement as long as she doesn't commit herself to open (analytic) discourse. If she can't do that, then I will cease all further attempts and consider the matter settled' (Ferenczi to Freud, 27 May 1912). Elma agreed – did she have any choice? But also, how could she respect this paradoxical contract? How could she get her analyst to recognize the authenticity of her love for him if he saw it as a transferential lie? The only way to convince him would have been to pretend that she did not love him, which she could not resolve to do: 'The analysis with Elma is going very, very slowly; she is clearly forcing herself to do it and is using (mostly ucs. [unconsciously]) every opportunity for obstruction' (Ferenczi to Freud, 10 June 1912). Ferenczi himself found it hard to resist love's temptation: 'I am (especially in the ucs.) not yet free of longingly libidinous feelings with respect to Elma, but I have this inclination under strict control; she, incidentally, expresses herself only at times, especially when I have to hurt her and bring her to tears' (18 July 1912). Freud, from a distance, encouraged Ferenczi not to give in: 'I am very glad to hear that you have remained consistently firm against Elma and have thwarted her tricks. It can only work in that way, if it works' (20 July 1912).

Finally, in August, Ferenczi scrupulously implemented 'the plan that originated in the Türkenschanzpark' (a park in Vienna where he and Freud had probably decided on an exit strategy from analysis). He informed Elma that he was ending the treatment and therefore also their affair: 'I did this with somnambulistic certainty, paying no heed to the painful uproar inside me. Elma was in despair; I accompanied her home and handed her over to her mother' (Ferenczi to Freud, 8 August 1912). Elma wrote him a long, heartbreaking letter:

Tuesday night. I promise you, Sándor, that I won't write to you anymore, not even on Sundays, never. Only today do I still want to speak to you. I understand completely that it had to come to this. I am writing you today because I feel that I will no longer be as close to you as I am today, and out of this closeness I would like to tell you what I am feeling. I don't know what my feelings mean. You probably know better than I, and this is why you wanted us to part. I know quite certainly that you will not come to get me. And yet I have such a terrible anxiety about it. This being alone that now awaits me will be stronger than I; I feel as if everything will freeze inside me. I will remain reasonable, but it will be so cold in me, I will freeze so much that I will also have to hate this last refuge, reason . . . I love you differently than anybody else who has been close to me up to now. I also feel really a little like your child, so much do I wish to be led by you . . . Perhaps, far away from you, I will gain the self-sufficiency that I lost completely with respect to you but can't do without at all . . . And thank you for everything. I often cannot talk because I have the feeling that I am living in you; everything that I am revolves around you (quoted in an undated letter from Ferenczi to Freud, presumably written after the breakup).

During the autumn, Ferenczi tried to convince Elma to marry a Viennese industrialist named Gratz. He told Freud that she would come to him for his 'permission' (31 October 1912): 'Please make it clear to her that it is actually *her* wish to get married and that she wants to do it (neurotically) in the form of a sacrificial act' (5 November 1912). However, neurosis or not, Elma was not ready to take her sacrifice that far: 'Of course, the best thing would be to get her married, but she is being difficult' (Ferenczi to Freud, 15 November 1912). Then, during the summer of 1913, Elma met Jan Nilsen ('J. Nilsen') Laurvik, an American art critic and curator of Norwegian descent who was attending an international conference where she was working as an interpreter (she was fluent in four languages). Laurvik was part of the Photo-Secession, the circle around the photographer and gallery owner Alfred Stieglitz, and he had just published a book on the European avant-garde: *Is It Art? Post-Impressionism, Futurism, Cubism*. He quickly proposed marriage to Elma, which caused a relapse into libidinal nostalgia on the part of Ferenczi (Ferenczi to Freud, 7 July 1913). Gizella, on the other hand, once again suggested that he should marry Elma: 'She claims that Elma loves me now as before. But I – now as before – have become sceptical about her capacity for love' (ibid.). The marriage to Laurvik took place in Budapest on 16 September of the following year, after which Elma and her husband left for Elizabeth, in New Jersey.

The marriage was not a happy one. Laurvik was unstable and violent, and Elma seems to have been afraid of him. After several separations, Elma returned to Budapest in 1924, where as an American citizen she worked at the American consulate until the Second World War. However, she never divorced Laurvik. Meanwhile, Freud, with whom Ferenczi had gone for several tranches of analysis between 1914 and 1916, urged him firmly to marry Gizella.

Portrait of
J. Nilsen Laurvik
by Alfred Stieglitz,
c. 1911.

Gizella, worried about her daughter's American marriage, resisted the idea because she did not want to put any obstacle in the way of a possible union between Sándor and Elma if the latter returned to Budapest. In the end, it was the shy and weak Géza Pálos who cut the knot by asking for a divorce. Almost fifteen years after the start of their affair and some inextricable analytical complications, Sándor Ferenczi finally married Gizella Altschul on 1 March 1919. Géza Pálos died the same day of a heart attack – unless it was a suicide; we do not really know. In 'Analysis Terminable and Interminable', Freud summed up this long story by saying that Ferenczi's analysis had had 'a completely successful result. He married the woman he loved.'

During the Second World War Elma Laurvik worked for the American State Department in Lisbon, then in Bern. Ferenczi had died in 1933 of a pernicious anaemia, full of bitterness towards Freud. Gizella, her sister Sarolta, and Magda and Lajos Ferenczi stayed in Budapest and found shelter in one of the houses of the famous Swedish diplomat-businessman Raoul Wallenberg during the Nazi occupation of 1944–5. After the war, Elma invited her mother and sister Magda to come and settle with her in Bern. Gizella died in 1949, at the age of 82, and the two sisters decided in 1955 to move to New York, where John Laurvik had left Elma an apartment when he died in 1953.

Elma, after all those years, continued to venerate the memory of Sándor – and also to protect that memory. Kurt Eissler, who tried to get her to relate her memories of Freud and Ferenczi in 1952, ran into a thick wall of silence. Elma went so far as to conceal the fact that she had been analysed by Freud: 'Eissler: On what occasions did you meet Freud? Elma Laurvik: I just saw him when we [Elma and her mother] visited Mrs. Freud . . . Eissler: Were you interested in analysis? Laurvik: Yes, very much. But I never took it up, other things happened' (24 July 1952).

When Ernest Jones wrote in his biography that Ferenczi had died a psychotic, she protested in the strongest terms to her friend Michael Bálint: 'It is horrible to make such a statement of a dead man, who cannot defend himself. Will somebody rectify it? Will something be written and done? Publicly, I mean. We are very, very sad that this could happen 25 years after Sándor's death' (11 August 1957). Elma clearly could not know that it was Freud, her ex-analyst, who was the source of this malicious rumour about Ferenczi. (After long negotiations with Jones, Bálint published an extremely diplomatic corrigendum, which went completely unnoticed.)

Along with Bálint, Elma also actively took care of the publication of Ferenczi's writings and in particular of his correspondence with Freud, despite her immense reluctance. She hoped, she told Bálint, that she would not still be alive when these letters appeared. Her wish was granted. She died on 4 December 1970, six months before Magda. The first volume of the Freud–Ferenczi correspondence, in which she occupies such a central place, did not come out until twenty years later.

31

LOE KANN

(1882–1944)

Born on 27 February 1882 in The Hague, Louise (Loe, pronounced 'Lou') Dorothea Kann came from a wealthy Jewish family in the Netherlands. She was an Anglophile, and came to settle in London. Everyone agreed that she was pretty, lively and witty, and few men could resist her charm – starting with her analysts. She suffered from acute abdominal pain as well as kidney stones, for which she had undergone several operations, and had developed an addiction to the morphine she was taking for pain management. She was also anorgasmic, it seems, and prone to mood swings. In 1905 she went to consult Ernest Jones, who was at the time a young psychiatrist starting out with an interest in psychoanalysis. Less than a year later they were living together in Loe's apartment, and she was introducing herself to everyone as 'Mrs Jones'.

In 1908, having been dismissed from the West End Hospital in London because, as a good Freudian, he had taken the sexual questioning of a patient a little too far, Jones accepted the post of director of a psychiatric clinic that had just been created in Toronto. Loe reluctantly followed him, fearing Canadian Puritanism and provincialism. She was right: the people of Toronto were not ready for psychoanalysis. Soon, scandalized rumours circulated about this illegitimate couple, as well as about Dr Jones's bad influence on his patients. Two husbands publicly complained that the analysis had pitted their wives against them. In 1911 a female patient accused Jones of engaging in sex with her, despite Jones trying to bribe his accuser's silence with $500, and a moral league called for his expulsion from the country. Fortunately for the doctor, the Toronto medical school supported Jones. Enraged, his

Ernest Jones, 1909.

accuser took a shot at him with a revolver but missed.

Loe was terrified and wanted to leave Canada and return to London. She also wanted Jones to abandon psycho-analysis, towards which she displayed complete scepticism. Jones's response was to persuade Freud to analyse her, in order to cure her of her scepticism and her various problems. Loe accepted, conditionally: 'She said she would do anything, so long as she wasn't expected to believe things she couldn't believe (i.e. to have ideas forced on her against her will)' (Jones to Freud, 17 October 1911).

The treatment began on 16 June 1912, two weeks before Freud's long summer holiday, at a rate of one session per day. It resumed in earnest in September, and Loe rented an apartment in Vienna where she settled with her maid Lina. Jones, who accompanied her, was asked by Freud to keep his distance during the analysis and he took the opportunity to visit Italy over the next three months. Freud was immediately won over by Loe: 'She is an extremely intel-ligent, deeply neurotic Jewess, whose case history is very easy to read. I will be very pleased to be able to expend much libido for her' (Freud to Sándor Ferenczi, 23 June 1912).

At first, the treatment looked promising. In November, however, Loe again experienced abdominal pain. A diagnosis of pyelone-phritis (bacterial infection of the upper urinary tract) had been made in London, but Freud decided that it was hysterical pain and refused to change his mind, even after a medical examination in Vienna had confirmed the original diagnosis. Loe, who had no reason to doubt the somatic nature of her pain, felt 'forced, bullied' by Freud's insistence on seeing it as a neurotic symptom. Jones, who kept Freud informed of all of Loe's epistolary confidences, reported that 'she complains bitterly about you, that you do not trust her, do not believe her statements, and twist everything until she is quite confused in her mind . . . She is beginning to feel the treatment as an attack on her personality' (13 November 1912). This conflict over the somatic or psychological character of Loe's pains would con-tinue until the end of the treatment, without ever being resolved.

The next month things got better again. Loe's abdominal pain subsided and she was able to gradually reduce the doses of morphine – at least, that is what she told Freud. Freud therefore decided to attack the issue of her frigidity. When Jones returned to Vienna in early January 1913, Freud recommended avoiding intercourse during the analysis. (Freud was used to this sexual interventionism, which also had to be endured by Sergius Pankejeff, Maggie

Loe Kann, undated.

Haller, Monroe Meyer and Edith Banfield Jackson.) Jones respected the Freudian ban, but could not help going to bed with Lina, Loe's maid. Loe was furious, both with Jones and with the analysis. The doses of morphine increased again, and Freud found it extremely difficult to persuade Loe not to stop the treatment.

Loe had a good reason to stay in Vienna, however. She had just met Herbert 'Davy' Jones, a 25-year-old American millionaire (she herself was 31). Davy Jones, whose family owned zinc mines in Wisconsin, had literary ambitions and toured the old cities of Europe after finishing his studies at Princeton. Passing through Vienna, he met Loe and immediately fell in love. One of his poems, 'O Mistress Mine!', describes his bedazzlement:

A sound of rapid steps: the door flew wide:
And all the room was light when she was in it.
– A beauty? Never. Something far more rare:
A spirit bright and flame-like, straight and clear,
That shone from laughing eyes and filled the air
Around her: knowing neither doubt nor fear; –
A little out of breath, with glowing cheeks,
As if the sun and tingling frost were brought
Into the room with her –

Loe took 'Jones II' into her bed while Jones I sheepishly returned to London to settle there as a psychoanalyst. Freud, usually indiscreet, said nothing to Jones about what was going on with his young namesake. Jones, who had been accused of destroying marriages, was going to learn the hard way what psychoanalysis does to a couple. Loe was in love. In March 1913 she briefly left Vienna with her young lover and wrote to tell Freud how happy she was, even though orgasm was still lagging. On her return, she invited Freud, Otto Rank and Hanns Sachs to dinner with Davy. Freud was more and more charmed by his patient: 'This Loe has become extraordinarily dear to me, and I have produced with her a very warm feeling with complete sexual inhibition, as has rarely been the case before (probably owing to my age)' (Freud to Ferenczi, 9 July 1913).

Jones eventually learned of his rival while he was on his way to Budapest to be analysed by Ferenczi. Freud and Ferenczi communicated regularly about their two patients, who were therefore analysed in parallel by two therapists at the same time. Freud forbade Loe to go and see Jones in Budapest. Ferenczi, for his part, asked Freud not to share with Loe what he told him about Jones's analysis. Finally, Loe and Jones returned to London together in August 1913 so that Jones could settle down in his apartment. Before starting her analysis, Loe had promised Jones that she would support him financially for at least three years while he built up a clientele in London and she took advantage of Freud's holiday to help him furnish his lodgings. Davy Jones, who returned to the United States in May, came to London to see her. Neither of them knew whether their affair had a future and Loe went through ups and downs, wondering if she had the right to be 'spoiling a young life' (Ernest Jones to Freud, 18 August 1913). She even thought of suicide. As was to be expected, her morphine intake increased again.

Freud, meanwhile, was impatiently waiting for her in Vienna so that he could resume her analysis after his holiday and give her the gifts he had bought for her in Italy. But Loe always found another pretext to delay the departure – a piece of furniture to buy, errands to do, great fatigue. To punish her, Freud gave the hours he had reserved for her to another patient, which angered her. In early December she finally returned to Vienna, where she was received coldly. Freud 'gave her 2 hours a week to help her in clearing the darkness of the last London events and freeing herself again from Morphia' (Freud to Jones, 4 December 1913). Freud found her in a 'deplorable condition' and 'nearly inaccessible' to analysis. She did not understand, he wrote to Jones, 'what we [!] want her to do or to find' (14 December 1913).

In early January 1914, however, Freud was able to announce to Jones that 'Loe has just given in and will take a daily treatment.' Davy Jones had just arrived in Vienna, which made the rest of the treatment much less confrontational. On 2 June 1914 Freud told Jones that he had just returned from Budapest where he and Otto Rank had been witnesses at Loe and Davy's marriage, with Ferenczi acting as translator (Jones must have appreciated this gesture from his analyst): 'I am sure it must be hard for you, and so it is for me when I remember the series of events from the evening in the Weimar coffeehouse when you offered me her treatment to the moments when I assisted to her wedding with another.'

Immediately after the wedding, Loe resumed the analysis. There was not much time left before Freud's holiday and he therefore concentrated his efforts on Loe's morphine addiction. Shortly before the end of the treatment, however, Freud confessed to Jones that the 'campaign against morphine' had failed. On 10 July 1914, the day of Loe's last session, he added: 'I will take leave tomorrow from Loe. She recovered instantly after taking more morphia and I see no way to wrench it from her at the moment. She has become no believer in Psa [psychoanalysis] yet, but she is charming with all her faults, which are more than outweighed by her excellent qualities. There is light and shadows.' At the end of 392 hours of treatment, Loe Kann was therefore still sceptical of psychoanalysis, a morphine addict and probably still anorgasmic. But her name was now Mrs Jones – officially.

War broke out soon after Loe and Davy's return to London. Still an Anglophile, and now married to an American, she immediately participated in the war effort against the Germans: 'Loe is buying up large quantities of morphia to send to foreign armies, because when the supply of morphia runs short it will be given only to those likely to recover, while the hopeless must die in pain. Isn't she wonderful?' (Jones to Freud, 3 August 1914). Loe now hated everything that was German and vowed never to set foot in a 'Germanic' house again, not even Freud's. As she nevertheless continued to feel affection for her ex-analyst, she suggested at the end of the war that he come and live permanently at The Hague in the house of her brother Kobus, who had emigrated to Palestine. Freud politely declined, while asking her how she, a Jewess, could feel so much hatred.

Loe remained a morphine addict until the end of her life. In 1938 she and Herbert 'Davy' Jones divorced in Reno, Nevada. Shortly thereafter, in May 1938, Herbert married Olwen Pritchard, a Welsh woman with whom he had two children. In early 1944 Anna Freud told Ernest Jones that Loe had just died. She was 62 years old.

32

KARL MEYREDER

(1856–1935)

Karl Meyreder was one of the most prominent architects in Vienna at the turn of the century. He had been the student of the great Viennese builder Heinrich von Ferstel, Marie von Ferstel's stepfather, and he was part of the architectural avant-garde of the time (Adolf Loos worked in his office for a time, and he had Richard Neutra as a student). Besides his private practice, he exercised multiple official functions in the urban community of Vienna and taught at the Technische Hochsule, the most prestigious polytechnic school in the Austro-Hungarian Empire, of which he briefly became rector in 1922–3. His wife, Rosa Meyreder (née Obermayer), was, along with Auguste Fickert, Marie Lang and Marianne Hainisch, a pioneer of the Austrian feminist movement and the author of influential books on women's issues, including *For a Critique of Femininity* (1905) and *Sex and Culture* (published in 1923, but mostly written earlier, in 1915).

The Mayreders were closely linked to Friedrich Eckstein and his sister Emma, and their network of friends therefore overlapped with that of Freud. Fritz Eckstein introduced them in the late 1880s to a circle of artists, reformers and theosophists who gathered around the charismatic feminist activist Marie Lang at Villa Bellevue (a holiday residence near Vienna also frequented at the time by Freud; it was here that he had his famous 'Irma dream'). The circle included, among others, the anthroposophist Rudolf Steiner and the composer Hugo Wolf, for whom Rosa composed the libretto of the opera *Der Corregidor* (1896).

The Mayreders had no children (Rosa had a miscarriage in 1883). However, they were a very close couple, despite Rosa having had two extramarital affairs. Karl unconditionally supported Rosa in all her literary and political endeavours, for which she was grateful. Their marriage was put to the test from 1912, however, when Karl developed a severe melancholic depression that was to last, with a few interruptions, until his death in 1935. The diary kept by Rosa Meyreder during these years returns again and again to the exhausting illness suffered by Lino (the diminutive she used for Carlino, 'little Karl'). Any illness, she wrote, is terrible, but this one undermined the very foundation of their marriage because it changed the 'personality' of her husband and 'the love it inspires'. Karl kept crying, had fits of anxiety, made delusional reproaches. At times he also became agitated and aggressive towards her: 'This morning Lino's fits of agitation intensified into a kind of madness: he declaims, sneers, expresses thoughts of suicide, hides in the closet, says he would like to beat me to give vent to his resentment against me' (6 November 1912). While regularly harbouring thoughts of flight, Rosa stayed with her husband until the end, desperately seeking help from one doctor after another. There were 59 in all, over a period of thirteen years.

Freud was the 25th. One day, out on the street, Rosa had met Paul Federn, the brother of her friend the feminist Else Federn, and he had urged her to consult Freud. Freud was of course known to the Mayreders (Rosa had even written a glowing review of the *Three Essays on Theory of Sexuality* in 1906). So Rosa went to see Freud with Karl and the treatment began the next day, 21 January 1915. It was to last only ten weeks.

On 14 February Rosa confided to her diary that Freud had told Karl she was not 'the woman he needed' and 'that a sense of coolness and distance towards me had taken place in him long ago. This was nothing new to me; like all the doctors, I understood this as a side effect of his illness.' Then Freud had been more precise: according to him, Lino's disease had started during Rosa's menopause, when the hope of any offspring had definitively vanished. Rosa was outraged to be made responsible for her husband's illness. During a scene between them, she let him know that all her doctors had certified to her that she could give birth despite her miscarriage and that if they had not had children, it was simply because he had never expressed the desire to have one. 'His life had been so absorbed by his work that in moments of anger I had said to him several times: "Still, it's lucky that we don't have children, because the truth is they wouldn't have had a father!"'

When Karl reported this conversation to Freud, Freud scolded him for speaking to his wife about what was said in the secrecy of the consulting room. The wall between analysis and the outside world was supposed to remain perfectly sealed. Rosa, for her part, was more and more upset by Freud's imputations. She thought of leaving her husband: 'I really can't stand the idea that it is his relationship to me that should in some way be blamed for Lino's disease. The attraction of common sexuality . . . is going to be the pivot of Freud's theory, I can see that coming, although apparently he hasn't emphasized this aspect of Lino's psychical life. But why does he avoid asking me too? Is he satisfied with the unilateral presentation of the facts by a patient? And can what he draws from Lino's "unconscious" replace what only I know and have experienced? No matter – I'm at the end of my tether.'

Karl seems to have relayed Rosa's complaints to his analyst, because the latter denied intervening in their married life: 'Freud explained to Lino that I was mistaken about his position in sexual matters; he has never advised a patient to change their sex life if the patient had not expressed a desire to do so, since he never gives the patient instructions on how to lead his life.'

Unconvinced, Rosa went to see her friend Emma Eckstein at her home: 'I spoke again in detail with [her] about Lino and Freud's treatment.' Freud now attributed Karl's lack of confidence to a latent conflict with his father, the hotelier Leopold Mayreder – a conflict, said Rosa, 'of which no one had hitherto noticed the slightest trace'. The diary does not say what Emma's reaction was, but a few days later, on 11 March, her brother Fritz came to visit Rosa and advised her not to let Karl see Freud beyond Easter. Evidently, the Ecksteins were no longer convinced of the therapeutic talents of their friend Sigmund.

Rosa followed Fritz Eckstein's advice and treatment stopped a week before Easter, on 27 March 1915. On the same day Freud wrote to his disciple Karl Abraham: 'I found confirmation of the solution to melancholia in one case that I studied for two months, although with no visible therapeutic success, which, however, may follow.' Freud is here referring to his article 'Mourning and Melancholia', which he had started writing in February 1915, precisely when he attributed Karl Mayreder's melancholy depression to a cooling of love for Rosa. The thesis of this famous and extraordinarily influential article is simple: melancholia is due to the pathological 'mourning' for an object from which the subject has had to withdraw his libido and with which he has regressively identified, now addressing to himself reproaches intended in fact for the lost object. This, then, is the theory that the Mayreder case (and this case alone, apparently) had 'confirmed': Karl Mayreder had fallen ill when he withdrew his love from his wife because she had reached menopause and could no longer give him a child. The reproaches he heaped on himself were in fact aimed at Rosa.

This 'solution' to the problem of melancholia did little to help Mayreder, whose condition remained unchanged. He unsuccessfully consulted dozens of other specialists over the years, including Alfred Adler, Paul Federn, the future Nobel Prize winner in medicine Julius Wagner von Jauregg, who recommended hormone therapy, and Eugen Steinach, who attributed the disease to insufficient glandular secretions. 'Fifty doctors,' exclaimed Rosa in 1927, 'and not a single correct diagnosis! Is it any wonder that in view of such "scientists" people turn to charlatans?'

Still, Freud's oracles continued to haunt the Mayreder couple for many years. In 1916 Rosa learned from Mitzi, Karl's sister, that Karl had confided to her that 'Freud considered his unrecognized hatred towards me as one of the causes of his illness.' Once again, Rosa tried to convince Karl of the absurdity of the Freudian explanation. Freud confused the effect of the disease (his aggressiveness towards Rosa) with its cause: 'The fundamental error of Freud is that he confuses the psyche of the neurotic with the healthy psyche and uses the processes of the former to explain the latter – instead of the other way round, explaining the sick person by the deviations

Reverse side of Austrian 500 schilling note.

of the healthy person. He makes side effects into efficient causes; moreover, he does not realize that he puts no limits to his brilliant art of interpretation.'

Karl did not know what to say. 'And yet the suggestion of Freud's authority is still so strong that at each objection [from Rosa] he replies: "Go and talk to him and he will refute everything in the clearest way" – of which I have no doubt, precisely because he is such an excellent dialectician of psychology and moreover a monomaniac of his system.'

On 5 July 1923 Rosa noted again in her diary: '"I have written my obituary," Lino said at breakfast. And after a break, he added: "Its title is: Death of Rosa Meyreder's husband". At first I laughed, but then I saw that it confirmed Freud's opinion that he suffers from my personality, because it removes his male prerogative . . . If I had to admit it, this would be for me the ultimate martyrdom, the complete loss of everything that made our life together precious.'

Rosa and Karl Mayreder now rest side by side in the central cemetery of Vienna, united in death as they were in life, despite all the difficulties and the blows of fate. In 1997 the Austrian government printed a banknote of 500 schillings on which they both appear, alongside a photo of the participants in the Federal Convention of Associations of Austrian Women in 1911.

33

MARGARETHE CSONKA
(1900–1999)

argarethe Csonka seemed destined for a dream life. Her father, Arpad Csonka, was the biggest oil importer in the Austro-Hungarian Empire, as well as being a partner of the Rothschild bankers. Of Jewish origin, but converts to Catholicism, the Csonkas were part of the Austrian upper classes. Margarethe's mother was far from indifferent to the attentions of men; it was rumoured that Paul Csonka, one of Margarethe's brothers, was the illegitimate son of Emperor Franz Joseph. Margarethe and her three brothers led the carefree life of the Viennese gilded youth: parties, beautiful cars, castles and palaces. In summer, they gathered in Brioni or in Semmering with the Wittgensteins, the von Sturgkhs, the von Ruesslers or the von Ferstels (one of Margarethe's friends, Ellen von Schoeller, would marry the nephew of Marie von Ferstel). Paul Csonka, however, escaped from this world and became a renowned composer and conductor, the friend of Karajan, Toscanini and Klemperer.

Margarethe had always been attracted to women. She fell in love with them one after another, ideally and platonically. It was female beauty that fascinated her, not carnal intercourse (for instance, she rejected the advances of her friend Christl Kmunke, who was an open lesbian). At seventeen, she fell in love with the sulphurous Baroness Leonie von Puttkamer. Leonie was a member of the Prussian nobility, a *demi-mondaine* who lived off men while flaunting her liaisons with women. In the early 1920s she was to have a rowdy affair with the nude dancer Anita Berber, and she was accused by her husband, David Gessmann, the president of the Austrian Chamber of Agriculture, of trying to poison him (she was released after spending some time in prison, where Margarethe went to visit her). Margarethe had a real relationship of courtly love with her, serving her as her 'lady' without hoping for anything in return. For her part, Leonie tolerated this young admirer and dragged her along to cafés and shops, much like one drags along a poodle.

Margarethe's parents, especially her father, were worried about this infatuation, which might damage their daughter's reputation. One day when Margarethe and Leonie were walking arm in arm in the street, Margarethe saw her father on the pavement opposite, talking to a colleague. In the article he devoted to the case of Margarethe Csonka ('Psychogenesis of a Case of Homosexuality in a Woman'), Freud writes that the father 'passed them with an angry glance which boded no good', whereupon the young girl, distraught, 'rushed off and flung herself over a wall down the side of a cutting on to the suburban railway line which ran close by'. In reality, according to the story told later by Margarethe Csonka to her biographers Diana Voigt and Inès Rieder, she had moved away from Leonie as soon as she saw her father and started running in the opposite direction to escape his gaze. Glancing over her shoulder, however, she realized that her father had not noticed her and was getting on a tram. She then returned to the baroness, but Leonie, annoyed that the young girl had not had the courage to show herself with her, dryly told her that she did not want to see her anymore. It was only then that Margarethe made her suicide attempt, which was thus not motivated by shame at having been discovered by her father but by a desire to prove to the baroness the depth of her love.

Alarmed by his daughter's suicide attempt, Arpad Csonka decided to send her to Freud to put her back on the straight and narrow path of heterosexuality. Freud did not promise anything, well aware

A young Margarethe Csonka.

that such a goal was unlikely to be achieved, but he nevertheless agreed to take Margarethe on for treatment for a certain time. In those times of political and economic breakdown, inflation had become rampant and Arpad Csonka could pay in foreign currency ($10 an hour). Freud made Margarethe promise that she would no longer see Leonie von Puttkamer during the treatment period (Leonie, moved by the girl's suicide attempt, had in the meantime agreed to resume relations with her). Margarethe went along to please her father, but she obviously had no intention of respecting the contract that had been imposed on her.

Every day, in the middle of the afternoon, she went to 19 Berggasse and politely bowed to the ritual of analysis: 'The analysis went forward almost without any signs of resistance, the patient participating actively with her intellect, though absolutely tranquil emotionally. Once when I expounded to her a specially important part of the theory, one touching her nearly, she replied in an inimitable tone, "How very interesting," as though she were a grande dame being taken over a museum and glancing through her lorgnon at objects to which she was completely indifferent.' After which, Margarethe met up with her dear Leonie in a *Kaffeehaus* and the two friends cheerfully chortled over the doctor's absurd oracles: Margarethe, he claimed, had turned away from men out of spite because her beloved father had given a child to her mother, whom she unconsciously hated!

Margarethe was later to tell Kurt Eissler how she had led Freud down the garden path during the treatment. One day when she had inadvertently mentioned one of her illicit meetings with Leonie, she corrected herself and with aplomb pretended that it was a dream. Freud had not seen through her game, and so Margarethe had continued – though she never dreamed – to serve him custom-made dreams in order to be left alone. After a while, Freud still ended up suspecting that there was something wrong with these too perfect dreams: 'At a certain period, not long after the treatment had begun, the girl brought a series of dreams which, distorted according to rule and couched in the usual dream-language, could nevertheless be easily translated with certainty. Their content, when interpreted, was, however, remarkable. They anticipated the cure of the inversion through the treatment, expressed her joy over the prospects in life that would then be opened before her, confessed her longing for a man's love and for children, and so might have been welcomed as a gratifying preparation for the desired change.' These dreams, continued Freud, were 'false or hypocritical, and . . . she intended to deceive me just as she usually deceived her father'.

Freud did not deduce from this, however, that he had been deliberately fooled by the girl. A good unconscious cannot lie: these deceptive dreams, according to him, were due to a positive transfer to his person and to Margarethe's unconscious desire to please the father-analyst. This positive transfer was not, however, sufficient to overcome the negative transfer that the patient simultaneously fostered towards him. She had transferred to him 'the sweeping repudiation of men which had dominated her ever since the disappointment she had suffered from her father' and suddenly resisted treatment. Freud therefore decided to end the analysis, much to Margarethe's relief. The treatment had failed, but at least the clinical material gleaned from it would allow the analyst to write a brilliant article on the psychogenesis of female homosexuality.

As for Margarethe, happy to get off the analytic hook, she resumed her frivolous life. After Leonie, she fell in love with many other women and even sometimes with men, always in the same ideal and aesthetic fashion. The flesh disappointed her most of the time. She made two more suicide attempts, again for reasons of love. In 1930 she married Baron Eduard Rzemenowsky von Trautenegg, an ex-fighter pilot more interested in the fortune of the Csonkas than in his wife. Heterosexual respectability was well worth a mass – or, in this case, a conversion from Catholicism to her husband's Protestantism.

Margarethe Csonka paid no attention to the dark clouds coming from Germany. She lived in her enchanted world and was not particularly interested in politics. When her husband, nostalgic for the Austro-Hungarian Empire, flirted with the National Socialists, she saw nothing to complain about. She herself, although of Jewish origin, was spontaneously antisemitic: 'We have nothing to do with these people!' After the Anschluss, the Nazis undertook to enlighten her on the reality of her situation. Her marriage to the Aryan Eduard von Trautenegg was annulled on the grounds of race, and her ex-husband took control of her property and her fortune. Her Jewish and homosexual friends were arrested and deported one after the other. Her mother joined her younger brother

Walter in Paris. Paul Csonka and her other brother took refuge in Cuba, like so many other Jews at the time (Paul assumed the direction of the National Opera of Havana, as well as that of the National Orchestra, before fleeing again in the United States in 1963 after Castro's takeover).

Margarethe, meanwhile, waited until the very last moment to leave Austria. In August 1940, using with sangfroid her passport in the name of Baroness von Trautenegg, she went to Berlin and from there took one of the last trains to Moscow. After a five-month journey through Russia, Manchuria, Japan, Honolulu and San Francisco, she finally arrived in Havana, where Paul welcomed her in the house he had built.

There thus began a long existence of permanent exile. She was at home nowhere. Her world was gone, engulfed by the war and the camps. As the Csonka fortune had evaporated, she had to work the rest of her life as a lady companion or governess for wealthy families. In 1947 she left Cuba for the United States, then returned in 1949 to Europe and finally to Vienna. She had a great love affair with Wjera Fechheimer, a friend whose husband had died in Dachau, but who eventually left her. Then, from 1960 onwards, she went to Thailand, Spain, the United States (again), Spain (again), Brazil and finally Vienna, where she returned to

Margarethe Csonka in Havana, early 1940s.

settle in 1973. She died during the summer of 1999 in the twelfth district of Vienna, in the retirement home where she ended up at the close of a century that she had lived through from start to finish.

Meanwhile, several researchers had finally discovered that this lively and distinguished old lady was none other than the famous case of female homosexuality immortalized by Freud. During the 1990s Diana Voigt and Ines Rieder collected the story of her life as a 'lesbian in the world' and wrote a richly documented and illustrated book on her, which came out in 2000. Others, such as Kurt Eissler and the psychoanalyst August Ruhs, were primarily interested in her analysis with Freud. The problem is that she had little to say about this. A year before her death, she confided to Ruhs: 'Yes, well, I didn't really think much of Doctor Freud. It didn't help either, I thought he was an uninteresting old man . . . One day, he said to me: "I am putting you in touch with the deepest motions of your soul and you behave as if I was just reading out something from the newspaper . . ."'

34

ANNA FREUD

(1895–1982)

Born on 3 December 1895, Anna Freud was the sixth and youngest child of Martha and Sigmund Freud, and she was not wanted. Martha, as was her habit, did not breastfeed her daughter (Anna was given Gartner's milk, a new baby formula). Later, Anna would remember a rather unhappy childhood. In the domestic economy of 19 Berggasse everything revolved around 'Sigi'/'Papa', and Anna was jealous of the other women in the family – Martha, Tante Minna (Minna Bernays) and in particular her sister Sophie, the prettiest daughter and favourite of the parents (in a letter of 1913 Freud mentioned her 'always being jealous of Sophie'). Anna was a problem child, tirelessly demanding and 'unreasonable'. She also had periods of apathy, during which she felt sad and *dumm* (stupid). Concerned about her physical and mental health, her parents regularly sent her to the countryside or to health resorts to rest and gain weight.

During her dreary phases of 'stupidity', Anna took refuge in intense fantasizing and masturbating. From the age of five or six, she started telling herself 'nice stories' in which a young man who clearly represented her was 'beaten' or humiliated by an older man. These fantasies of humiliation and beating, which continued until adulthood, were regularly accompanied by masturbation, when they did not replace it as a path to orgasm. Anna also had dreams in which she served or defended a father figure: 'Recently I dreamed that you were a king and I was a princess, and that someone wanted to separate us through political intrigues. It was not at all nice but quite thrilling' (Anna Freud to her father, 6 August 1915).

Anna, who had started attending meetings of the Vienna Psychoanalytic Society at the age of fourteen, told her father everything. In a letter of January 1913 from Meran, where she had been sent for a health cure, Anna talked in veiled terms about the feelings of guilt that 'it' caused her – that is, the masturbation that her father seemed to have prohibited or recommended that she abandon: 'When I have a stupid (*dumm*) day everything looks wrong to me. Today, for example, I cannot understand how it can be so stupid sometimes. I don't want to go through this again because I want to be or at least become a sensible person but I can't always help myself alone.'

Anna had at least become 'sensible' enough in 1914 to start studying to become a teacher. She was eighteen years old. During the summer, she went to England, where she was courted by Ernest Jones. Freud sent her an alarmed letter to warn her against his advances. To Jones, he wrote: 'She does not claim to be treated like a woman, being still far away from sexual longings and rather re- fusing man. There is an outspoken understanding between me and her that she should not consider marriage or the preliminaries before she gets 2 or 3 years older' (22 July 1914). In fact, Freud had nothing to worry about: Anna was much more interested in Loe Kann, Jones's beautiful ex-mistress (and one of her father's ex- patients, of whom he was very fond). 'I dream terribly often of her [Loe], last night too . . . You know that I am extraordinarily fond of her.' However, the war broke out and Anna had to rush back to Vienna, where she spent the next four years training as a teacher while continuing to take an interest in psychoanalysis.

In October 1918, at the age of 22, Anna began analysis sessions with her father. It was not the first time that Freud had analysed one of his children, because it seems that he did the same with Sophie. Why did Anna decide to lie on the couch? She was proba- bly thinking of training in psychoanalysis, which she intended to apply to pedagogy, but many personal factors definitely also came into play. In his article 'A Child Is Being Beaten', which is based largely on Anna's analysis, Freud speaks of a case that 'had come to be analysed merely on account of indecisiveness in life, [and] would not have been classified at all by coarse clinical diagnosis, or would have been dismissed as "psychasthenic"' (these days we would call it depression). Anna – for it is her case that is most likely being discussed – was ill at ease in life and in her sexuality. There was no shortage of suitors, whether they had declared themselves or not (Hans Lampl, August Aichhorn, Siegfried Bernfeld, Max Eitingon, to name a few), but Anna could not separate herself from her father and confront what Freud called 'genitality'. Freud expressed his worries to his friend and disciple Lou Andreas-Salomé, while admitting to her that if Anna were to leave him one day, he would experience a feeling of deprivation 'as I should do if I had to give up smoking!' (13 March 1922).

In December 1918, just a few weeks after Anna's analysis began, Freud began to write 'A Child Is Being Beaten', in which he provided the Oedipal key to his daughter's masturbatory fantasies: the beaten boy was Anna herself, and the elderly man who humiliated or castigated him was Freud, the father, who was punishing her, in her fantasy, for wanting to sleep with him. She had sadistically wanted him to beat another child (Sophie) with whom she was competing for his exclusive possession and now she had to enjoy masochistically being beaten by him. (We can imagine the scene: 'Papa' smoking a post-prandial cigar and offering this interpretation to his daughter as she lay on the couch . . .) Anna took up the interpretation in the essay 'Beating Fantasies and Daydreams', which she read to the Vienna Psychoanalytic Society in May 1922 with a view to becoming a psychoanalyst, but without revealing that the case she was describing was in fact her own, analysed not by her but by the honorary president of the jury that would be approving her candidacy.

The paternal analysis had lasted four years. Meanwhile, Anna had started to analyse Sophie's boys after the latter's death in 1920, thus continuing the tradition of the Freud family into the next generation. In 1923, after the discovery of cancer in Freud's jaw and his first surgical operation, Anna vowed that she would never leave him – a vow that received the blessing of Lou Andreas-Salomé, with whom she had been pursuing a kind of parallel analysis since 1921. Now supplanting her mother and Tante Minna vis-à-vis her father, Anna became the Antigone of the ageing Oedipus, in a sort of Viennese remake of the tragedy of the House of Atreus.

The following year, she returned to Papa's couch. As she explained to Lou, she was again beset with fantasies that left her *dumm*, as in the past, and she experienced 'an increasing intolerance – sometimes physical as well as mental – of the beating

Anna Freud,
1915.

fantasies and of their consequences [that is, masturbation] which
I could not do without.' Freud took the opportunity to write a
second article, based, in all likelihood, on the analysis of his daughter: 'Some Psychical Consequences of the Anatomical Difference
between the Sexes' (1925). Freud deepened his analysis of jealousy,
which was Anna's main character trait: what the little girl is really
jealous of is the penis that she 'envies' in boys from the moment
she realizes that she does not have it. Expanding on his essay
'A Child Is Being Beaten', Freud proposed to see in the beaten
boy the clitoris-penis being masturbated during the little girl's
phallic phase: 'Masturbation, at all events of the clitoris, is a masculine activity and . . . the elimination of clitoridal sexuality is a
necessary precondition for the development of femininity.' Freud
added, more generally, that the female Oedipus complex was a
result of the little girl replacing her penis envy with the desire to
have a child – hence her love for her father and her jealousy of
her mother. And finally this: 'When the girl's attachment to her
father comes to grief later on and has to be abandoned, it may
give place to an identification with him and the girl may thus
return to her masculinity complex and perhaps remain fixed in

it.' During the International Psychoanalytic Congress held in Bad Homburg in September 1925, Anna read out this Oedipal oracle in her father's place, as he was too ill to give the paper himself. Like all oracles, this one was coming true.

Earlier in the year, while Anna was still on his couch, Freud had complained that he could not detach Anna from him: that is, he could not get her to resolve her Oedipus complex. At the end of March, he wrote to Anna von Vest: 'The girl doesn't want to get married.' And to Lou, on 10 May 1925: 'I fear that the suppressed genitality will play her a nasty trick some time. I cannot get her away from me, but then nobody is helping me with it.' The arrival of Dorothy Burlingham in Vienna would change things, while verifying Freud's prediction about the return of the little girl (*his* little girl) to the 'masculinity complex'.

Dorothy Tiffany Burlingham, born on 11 October 1891, was a wealthy American whose grandfather had founded the Tiffany department store in New York. Her father, Louis Comfort Tiffany, was the creator of the famous Tiffany lamps. In 1914 she married

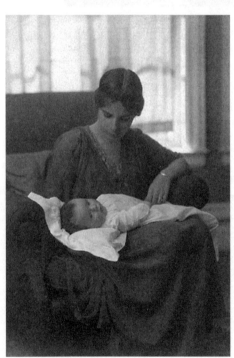

the surgeon Robert Burlingham, son of the great New York lawyer and bigwig of the Democratic Party Charles Culp Burlingham. The couple had four children – Bob, Mabbie, Tinky and Mikey – but it soon became apparent that Robert Burlingham was suffering from manic depression. Dorothy, exhausted by her husband's constant breakdowns and worried about the psychological balance of her children, decided in 1925 to take them to Vienna to have them psychoanalysed by Anna Freud. During a preliminary interview in the summer of 1925, Anna agreed to accept Bob and Mabbie for analysis (and a little later Adelaïde Sweetzer, the daughter of a couple who were

Dorothy Burlingham with her son Robert ('Bob') Jr.

friends with Dorothy). She also arranged an analysis with Theodor Reik for Dorothy. In September, just as Anna was reading her father's text out at the Bad Homburg Congress, Dorothy and the children moved to Vienna and settled into the luxurious house of a Hungarian prince.

Anna was immediately seized with a compelling desire to 'have' the Burlinghams for herself – the children, but also their mother. The two women met constantly to talk about the children and quickly became inseparable. They spent their free time exploring the surroundings of Vienna together in Dorothy's Model T (a rarity in Vienna in these times of scarcity), often with Papa in the back.

Anna was ashamed of her possessiveness towards Dorothy and her children, 'especially in front of Papa', as she wrote to Max Eitingon on 5 February 1926. Unable to talk about this directly to her father on the couch, she had set up Eitingon as a confidant/analyst – and Eitingon, of course, kept Freud informed about all this. Freud was very fond of Dorothy and the dog she had given him, a chow named Lun Yu. In a letter to Lou of 11 May 1927, he bizarrely described her as an 'unhappy virgin', which seems to indicate that in his mind he identified this mother of four children with his unmarried (if not asexual) daughter.

Anna and Dorothy spent their weekends in a house they had rented in Neuhaus before buying a small farm together in Hochrotherd, near Vienna, with cows, chickens and a vegetable patch. The Freud and Burlingham families also spent their holidays together. In the autumn of 1929 Dorothy and her four children moved to an apartment above that of the Freuds at 19 Berggasse, which was very practical since Anna, as early as 1927, had made sure that Dorothy would leave Reik's couch for Freud's instead (Dorothy was to remain one of Freud's patients practically until Freud's death). So Dorothy had only one floor to go down for her daily session of therapy, while her children were psychoanalysed by Anna, who herself was being analysed episodically by her father. Dorothy also had a direct telephone line installed between her bedroom and Anna's so that they could speak at night. In this family-analytic atmosphere, it is not surprising that the unconsciouses of these different people would communicate telepathically. In his essay 'Dreams and Occultism', Freud recounts how one of

Dorothy's sons had once brought her a gold coin when she had just been telling her analyst about a certain gold coin that had played a role in her childhood. As Freud wrote to Ludwig Binswanger in 1929, 'Our symbiosis with an American family (without husband), whose children my daughter is bringing up with a firm hand analytically, is getting more and more established' (11 January 1929).

Anna, in a total identification with her father, occupied vis-à-vis the Burlingham children both the position of analyst and that of 'paternal' and educational authority in the couple she formed with Dorothy. Under her aegis and in collaboration with Eva Rosenfeld, another friend of Anna, Dorothy had in 1927 founded a private – very private – school for her own children and other young patients of Anna's, such as Ernst Halberstadt-Freud (Sophie's son), Adelaïde and Harold Sweetzer, Peter Heller and Victor Ross (Eva Rosenfeld's son). In reaction against the rigid Austrian education of the time, anti-authoritarian, sexually 'enlightened' and psychoanalytic educational principles were applied in this tiny institution, nicknamed the 'Matchbox School'. Once he had become an adult (and Dorothy's son-in-law), Peter Heller would express mixed views about this radical educational experiment, for which he himself had paid the price: 'Most of us had a difficult time meeting the requirements of public education once our special school was dissolved; and some, I believe, never acquired the discipline necessary for a substantial professional contribution.' Heller also stated that 'one older student committed suicide, an event hardly even mentioned, let alone discussed, in this liberally "open minded" educational community.'

Meanwhile, Robert Burlingham, who was a devoted father and husband when he was not going through one of his breakdowns, was desperate to see his wife and children again. Convinced that Dorothy and the children would return to the United States after their analysis was complete, he had started looking for a house for them to return to, but eventually he was forced to realize that Dorothy had no intention of leaving Vienna and her new family. According to one of his female friends, Robert 'was terribly sad at times but tried . . . to keep on hoping and not to slide into a depression . . . But soon he very clearly started to decline.' Robert and his father came to Vienna several times to collect the children and wrest them from the influence of the Freuds, thus creating intense conflicts among the four little Burlinghams, torn between their father, their mother and their analyst. Robert Burlingham was, however, persuaded to seek treatment from George S. Amsden, an American analyst in Budapest who had been recommended by Ferenczi. According to Elisabeth Young-Bruehl, Anna Freud's biographer, 'the Freuds pressured both Amsden and Ferenczi to do their best to keep Burlingham in Budapest and to convince him not to sue for custody of his children.' Finally, Dorothy won the battle and Robert Burlingham was only allowed to see his children during the holidays – and never all at the same time, for fear that he would kidnap them. In May 1938 Robert solved the problem for everyone: he threw himself from the fourteenth floor of the building in which he lived in New York.

Shortly thereafter, on 4 June 1938, the Freud family emigrated to London, to 20 Maresfield Gardens in the upscale area of Hampstead. True to her vow never to leave her father, Anna decided to stay there after his death, along with Martha, Tante Minna, the faithful maidservant Paula Fichtl – and Dorothy. Momentarily trapped in New York by the war, Dorothy had harboured romantic feelings for the psychoanalyst Walter C. Langer (an analysand of Anna's), but after an exchange of letters made her fear losing Anna, she returned to settle permanently with her in March 1940: 'I know life without you would be quite without sense,' she wrote to her in alarm.

The two now formed a couple, continuing their analytical work with the children, first in the Children's Rest Centre, a war kindergarten during the Blitz, then, after the war, in the famous Hampstead Child Therapy Clinic. The four Burlingham children had married in the meantime and no longer lived with them. When they came to visit their mother, they had to lie down simultaneously on Anna's couch, as the latter was still their analyst (the spouses could not stay at 20 Maresfield Gardens, as they needed to abide by the separation between analytical space and the outside world). Bob Burlingham, who with his brother and sisters was one of the ten cases on which Anna based her *Introduction to the Technique of Child Analysis*, was in analysis with Anna for 45 years, right until his death. He suffered from the same manic-depressive cycles as his father, but Anna refused to let him take medication. He died at the age of 54. His sister Mabbie, whom Anna had considered the 'most successful' of the ten cases in her book, committed suicide with barbiturates one evening while she was at 20 Maresfield Gardens. This did not prevent Dorothy from taking a client for analysis the next day: '*Messieurs, la séance continue!*'

After Dorothy died on 19 November 1979, Anna carried on. Right up to the end, and just as in her girlish dreams, she defended her father against his adversaries and the ignominies spread by historians of psychoanalysis such as Paul Roazen or Peter Swales: 'It was not at all nice but quite thrilling.' She died on 9 October 1982 from a stroke. Antigone remained virgin and faithful.

35

HORACE FRINK
(1883–1936)

U nlike most of Freud's patients until the end of the First
World War, Horace Westlake Frink was neither Jewish,
nor Viennese nor wealthy. He belonged to another world,
that New World which Freud sought to conquer while cordially
despising its materialism and philistinism. His father, George S.
Frink, owned a modest foundry in Millerton, a small town north
of New York. When Horace was eight years old, the foundry was
destroyed by a fire and his parents left to start a new life in the
West ('Go West, young man'), leaving Horace and his younger
brother with their maternal grandparents in Hillsdale, New York.
Horace was never to live with his parents again. His mother,
Henrietta Westlake, died of tuberculosis when he was fifteen and
Dr George Westlake, his grandfather, became his legal guardian.
George Westlake held George Frink responsible for the death of
his daughter and agreed to take care of the two boys only on the
condition that their father never communicated with them again.

A brilliant student and accomplished athlete, Horace Frink
studied medicine at Cornell Medical College in New York where he
befriended Clarence Oberndorf and Swepson J. Brooks. Appointed
to Bellevue Hospital in New York after obtaining his doctorate in
medicine in 1905, he hoped to become a surgeon, but an infection
contracted on the right index finger during an operation in 1907
meant that he could no longer bend it, thus ending his surgical
career. In 1908 he returned to Hillsdale, where his grandfather had
just died, and experienced his first episode of depression, which he
treated with swigs of whisky. A childhood friend, Doris Best, took
care of him. Probably as a result of this personal experience, he
moved into psychiatry and started to take an interest in hypnosis

– which he practised successfully on some of his patients when he returned to New York in 1909 – as well as in psychoanalysis.

In New York he met Abraham Arden Brill. Brill, an Austro-Hungarian by birth, had just returned from an internship at the Bürghölzli psychiatric hospital in Zurich, where he had been trained in psychoanalysis by Eugen Bleuler and Carl Gustav Jung. He had won Freud's trust when the latter came to Clark University in 1909 and became his de facto representative in the United States. Eager to be trained, Frink started an analysis with him at a rate of one session a week. Brill's treatment consisted essentially of an analysis of Frink's dreams, which was usual at the time in terms of training analysis (though this term did not yet exist).

In 1910, having married Doris Best, Frink set up shop as a psychoanalyst in New York. A founding member of the New York Psychoanalytic Society with Brill and Oberndorf in 1911, he was elected as its president for the first time in 1913, replacing Brill. In 1915 Frink, Oberndorf and Thaddeus H. Ames, another Freudian, took over the teaching of neurology at Cornell Medical College and made it a springboard for the dissemination of psychoanalysis. Among their students were Abram Kardiner and Monroe Meyer, both of whom Frink also analysed. In 1918 Frink published *Morbid Fears and Compulsions* in collaboration with the journalist Wilfred Lay. Written in an alert and reader-friendly style, this was the first presentation of psychoanalysis to an American public. The book was highly successful and contributed decisively to the popularization of psychoanalysis in America. In less than ten years Frink had managed to establish himself as the most prominent psychoanalyst in the United States.

His private life was less glorious. In 1913 he underwent a new analysis with his colleague Thaddeus Ames, probably to solve some conjugal issues. His marriage to Doris Best was not happy – more his fault than hers: Doris seems to have been very devoted to him, but he was aggressive towards her and cheated on her. From 1915 he began again to have episodes of depression, which culminated in 1916, the year in which his son John ('Jack') was born. Frink had thoughts of suicide, and considered leaving his family. Then, as he recounts in a self-report written later for psychiatrist Adolf Meyer, the depression suddenly gave way to aggressivity and a feeling of omnipotence.

This was the first sign of a manic-depressive oscillation that was to last nearly a decade, but Frink himself was baffled: 'There was nothing to suggest that this was a hypomanic manifestation in this period itself. Only upon viewing it in connection with the previous mild depressions and the present attack does this suspicion arise' (self-report, 1924). In 1918 depression came back after the publication of *Morbid Fears and Compulsions*. Despite the very positive reception given to his book, Frink felt as if he had been ignored and developed 'toxic headaches' that he went to treat on a ranch in New Mexico. (In the land of cowboys, ranches often substituted for the spas and sanatoria of the European elite.)

Then there was the psychoanalytic and conjugal imbroglio. In 1912 Frink had taken into analysis a wealthy heiress, Angelika ('Angie') Wertheim Bijur, whom Brill had sent him. Angie, who was 28 at the time, was part of New York high society. Her father, Jakob Wertheim, had made his fortune in the tobacco industry and chaired the United Cigar Manufacturer Company, while also being director of General Motors and the Underwood Typewriter Company. He was additionally the founder of the Federation for the Support of Jewish Philanthropic Societies. Angelika's brother, Maurice Wertheim, was to set up one of the most important investment funds in the United States, Wertheim & Co. In 1907 Angelika had married a tobacco importer some ten years older than she was, Abraham Bijur, who was also descended from a prominent Jewish family (his cousin, Nathan Bijur, was a member of the United States Supreme Court). The couple had adopted two children, Elizabeth ('Betty') and Dorothy Louise, but the marriage was not very happy.

Brill knew the Wertheim family personally and preferred to direct Angie to Frink rather than take her into analysis himself. Abraham Bijur also spent some time on Frink's couch, but in 1917 the latter sent him to continue his analysis with Thaddeus Ames. Frink also sent his wife to Ames, who therefore found himself at the centre of the affair that was brewing. The Frink and Bijur couples met each other socially outside of the analyses, and what had to happen happened: according to the account given by Frink to Adolf Meyer, he fell in love with Angie in 1917 (thus during his hypomanic period) and started an affair with his patient. Doris Frink seems to have tacitly accepted the situation, but Bijur was furious with his wife, because they had just adopted the young

Freud's bill for Frink's treatment, April and
May 1922.

girls Betty and Dorothy (Thaddeus Ames, interview with Kurt
Eissler, 3 July 1952). Angie, meanwhile, was discovering an intense
sexuality. As she was to write later to Meyer: 'Dr F's lovemaking
freed me from the prison in which I had shut myself.'

In 1920 Angie told Frink that she loved him and clearly raised
the question of divorce. Frink was reluctant to abandon his wife
and two children (his daughter Helen had just been born that
same year). So he decided to consult Freud to help him solve his
dilemma: did he really love Angie? This was the time when all the
young New York psychiatrists – Clarence Oberndorf, Thaddeus
Ames, Abram Kardiner, Adolph Stern, Leonard Blumgart, Monroe
Meyer – were travelling to Vienna to train with the master. Frink
wrote to Freud in July 1920, who replied that he would be delighted
to receive him on his couch between March and mid-July of the
following year: 'My fee is the same for physicians as for ordinary
patients, #10 an hour to be paid not in austrian [sic] crowns but
in your money. You know how desolate our condition here is' (to
Frink, 10 October 1920).

At the end of the war, inflation was indeed galloping and the
Austrian crown was worth almost nothing. Even the prohibitive
prices charged by Freud were no longer sufficient to maintain his
family's standard of living and so he would only take on patients
who could pay in dollars. As Oberndorf remembered, this very
much worked to his advantage: 'He [Freud] would only accept
American money . . . When I first went to Vienna [in 1921], I think
the Crown was about three thousand for a Dollar. Before I had

left, it had gone to a hundred thousand for a Dollar. And so . . .
I presume that one hour paid his rent for several months' (interview with Kurt Eissler, 1 October 1952). To avoid the Austrian tax authorities, checks were to be made payable to Dr Ernest Jones and sent to his open account with Messrs Lippman, Rosenthal & Co., bankers in Amsterdam. Leonard Blumgart (who paid $15 per hour) recounts: 'And I didn't pay him [Freud] but I drew up a check [to] Ernest Jones and sent it to Holland; for some reason he wanted that arrangement made' (interview with Kurt Eissler, 11 September 1952). Nobody complained. Kardiner, who was in analysis with Freud at the same time, had never been so rich in his life: 'I was a millionaire with a few dollars in my pocket.' Even more so Freud himself: according to Adolph Stern, '$10 in Vienna was a lot of money, and when he [Freud] had as many as four or five Americans at one time he was making more money than the Kaiser' (interview with Kurt Eissler, 13 November 1952).

In any case, money was no problem for Frink. Angie, who was impatiently awaiting Freud's oracle, would pay for his trip and his analysis. She had also promised to cover the costs of the analysis of Monroe Meyer, whom Frink intended to take as partner after returning to New York.

Frink arrived in Vienna on 27 February 1921 and settled with Monroe Meyer in an apartment that the latter had rented for them on Laudongasse (Meyer had preceded him and had already

Horace Frink sitting with Monroe Meyer (?) in a Kaffeehaus
in Vienna, 1921 or 1922.

started his analysis with Freud). Freud had jokingly asked Frink 'to bring some bit of neurosis of your own, on which your analysis could stand' (5 August 1920). Frink brought him a psychosis. He was again in a hypomanic phase and could no longer sleep. Everything felt unreal to him, Vienna seemed like a dream. In his self-report to Adolf Meyer, he writes: 'I was very happy, and more talkative and full of fun than ever in my life before, though I have always loved fun and had a great sense of humour.'

Freud was delighted to find in Frink a witty man with whom he could compete in humour: 'Your repressed sadism is coming up in the shape of excellent grim humour but harmless too. I was never afraid of it' (20 February 1922). In an unpublished portrait of Freud written at the same time, Frink insists at length on this aspect: 'He is a great lover of fun and a most gifted humourist . . . He enjoys a joke the way a Frenchman enjoys a bottle of wine, quietly, expertly, contemplatively, with cultivated awareness of all the nuances of the flavour.'

Inevitably, Freud and Frink fell for each other's charms. Freud much preferred the lively and witty (and hypomanic) Frink to the 'boring' Adolph Stern or the 'arrogant' Clarence Oberndorf, who did not accept his interpretations. He immediately decided to make Frink his representative in the United States, encouraging him to supplant his friend and ex-analyst Abraham Brill, with whom Freud had disagreements. 'The plan', remembered Angie, 'was to make out of Frink the leading and greatest analyst of the United States. He should even supersede Brill' (interview with Kurt Eissler, 19 June 1952). As Mark Brunswick (another American in Vienna) told the historian Paul Roazen, Freud made 'a complete transference' onto Frink. Frink made a no less complete transference onto Freud. As an ex-practitioner of hypnosis, he had no trouble recognizing the hypnotist in Freud: 'Freud knows how to hypnotize, and this shows in his psychology.' But that did not stop him from falling under the hypnotist's spell himself. Angie was later to write to Adolf Meyer that Frink's attitude towards Freud 'was that of a child to an all-wise father as demonstrated by his acceptance and obedience to Freud's views' (letter to Adolf Meyer, June 1924).

Predictably, Freud diagnosed in Frink a repressed homosexuality. Kardiner, who was being analysed by Freud at the same time, recounts in his book of memories that this was standard operating procedure: 'In comparing notes with other students, I discovered that, as with the Oedipus complex, unconscious homosexuality was a routine part of everyone's analysis.' Frink, just as predictably, resisted the idea. Freud therefore encouraged him to get divorced and marry Angie Bijur so as not to get stuck in a sublimated homosexuality. Angie, whom Freud did not yet know, was supposed to get divorced too. Frink, for his part, was still in a hypomanic state. As he says in his self-report: 'I went through it all while definitely sick and no master of my faculties.' He wavered between love for Angie and utter lack of interest: 'It was as if she, too, was part of a dream.'

Finally, after much hesitation, Frink decided 'more or less' to follow Freud's advice. Whereupon the hypomanic state faded again. When Angie Bijur, who was in Paris with her husband, joined him in early July, she found him 'immersed in what I now know as a depression. When I saw Freud, he advised my getting a divorce because of my incomplete existence . . . and because if I threw Dr Frink over now, he would never again come back to normality, and probably develop into a homosexual, though in a highly disguised way' (letter to Adolf Meyer, June 1924).

With Freud's blessing, Frink and Angie therefore returned to Paris in July to inform Abraham Bijur of their decision. Bijur was flabbergasted and flew into a rage. Just a few days earlier, he and Angie had made love and she had offered him a pair of pearl studs worth $5,000 as a token of her affection. During the whole of the argument between him and Angie, Frink stood in a corner, as if he were not there. Then everyone returned to New York separately. As soon as he came off the boat, Frink announced to Doris that he wanted a 'quick divorce'. Doris was devastated. After Frink had announced the news to her, she wrote him a letter telling him that she did not agree with Freud's recommendation, but that she would acquiesce if this was what he wanted: 'I feel that you have had great unhappiness and I am anxious that you should have just as great happiness. I cannot feel that it lies where Freud thinks it does . . . To be to you what you desire would give me absolutely the greatest joy in the world.' As her sister was to say much later to her daughter Helen, she knew that Frink suffered from a mental illness: 'She understood something Freud didn't understand.' She was not the only one: as Adolph Stern related: 'It was unavoidable – you couldn't possibly mistake his [Frink's] sickness. I don't see how anyone could have – I mean a psychiatrist – help but see that. I frequently thought of that – how Freud didn't see that . . . it was so apparent and it was evident to those who knew him – like Oberndorf who knew him – Brill [who] knew him' (interview with Kurt Eissler, 13 November 1952).

Confronted with the damage they were creating all around them, Frink and Angie themselves very quickly began to doubt the wisdom of their decision. Frink, in particular, once again started to wonder how real his romantic feelings towards Angie actually were. Relations between them were tense and Angie sought aid from Adolph Stern, on whose couch she was for several months. At the beginning of September, she sent a long and desperate cablegram to Seefeld, where Freud was spending his holidays, to ask him if he had not been mistaken and if he was quite certain that they ought to get married (Freud to Frink, 12 September 1921). Brill, who happened to be visiting Seefeld and who knew the parties intimately, tried to convince Freud of the madness of this marriage project. Freud went ahead anyway and wrote a terse cablegram which he asked Brill to send from Innsbrück: 'NO MISTAKE. BE KIND AND PATIENTS [sic].' Brill complied, with the greatest reluctance. Freud also wrote to Frink to confirm: 'I have not changed my mind about your affair . . . I know that I am right. I should cling to what I consider the truth . . . I even cling to my words that your case is complete' (12 September 1921). The letter swept aside Frink's hesitations, and he sent a copy to Angie: 'I am enclosing a copy of the Freud letter which I hope may be as much of a comfort to you as it has to me. I want to preserve the original. Our grandchildren may be interested to read it sometime. I am very, very happy.' Angie was too. As she would say to Adolf Meyer, 'I at the time felt Freud to be the greatest authority we could trust and was happy.'

Meanwhile, rumours about the affair were circulating in New York, and Frink's colleagues began to get seriously worried. Abraham Bijur was fuming and threatened to cause a scandal. He had written an open letter to Freud that he intended to publish as a full page advertisement in the *New York Times*, in which he denounced his transgression of medical ethics: 'Dr Freud: Recently . . . two patients presented themselves to you, a man and a woman, and made it clear that on your judgment depended whether they had a right to marry one another or not. The man is at present married to another woman, and the father of two children by her, and bound in honour by the ethics of his profession not to take advantage of his confidential position toward his patients and their immediate relatives. The woman he now wants to marry was his patient. He says you sanction his divorcing his wife and marrying his patient, but yet you have never seen the wife and learned to judge her feelings, interests and real wishes. [In fact, Angie had met Freud in Vienna, as we have seen.] The woman, this man's patient, is my wife . . . How can you know you are just to me; how can you give a judgment that ruins a man's hope and happiness, without at least knowing the victim so as to see if he is worthy of the pun-ishment, or if through him a better solution cannot be found? . . . Great Doctor, are you a savant or charlatan? *Doktor,* please write me the truth. The woman is my wife whom I love . . .'

Psychoanalysis in the United States would undoubtedly not have survived such a publication. Thaddeus Ames, who was the analyst of Abraham Bijur (and of Frink, and of his wife), forwarded a copy of Bijur's letter to Freud and Ernest Jones, then president of the International Psychoanalytic Association. In his capacity as president of the New York Psychoanalytic Society, Ames warned Freud that, because of Frink's ethical transgressions, 'the whole psychoanalytic movement in America is liable to serious attack.' To avoid scandal, he proposed to take drastic action: 'My present plan is to ask Frink to give me personally a letter of resignation from the Society, and I will assume the authority of the Society as President, of accepting it, and I will then not record it in the minutes or present it to the Society unless necessary.'

Freud replied on 9 October 1921: 'As you are an analyst your-self [Ames had been trained by Jung in Zurich in 1911] I may trust you will not have thought it likely that I acted as an advice-giver to Frink or Mrs. B[ijur]. You know it is not the passion of analysts to give out advice and to direct people in the line of our own pref-erence. – I simply had to read my patient's mind and so I found out that he loved Mrs B, wanted her ardently and lacked the cour-age to confess it to himself . . . When he grew uncertain with his mind, I had to take the side of his repressed desires, and in this way become the advocate of his wish to divorce and marriage with Mrs. B. In a conversation with the latter I felt entitled to guarantee the intensity and truthfulness of Frink's affection for her . . . I think the analysts of New York ought to stand by him and make it easy for him as possible, without being afraid of a passing tempest in a corrupt and vile press.'

Probably under the influence of Ames, Abraham Bijur seems to have given up his plan to publish his open letter, because in a letter to Frink of 27 October Freud said he was relieved to learn that 'the big scandal could be avoided'. American psychoanalysis was saved. In the same letter of 27 October, Freud acknowledged receipt of two photos that Frink had sent him. One showed Frink before his analysis, the other after, haggard, emaciated, twenty years older: 'Here is what analysis does to you!' Freud found the joke excellent (he told it to Kardiner, who was still in Vienna): 'You are a naughty boy! I had my laugh at your photos . . . I rejoice in this trick of yours as a token of your good humour.'

Depressed, tortured by doubt and guilt towards his wife and children, Frink, however, was far from laughing. Three weeks later, Freud felt the need to cheer him up: 'I see as far as I can gather from your letters that you are not yet out of trouble and have not yet mastered all your secrets. May I still suggest to you that your idea that Mrs. B. had lost part of her *beauty* [Frink no longer had sexual desires for her] may be turned into her having lost part of her *money*. If so I am sure she will recover her attraction and neither you nor [Monroe] Meyer will be the losers. [Angelika Bijur had been slow to send the money promised for Monroe Meyer's analysis.] Your complaint that you cannot grasp your homosexuality implies that you are not yet aware of your fantasy of making me a rich man. If matters turn out all right let us change this imaginary gift into a real contribution to the Psychoanalytic funds' (17 November 1921).

It seems that Frink denied having this fantasy, because two months later Freud returned to the charge: 'It is very amusing you should mention Mr. Rosenberg [another American that Frink had sent to Freud] . . . just after denying your fantasy of giving me a lot of money' (15 January 1922). But it was not a fantasy, and they both knew it. According to Thaddeus Ames, 'Mrs Bijur . . . promised him [Freud] enough funds to publish all that could be written on psychoanalysis and put it on the market. And Freud very promptly thought she was a wonderful person . . . Frink told me this afterwards' (interview with Kurt Eissler, 3 July 1952).

In March Doris left with the two children for New Mexico and Nevada, two states that permit quick divorces. At the instigation of Angie's lawyer, Charles Riegelman, she had said nothing to anyone about her trip for fear of creating a scandal, and she sent her mail to her relatives through Thaddeus Ames so as not to reveal where she was. She was sad, resigned, exhausted: 'I do hope you are feeling better,' she wrote to Frink from Albuquerque. 'I seem to have lost my grip entirely since I arrived here. I never wanted to be looked after so much in my life.' Angelika likewise travelled to Reno, Nevada, to ask for a divorce. Frink, meanwhile, was feeling worse. To Brill, he confided that he did not like Angie, to which Brill, exasperated, replied: 'Well, then you should not marry her!'

To get a clearer view, Frink returned to Vienna for a second round of analysis with Freud from April to June 1922, still at Angie's expense. He had 'queer feelings', as if he were in a fog. Angie appeared to him 'queer, like a man, like a pig'. Meanwhile, as luck would have it, Abraham Bijur died of cancer on 1 May 1922, leaving the way open for Angie to rejoin Frink in Vienna via the Hotel Plaza Athénée in Paris, where she liked to spend her summers. From the town of Minden, Nevada, where she was lying low, Doris wrote to H. W. Frink, c/o Prof. S. Freud, Berggasse 19, Vienna, IX, Austria: 'I understand that Mr. B. died May first. I really feel quite badly about it, though it will make matters much easier for you and A. Let me know how you are. As soon as you are willing, I shall let people know where I am because the mystery is rather difficult and unpleasant to me' (16 May 1922).

The situation became more and more distressing for her, especially since little Jack, disoriented by their constant movements, kept having temper tantrums and had become 'absolutely unmanageable'. In September she admitted to wanting to end it all: 'I am so entirely discouraged with life that I'd end the whole thing right now if I knew just the right person to leave Helen to' (14 September 1922). Frink replied from the Bristol Hotel in Vienna, where he was staying with Angie. He had asked Freud for advice about Jack: 'The complete explanation he gave is too complicated to repeat here . . . His advice is that if this keeps up, it would be the best thing for Jack to send him away to [boarding] school for a time . . . He feels that Jack gets some sort of sadistic gratification out of his present behaviour . . . If you take away the object of this gratification (yourself) by sending him to school, he may then give up this attitude for a more desirable one' (9 October 1922).

From New York, Thaddeus Ames watched these developments with dismay. He felt bad for not having been able to prevent them – after all, he was the analyst of three of the people involved. In July he wrote to Freud asking him to take him into supervision and explain how he had erred, enclosing a letter from Doris to tug at his heartstrings. Freud replied positively and gave him an appointment for a first session in early October, when they had returned from the Berlin Congress, which they were both going to attend. But when Ames appeared on the appointed day at 19 Berggasse, Freud announced on the doorstep that he would not be able to see him. Ames was stunned: 'But what am I to do? I have come from America to be analysed!' Freud replied: '"See Rank." And then he shut the door.' It was only later that Ames learned from Frink that the latter, furious at his meddling in his affairs, had threatened Freud to stop his own analysis if Freud took on Ames as a patient. Freud was certainly not going to jeopardize his elective relationship with Frink for Ames: 'From what Frink told me afterwards ... Freud had had a positive transference to him, to Frink. Frink later saw through that and he said that Angelika had promised him [Freud] all the money that was necessary to put psychoanalysis on the market and that Freud fell for it, and he was all for Frink and therefore against me. Frink told me he was very sorry for his having told Freud he wouldn't stay with Freud if Freud took me' (interview with Kurt Eissler, 3 July 1952).

Meanwhile, Frink was still in Vienna with Angie, who had joined him from Paris. His analysis had finished at the end of June due to Freud's holidays in Bad Gastein and then in Berchtesgaden, but he and Angie remained in Vienna. Angie had now become very close to Freud. Kurt Eissler, who interviewed her in 1952, reports: 'Professor Freud was very much in favour of Dr Frink's marrying Mrs. Frink [who was still, at the time, Mrs Bijur]. Mrs. Frink was accepted in the house of Freud like a member of the family. She followed the Freuds to Berchtesgaden [with Frink] and spent the summer with them.' From there, she and Frink went on an excursion with the Freud family to Munich: 'She remembers one incident when they were dining in Munich and she suddenly had the idea to go to a night-club. Miss Anna Freud nearly fainted at the idea

... but he [Freud] was quite ready ... But when they came there, the night-club was closed.' Then everyone went to the seventh International Psychoanalysis Congress in Berlin at the end of September, where Angie listened to Freud reading his famous essay 'The Ego and the Id'. Freud gallantly offered Angie Bijur a photograph of him dedicated 'To Angie Frink, in memory of your old friend, Sigmund Freud, Sept. 1922' (we doubt it was a Freudian slip). He also gave her a small Greek statue that was on his desk. 'Only later,' reports Eissler, 'did [Angie] recognize what was going on and ... she dropped the remark that her great wealth played a role in the way she was accepted by Freud' (interview with Kurt Eissler, 19 June 1952).

At the end of October, having returned to Paris with Angie, Frink learned from Doris that their divorce had been made final at last. Angie had her lawyer set up a $100,000 trust fund for Doris Frink, awarding her $460 child support per month for the rest of her life. In the event of her death, the contract stipulated that the fund would be transferred to her children or to their legal guardian until January 1941 (in her will, Doris had appointed as guardians her analyst, Thaddeus Ames, and a friend, Mary Hastings). Brutally forced to face the consequences of his actions, Frink decompensated. Leaving Angie at the Plaza Athénée, he went back to Freud between November and Christmas 1922. There he became delirious. He hallucinated on the couch, frantically paced up and down Freud's study following the patterns in the carpet, took his bathtub for a grave, went in rapid succession through the whole range of emotions, 'elation, depression, anger, fear' (self-report, 1924). Alarmed, Freud hired a doctor, Joe Ash, to watch over him day and night, but without informing Angie of the situation. On the contrary, he sent her innocent cablegrams to Paris assuring her that everything was fine.

Angie was never to forgive Freud for this betrayal, which she discovered only two years later. According to her half-sister, the psychiatrist and psychoanalyst Viola Wertheim Bernard, 'Angie seemed especially bitter about Freud's withholding from her the fact of Frink's acute psychotic break just before their marriage, when he required suicide precautions and care around the clock. Had Freud informed her of this, it would have confirmed the validity of her fears about the significance of Frink's moods to the point that she might well have broken off the plan to marry' (Viola W. Bernard MD, 'Explanatory Note on My Donation to the Freud Archives of Items Pertaining to the Freud-Frink-Bijur Events in the 1920s').

Taking advantage of a remission, Freud declared on 23 December that the analysis was definitively over and summoned Angie to Vienna. She later remembered this in a letter to Adolf Meyer: 'Freud said . . . that he [Frink] should get married, have children and that he would soon be well under the happy condition he had won for himself.' Frink and Angie married in Paris four days later and left to spend their honeymoon in Egypt until February 1923. Oberndorf, who was still being analysed by Freud, told him that in his opinion the marriage would not last, but Freud would not hear of it: Frink and Angie got along well sexually, so it would work. When Stern wrote to tell him that Frink was too unwell to marry, Freud likewise cabled back: 'NONSENSE.'

Under insistent pressure from Freud, Frink was re-elected president of the New York Psychoanalytic Society while he was still on honeymoon. On 28 February, however, he asked Freud to return to Vienna so that he could embark on a fourth round of analysis. (Freud agreed, but the plan did not come to fruition.) As Frink was to reveal in his 1924 self-report, he now had feelings of hatred and persecution towards Angelika and most of the time had no sexual desire for her. According to a letter from Freud of 25 April 1923, however, it seems that he obeyed the injunction to have children and that Angie became pregnant: 'I was prepared to your news, which to me appear [sic] rather full of promise. I knew you would not give in and I am sure you will conquer in the end. Let us hope that the pregnancy goes well and leads to a happy end.' (Due to either miscarriage or abortion, this pregnancy did not come to term.)

At the same time, on 26 April, Frink learned that Doris had contracted pneumonia and was dying in Chatham, New York. She died on 4 May without Frink being allowed to speak to her. Frink was deeply shaken. Ruth Best, Doris's sister-in-law, later told Helen Frink Kraft that he paid his respects to her body for thirty minutes, after which 'he left the house without speaking to us or looking at us and we never saw him or heard a word from him again . . . He took you both that day. We never saw the two of

Horace, Angie and little Dorothy in front of the Grand Hôtel de Cimiez in Nice on their return from Egypt, February 1923.

you again.' Under New York State law, Frink indeed became the legal guardian of his children, despite the stipulations of Doris's will. As such, he was now receiving the child support that Angie had planned for Doris. Jack was sent to boarding school, as Freud had recommended. Helen came to live with her father, Angie and Dorothy (the Bijur family, who were very angry with Angie, had obtained custody of Betty).

Overwhelmed with feelings of guilt, Frink constantly quarrelled with Angie, to the point of becoming physically violent with her. Angie wrote to Freud to inform him that their marriage was a failure. Freud cabled back on 1 June 1923: 'EXTREMELY SORRY THE POINT WHERE YOU FAILED WAS MONEY.' Did he mean to say that Angie had not fulfilled her husband's supposed fantasy of making Freud rich? Stung, Angie retorted that she had given no less than $100,000 (an extremely large sum at the time) to Doris to encourage her to accept the divorce Freud had suggested. On 5 June Freud sent a cable by return: 'DID NOT REALIZE YOUR SHARE UNTIL LATE INCAPABLE JUDGING PRESENT SITUATION.' However, in

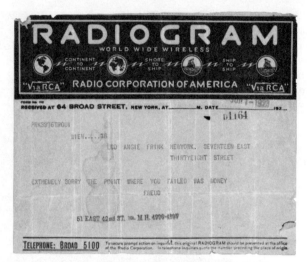

Freud's cablegram of 1 June 1923 to Angie Frink.

a letter sent the following year to Ernest Jones, Freud continued to attribute the failure of the marriage to Angie's refusal to share her fortune with Frink: 'On account of her hardness in regard to money matters, he did not get all the tokens he had pressed her for' (Freud to Jones, 25 September 1924).

At the same time, Frink's professional conduct was becoming increasingly erratic. On his return to New York, he behaved like Freud's 'satrap' (Clarence Oberndorf) and alienated all his colleagues by his authoritarian and contemptuous attitude. He wrote a particularly nasty review of a book by Brill, assumed the right to censor all communications to the New York Psychoanalytic Society and demoted Oberndorf in the Society's hierarchy. Oberndorf related: 'He met me in the hall, and he got me up against the wall . . . and put his hands over me, as though pinning me to the wall, and said – this man who had formerly been a very good friend of mine: "You're ignorant, incompetent, disinterested in psychoanalysis, and henceforth you've got to occupy an inferior place in psychoanalysis in America."'

Soon Frink even stopped attending the meetings of the Society of which he was president. In August 1923, unable to work, he closed down his practice. Angie placed him in Saint Vincent's Retreat for Nervous and Mental Diseases in Harrison, New York, a private clinic run by his friend Swepson J. Brooks. In a report written the following year for his colleague Frederic H. Packard,

Brooks writes: 'He was sent away with a nurse but chafed under it. Would not settle down and wished to change frequently. Contact with his wife always resulted in a relapse. He went from place to place getting better, then worse' (12 November 1924).

Freud, meanwhile, was beginning to realize the mistake he had made in imposing Frink as a leader on the New York psychoanalysts. By May 1923 he was already reproaching him for his plan to 'drive Brill wild'. He soon had to face the fact that Frink's colleagues had been right all along to warn him against his behaviour (which did not prevent him, later, from privately holding them responsible for his collapse). In March 1924 Brill read aloud to the New York Society a letter from Freud to another analyst in which he claimed that Frink could no longer remain president because of his 'mental illness'. Freud had spoken. A new president was elected to replace Frink.

Frink was not present at the meeting, but this disavowal of him by Freud devastated him. On 9 May 1924 he was admitted to the Henry Phipps psychiatric clinic at Johns Hopkins Hospital in Baltimore, directed by the great Swiss-American psychiatrist Adolf Meyer. Frink knew Meyer well because he had been his student at Cornell Medical College. Having familiarized himself with his patient-colleague's life history, as he routinely did, Meyer was quite disgusted. Frink's story was 'one of the most nauseating events in my psychiatric practice': 'The attitude of Freud was evidently one of encouragement and suggestion rather strongly in contrast to his usual pretention that these factors are left out of consideration.' The medical report drawn up by his assistant Friedrich Ignatz Wertheimer also mentioned that Frink himself now harboured 'strains and doubts about Freud's analysis and advice'.

Meyer diagnosed a 'reactive depression' (in other words, one caused by external events) with a constitutional manic-depressive background. Angie, meanwhile, was not well either. She was depressed, and was not leaving her apartment. Brill, from whom she had sought help, felt too involved to take care of her and sent her to the psychiatrist George W. Kirby, an ex-collaborator of Adolf Meyer and his successor at the New York State Psychiatric Institute, Ward's Island. Kirby would keep Meyer informed of his patient's mental state and Meyer would send him messages for Angie.

To Angie, who once again paid for Frink's stay and haughtily asked whether her investment was going to be more profitable than with Freud, Meyer explained that Frink might recover but that it would take time: 'It is a definite sickness and not merely a psychoanalytic tangle to be dispelled by more and more analysis . . . It is tremendously important to suspend all counting on fixed date' (12 May 1924). When Angie was allowed to see Frink in a hotel room in Baltimore in June, she found him even more depressed and indifferent than before: 'He showed no tenderness to me . . . What he told me was that he had discovered a fundamental fallacy in Freud's exposition of a certain problem and that he was going to stir this up (as he put it) by first printing (a book) and showing how erroneous were the conclusions he (Freud) drew' (letter to Adolf Meyer of 24 June 1924).

To soothe Frink's spirits, Meyer sent him to spend the summer at Bishop's Lodge, a health resort near Santa Fe, and then to a ranch in New Mexico. The physical activities practised there do not seem to have done him as much good as expected, however. To Wertheimer, Frink reported: 'Ever since I left Baltimore, I have been making irregular but continued progress in the direction of getting worse . . . The thing that worries me perhaps most is that I frequently get in a very suicidal frame of mind . . .' (August 1924). He also sent a disillusioned letter to Meyer about his future: 'I should hate to practice psychoanalysis again after what it has done to me. But there is no other way in which I could make a living. I'm too sick and depressed . . .'

Back at the Phipps clinic, on 11 September, Frink learned that Angie had asked for a divorce despite Meyer's appeals for more patience and understanding for her husband. Angie would not hear of it, and this managed to exasperate Meyer. On 12 August he had vented his anger in a letter to Kirby. Mrs Frink, he wrote, 'puts the entire matter on a vague and probably exaggerated notion of homosexuality on the part of Dr Frink. It makes me hot to deal with that kind of over-condensation of a much broader philosophy of domination which evidently she enjoyed when it was a question of mere husband-wife dominance but which I feel is more sweeping – I say "hot" at Freudianism rather than at Mrs F.'

As for Frink, he had suffered another breakdown and was crying day and night. According to Wertheimer, the patient told him: 'I wish I had stayed with my first wife. If she were alive, I'd return to her now.' The clinic's medical record states: 'Since then varying attitudes: to conform with Mrs. Frink's plans or to try to change them. During last ten days of stay in Clinic he was less depressed and in more aggressive mood. Could not be determined to stay.'

Frink left the Phipps clinic on 22 October 1924, after which he went to take refuge at Swepson Brooks's clinic. There he made a first suicide attempt with Veronal and Luminal on 27 October, then slit his wrists a few days later, when he was supposed to take a boat for France and complete the divorce formalities in Paris (it is in Paris, we remember, that the wedding had taken place two years earlier). At the request of Angie, Brooks sent him to Harvard's upscale McLean psychiatric hospital with a detailed medical report for the superintendent, Dr Frederic H. Packard. The latter wrote to Adolf Meyer shortly afterwards to inform him that Frink was improving: 'He is very bitter against Freud. He says that Freud does not at all understand psychoses, that the field of psychoanalysis is limited to psychoneuroses, that Freud himself knew this and never should have attempted to treat him when he was in a psychotic condition and that his treatment and advice was harmful and detrimental to his best interests . . . His wife is very bitter against Freud and in a way against Frink' (letter to Meyer, 2 December 1924).

Angie had indeed been copied into the report that Brooks sent to Packard, and she had thus learned for the first time that Frink was in the throes of a psychotic episode just before their marriage. The scales having fallen from her eyes as she realized what Freud's intentions towards her had been, she made copies of all the cablegrams and letters that Freud had sent her and gave them to her lawyer so that he could attach them to the procedural file of divorce as 'examples of Freud's participation in our affairs'. 'A ghastly affair,' she noted in the margin of her letter to Riegelman, the lawyer.

Frink left the McLean hospital in the spring of 1925, fully recovered. The divorce was finalized in July, in his presence and that of Adolf Meyer. Angie refused to shake hands with Frink. She resented him too for the way he had played along, she felt, with Freud's manipulation. The divorce decree stipulated that Frink would continue to receive the support initially intended for

Doris, but that this would cease on 1 January 1941 at the latest, and that Angie would then recover the entire trust fund.

Frink picked up Jack and Helen (Angie had looked after her during his illness) and moved with them to Southern Pines, North Carolina. There he remained for two years and, according to a handwritten note made by Wertheimer, had 'some sort of love affair; went into it for *therapeutic possibilities* [?] ♀ 33 yrs, gets awful irritable with her' (undated). In 1927 he tried to resume his activity as a psychoanalyst in New York, without success. As Wertheimer (who had meanwhile changed his name to Fredric Wertham) would scribble in 1975, in the draft of a text that he intended to entitle 'Freud's Mismanagement of a Case': 'When Frink wanted [to] start practice again, the organized psychoanalysts inexcusably act[ed] ag.[ainst] it.'

So Frink returned to Hillsdale, the city of his childhood. He was fully recovered and even serene. He never spoke of Freud or psychoanalysis, nor of the mother of his children (according to Helen, 'He never mentioned her, and we learned not to inquire'). He had dropped all contact with his former colleagues and friends, except for Wertheimer / Wertham and his wife, Florence Hesketh Wertham. He took care of the education of his children, hunted for bargains in second-hand shops, followed sports news closely and was much liked in the neighbourhood. In 1933 he moved to Chapel Hill to follow Jack, who was studying there, and took advantage of the opportunity to give occasional psychology les-sons and lectures at Duke University and the University of North Carolina. He also saw some patients in private at his home. According to a letter that Brill sent him to thank him for some books he had donated to the New York Psychoanalytic Society, he himself was in the process of writing a book (5 September 1933). In 1935 he married Ruth Frye, a schoolteacher whom he had met ten years earlier at Southern Pines (was she the enigmatic 'love affair' mentioned by Wertheimer?)

At the beginning of April 1936 he felt very tired (letter to Florence Wertham, 7 April 1936). He was also extraordinarily happy and let everyone around him know as much. He had a long con-versation with Helen during which he told her that he loved her and that there was a God. He also recalled a memory of his stay in Paris with Angie, when they were both gazing down on the city from the balcony of the Opéra Garnier. Angie was 'radiant in a red velvet cloak'. She had said to him: 'Horace, with your brains and my money, we can have the world.'

Then, on Monday 13 April, he asked Helen to call Dr Augustus Rose, a psychiatrist from Chapel Hill, and have him drive him to the Pine Bluff Sanitarium in Southern Pines, a clinic Frink had helped set up ten years earlier. In the car, he could not stop talking. Once he reached the hospital, his hypomanic excitement worsened. One of the doctors later told his wife that Frink was one of the most difficult-to-control patients he had ever had. He kept tearing his clothes and walking frantically up and down. On Saturday 18 April 1936, he suddenly fell to the ground, lifeless. His wife found his face to be extraordinarily tired and tense. His mouth was strangely drawn to one side. The death certificate indicates that he suffered from manic-depressive psychosis, generalized atherosclerosis and chronic myocarditis. In his bedside table was a bundle of letters that Doris had sent him in 1922.

Angelika Wertheim Bijur Frink died in 1969. While sorting through her affairs, her half-sister found, hidden in a drawer among yellowing photographs and newspaper clippings, the two cablegrams of June 1923 in which Freud attributed the failure of Angie's marriage to Frink to her lack of financial generosity. That was all that was left of the 'voluminous handwritten correspondence from Freud to Angie' (Viola Wertheim Bernard), because Angie had ordered that all these letters be destroyed when she died. On the back of the first cablegram, Angie had written in pencil: 'I wish I had the courage to publish this as an example of Freud's "therapeutics" in my case.' On the back of the second, she had written: 'What a frightful cable.'

36

MONROE MEYER

(1892–1939)

Monroe Abraham Meyer was a true New Yorker. He was born in Manhattan on 1 August 1892, the eldest son of Henry and Henrietta Meyer, and died there on 27 February 1939. A brilliant student, he received a bachelor's degree from Cornell University in 1913 and went on working towards an MD at the Cornell Medical College on the Upper East Side of Manhattan. There he studied neurology – in fact, Freudian psychoanalysis – under Horace Frink and Clarence Oberndorf, along with his fellow student Abram Kardiner. Oberndorf later told Kurt Eissler how he would be annoyed by this student who was always asking questions for which he did not have answers. Meyer was, he said, 'one of the brightest men with whom I had ever come in contact. His mind was so quick and so direct, that at times it was startling . . . His memory was phenomenal, his alertness was unusual' (24 September 1952).

Oberndorf was therefore stunned when, shortly after Meyer had received his MD in 1916, he met his student on the grounds of the Bloomingdale Insane Asylum, where he had come to visit one of his patients: 'I thought he was up there to see a patient, like myself. But he appeared very much embarrassed and finally he said, "You know I'm a patient here myself."' The young psychiatrist was suffering from recurring bouts of depression – 'melancholic spells', as he called them. Once out of the hospital, Meyer went to see Frink and started an analysis with his former teacher. Probably because he recognized himself in Meyer's predicament, Frink took him under his wing, going as far as taking care of him in his own home. According to Adolph Stern, 'Monroe Meyer lived with Frink at one time – he was in a state of depression and he lived in Frink's house with his family for a good number of months' (interview with Kurt Eissler, 13 November 1952). This was the time when Frink himself was going through episodes of depression. Meyer and Frink were a perfect match, the blind leading the blind.

Left to their own devices during the war, the members of the little New York Psychoanalytic Society had basically learned their trade by analysing each other, with uncertain results. Now that communications had been re-established with Vienna, they felt the need to travel to The Source, all the more so as the word was out that Freud was welcoming requests for training analysis from foreigners. In 1920 Oberndorf, Frink, Kardiner, Leonard Blumgart, Albert Polon and Adolph Stern all sent in their applications. All were accepted. In his reply of 5 August 1920 to Frink's letter, Freud also agreed to see a 'young analyst, to whom you can lend your protection in his beginnings'. The young analyst in question was Monroe Meyer, whom Frink planned on taking as partner in his private practice upon their return from Vienna. The costs for Meyer's analysis and stay in Vienna were to be borne by Frink's patient and lover Angelika Bijur, who was also underwriting Frink's own analysis with Freud.

Meyer arrived in Vienna in early autumn 1920, ahead of Frink, who was scheduled to start his treatment at the beginning of March 1921. Oberndorf, Blumgart, Kardiner and Stern were also there (Stern only for three months). Not having much to do beyond their daily appointments at Berggasse 19, 'the Americans', as Freud called them, would spend their time together in the Vienna *Kaffeehäuser*, comparing notes about their treatments and gossiping about the old man. Freud himself, however, was not beyond some gossiping and leaking of his own. Oberndorf's analysis, he told Meyer, had 'brought him off his high horse', and he approved of Meyer's 'taking up the task of showing Obie [Oberndorf] what he doesn't know about analysis' (Meyer to Frink, 20 January 1921). With Frink he shared his negative diagnosis of Adolph Stern's personality: 'What is mostly wrong in him is the passive and feminine attitude towards man' (10 October 1920). Of the whole group, he wrote to Frink that he felt 'rather disappointed' (27 October 1921); 'Their level is low . . . Courses of lectures have been arranged for them given by all the abler members of the [Vienna Psychoanalytic] society to promote their scanty theoretical knowledge and to take away some of the evenings which they were inclined to spend in a rather frivolous manner ("Have a good time", you know)' (17 November 1921).

The Americans surely enjoyed their time in Vienna, far away from the puritanical mores of the East Coast. None of them seem to have respected the sacrosanct psychoanalytic 'rule of abstinence'. Oberndorf told Eissler that he and Frink would share the favours of Elie, a technician in the psychiatrist Julius Wagner-Jauregg's laboratory: 'Elie was the kind of girl who could go from person to person that way' (24 September 1952). Meyer, who had left behind a 'Phila.[delphia] lady' who was pregnant by him, soon forgot her with Ilse, a young Viennese woman to whom he got engaged barely a few weeks after his arrival (Meyer to Frink, 20 January 1921).

With the exception of Oberndorf, the other Americans were quite fond of Ilse – 'Blumgart is forever asking her if she hasn't a twin sister for him!' (Meyer to Frink, 27 December 1921). Freud, on the other hand, disapproved of Meyer's choice and immediately told Frink, who was at that time still in the United States. When Frink, alarmed, inquired from New York about the 'famous bride', Meyer reassured him: 'My matter with Ilse stands so: Freud has directed me to continue my engagement until the analysis is finished and then to see what I want to do. Accordingly I am following his instructions. Since I do not use any of your [that is, Angie Bijur's] money to buy her things comfortable to the dictates of my sense of honesty it costs me no more to go around with her than with any other girl . . . I consider myself in no way bound to marry Ilse – I think the problem will with full analysis solve itself. Regarding my getting engaged as a symptom in analysis, the question to be answered is: What was the immediate motive, what infantile situation did I attempt to produce, what peculiar characteristics in Ilse reminded me of certain traits that I ascribed to my mother when I was little, what component of my own narcissistic ego ideal do these traits form? Some of these questions Freud has already answered, the others will come soon to an answer in turn.' At any rate, the 'old man' was expecting Meyer to be 'in shape to return April 1st . . . to start on the patients that you have so kindly dated up for me', so Frink had nothing to worry about (20 January 1921).

But when Frink arrived in Vienna at the end of February, Meyer was still struggling to find the answers to his questions.

So the analysis continued, while Frink moved in with him in the apartment he had rented on Laudongasse, in Vienna's eighth district. Meyer must therefore have witnessed his roommate's hypomanic state at first hand, followed by the usual depression before Frink returned to New York via Paris at the beginning of July. Meyer himself remained in Vienna and Oberndorf took over from Frink at the Laudongasse apartment when he came back from the summer break to resume his analysis.

Oberndorf was taken aback by the change from the Meyer he had left a few months before: 'I found Monroe Meyer, who had been there over a year then, in an extreme depression. He spoke very little, had a very glum face . . . He was then in the throes of a love affair with a girl who was not at all worthy of him . . . Sometimes he would come in and not utter a word; sometimes for days, "Hello," with this sort of blank, dull expression on his face . . . It was probably the same kind of depression which he had up at Bloomingdale some two or three years previously, which his treatment by Frink did not alleviate' (24 September 1952).

According to Oberndorf, 'with Meyer, Freud adopted an extremely active therapy, forcing him into situations which he thought would bring out reactions . . . which, according to my psychiatric experience, was a very bad thing to do . . . At all events, during the time I was there, Meyer did not improve. But, for instance, one night Meyer – we were in the room at about half past 11, Meyer gets up without a word and puts on his hat. I said, "Where are you going?" He didn't answer. About half past 12, he came back, and I said again, "Where've you been?" He was quivering and white as a sheet. He said, "I've been out to the graveyard." I said, "What for?" He said, "Freud said I must go out there to overcome my fear of the dead and death"' (24 September 1952).

Freud also intervened very actively when Angie Bijur's money for Meyer's treatment did not arrive in a timely fashion. On 9 October 1921 Freud sent Frink a friendly payment reminder: 'I heard from Meyer about the delay in sending him the money promised for the prolongation of his treatment and staying here. I confess I find it an unnecessary aggravation of my hard work with him. You know how he is, subject to mistrust and pessimism owing to his earlier experience [with Frink] and that my therapeutic plan was built upon your friendly care for him and Mrs. B[ijur]'s generous offer . . . So I pray you will try to shorten this delay as much as possible and give him back his assurance.'

On 27 October came a second reminder: 'I have a bad time with Meyer. You remember I was of opinion that active interference was needed in this serious case and that I built my plan of reconstruction on the generous promise, which was to prove him, that he was esteemed and cared for by some people and had some chance in life. The delay in sending the rest of the money has shaken his confidence and given him a good pretence for closing his mind to the suggestions of the analyst . . . Could you not send it at once, the full sum? I would engage myself to keep it for him in order to save it from any foolish attempt at squandering it.'

Frink promptly sent two cables to Meyer to assure him that the cheque was in the mail, which according to Freud achieved the desired effect on the patient: 'Indeed he [Meyer] exclaimed today: Now I am sure I have got over my troubles. That is no effect of analysis but of "active" therapeutics in the sense of Ferenczi which I thought necessary to be applied to him so as to enable him to profit by analysis . . . He is a hard case but a good and clever boy' (17 November 1921). One month later, Meyer confirmed to Frink that he was indeed feeling better: 'Just a few lines to tell you that I am getting on quite well. My analysis is proceeding slowly but surely. I am now free of melancholy spells and so am free of what was a terrible burden. I am full of phobias and altho they are disagreable enough I rather welcome them as a good sign that I am going into the father identification, the solution of which will surely see me cured.'

Meyer took this opportunity to ask his mentor for advice: 'Given the circumstances of Miss R. [the 'Phila. lady'] and the illegitimate child, given the fact that I hope to practise analysis in NY and indeed your office, assuming that I recover here and then have a suitable girl and wish to marry, can I probably get away with it (and accomplish my professional aims in NY) despite such stink as Miss R. may raise ? Or am I tackling a problem that would beat a normal man? Would appreciate your opinion in this matter' (27 December 1921).

We do not have Frink's reply, but this question clearly became the main focus of the analysis from then onwards. Should Meyer be allowed to marry Ilse? On 15 January 1922 Freud conferred with

Frink: 'Meyer is progressing nicely, the next difficulty is in regard to his fiancée whom he picked up when he had no right to do so. You know her, what is your judgment? Mine from afar is rather unfavourable.' One month later, 20 February 1922: 'Meyer is very good, he would be all right at this time had he not provided fresh stuff for disturbance at the beginning of his analysis by his engagement. He now struggles to escape and maybe he will not succeed. I do not interfere with any pressure as the girl has some good points in her. She is nice, quick of intellect and may give up some of her whims when sexually satisfied. She loves him no doubt and has behaved rather bravely through his bad times.'

We do not know what happened next, for there is at this point a one-year hiatus in Freud's correspondence with Frink, due to Frink's presence in Vienna and Europe from April 1922 onwards. However, when Freud resumed the correspondence on 21 March 1923, he summed up Meyer's treatment in a long letter that reads like an anticipated obituary:

> Meyer is to leave this day week. I am sorry to say I cannot foresee in what condition he will arrive in New York or if he will arrive at all. It is always gambling va banque with these bad neurotics, but I think the attempt had to be made to help him from his misery. If he declines and prefers to perish I will feel nature has been too powerful and our means too inefficient . . . So let us remain cool about it whatever the result happens to be.
>
> You remember how he found that girl Ilse after a few weeks and recognized her with his sharp discernment for possible mischief as an excellent instrument either to spoil his life or his analysis. After he had got your money he made a splendid step, understood and overcame his melancholia (mother identification) and for a time showed all right. In my last letter I tried to adapt myself to the issue of his marrying her and accentuated her good and shining qualities. Soon afterwards her extravagances grew more conspicuous and the suspicion of her taking cocaine arose. [According to Blumgart, Meyer had taken morphine, not cocaine, while Freud was away on his summer holiday in 1922.] Meyer struggled to blind himself to all the tests. I made no prohibition

Monroe Meyer, undated.

but I requested 6 months respite and work in New York before marriage. Nearly on the same day your letter to him came demanding the same. So he gave in but developed a negative trans- ference, spiteful behaviour and most silly arguments against analysis even after he had recognised the girl's unworthiness. In these last days he started anew on the subject of leaving money to her which she seems anxious to extract from him. I resigned my last bill to be paid from NY in order to make it possible to him to give her about $200. Nevertheless he got very angry about this business, did not tell me the plain truth, fell back into the most childish gestures of resistance, etc. . . . today he did not utter one syllable during half an hour and then went to Kardiner to explode in invectives, threats and criticisms. There it stands. It may be all right in a few days or may lead to a disastrous end. Qui vivra verra.

Meyer did survive the trip back to New York, but barely. Oberndorf remembered how resentful his friend was at the way Freud had terminated the analysis: 'And with poor Monroe Meyer, after years there, Monroe Meyer told me Freud sent him back so sick it's wonder he survived the voyage on the ship over here, that Freud had no right to send him back as sick as he was.' But Mayer did follow the old man's instructions, leaving Ilse behind as he had left Miss R. before. Shortly after his return, he met and married Pearl Sherman, a young woman from Russia, with whom he had a daughter, Barbara, in 1925. He was still having the same 'melancholic spells' as before. According to his friend Adolph Stern, Meyer's two years of analysis with Freud had not brought any progress: 'All I know is that he came back as he went over' (Stern said the same thing about his own analysis) (13 November 1952).

Meyer began his private practice, all the while working as Adjunct Psychiatrist at Mount Sinai Hospital in New York. Mindful of the lecture courses that Freud had set up in Vienna for 'the Americans', he became intensely involved in the teaching of psychanalysis, first at the New York Psychoanalytic Society and then, from 1932 onwards, at its training Institute, of which he became the executive director. He was keen on replicating his own experience with Freud with others. His colleagues later reminisced that 'there was a touch of the crusader in Monroe Meyer, as indeed there had been . . . in his devotion to the interests of the New York Psychoanalytic Institute.'

On 27 February 1939 Monroe Meyer finally killed himself at the age of 47. 'Qui vivra verra,' Freud had said.

37

SCOFIELD THAYER
(1889–1982)

O
n 27 November 1920 Edward Bernays sent from New York a cablegram to his uncle, Prof. Dr. Sigmund Freud, Berggasse 19, Vienna, Austria: 'GENTLEMEN OF HIGHEST PROBITY INTERESTED IN PSYCHOANALYSIS URGE YOU TO COME TO AMERICA UNDER THEIR AUSPICES FOR SIX MONTHS TO . . . GIVE SEVERAL LECTURES IN AND NEAR NEW YORK PERIOD THEY GUARANTEE TEN THOUSAND DOLLARS IN ADVANCE PROVIDED YOU ARE WILLING TO DEVOTE AS MUCH AS YOUR MORNINGS TO PSYCHOANALYSIS AS THERE ARE PATIENTS WHOM YOU CONSIDER WORTHY OF A TREATMENT AT . . . TWENTY FIVE DOLLARS HOUR PERIOD . . . I BELIEVE THAT HALF THIS TEN THOUSAND WILL COVER ALL POSSIBLE EXPENSES . . . AND THAT YOUR NET PROFIT WILL BE SEVERAL TIMES THE REMAINING FIVE THOUSAND DOLLARS PERIOD I URGE YOU TO ACCEPT PERIOD . . . EDWARD BERNAYS.' At the bottom of the cable, Bernays indicated: 'Charge to Scofield Thayer, c/o The Dial, 152 West 13 Street, New York City.'

Bernays was the son of Eli Bernays, Freud's brother-in-law whom he had helped financially when Eli had emigrated to the USA after having gone bankrupt. Despite his young age, Edward was already a man of money and influence (literally: he is seen as the father of modern public relations, or 'propaganda', as he preferred to call it) and he had decided to sell his uncle to Americans in order to provide him with the dollars that Freud so desperately needed in Vienna. He had negotiated the sale of the translation rights for the *Introductory Lectures on Psychoanalysis* in the United States and had also managed to convince the magazine *Cosmopolitan* to offer Freud a lucrative contract for a series of articles on psychoanalysis intended for the general public. The invitation to come to the United States, which was extended by Scofield Thayer, the co-owner and editor of the prestigious literary magazine *The Dial*, was part of this vast promotional campaign.

Freud cabled back: 'NOT CONVENIENT'. In a follow-up letter, he explained that his health was not what it used to be and also, 'in the second place, the offer is not a very generous one . . . I communicated the conditions of your cable to two of my English patients here [Alix and James Strachey, presumably] and they gave the judgment that I had not to go, that the offer was far below my level, that they expected the guarantee to extend to a sum of $50–100,000 and I had better wait until the patients who needed me came over to Vienna . . . A last consideration could warn me, that if I brought back some thousand dollars from America I could not keep it a secret when I returned and had to pay a big portion to the tax here . . . With affectionate regards, Your uncle, Freud.'

Freud's response must have come as a huge disappointment to Scofield Thayer. Not only was he keen on associating his magazine with Freud's name, but he had hoped to benefit personally from his ministrations. He had been on the couch of the eminent Manhattan psychoanalyst Leon Pierce Clark since the previous year and felt that he was not getting much of a return on his investment ($25 an hour, $4,700 for nine months of analysis). So why not have the 'Great Master' come to him in New York? As he confided to James Sibley Watson Jr, his partner at the helm of *The Dial*: 'I am extremely eager to lay before him my troubles.'

Scofield Thayer, early 1920s.

Thayer was inclined to lavish money on people he admired, or liked. He was born into extreme wealth and was extremely generous with it, contrary to what Freud implied. One year before buying *The Dial* with his equally wealthy friend Watson and sponsoring the entire roster of European and North American modernism, he made out a cheque for $700 to James Joyce, whom he had heard needed money. The cheque was forwarded to Joyce by his publisher with the comment: 'Please don't imagine that America is full of rich young men of that kind!' (But when subsequently Joyce came back asking for more, Thayer declined, arguing that he was already losing a lot of money on his magazine. As generous as he could be when people didn't ask him for anything, he was wary of people patronizing him for his money.)

Thayer was born on 12 December 1889 in Worcester, Massachusetts, the lone heir to three generations of successful textile manufacturers. Across the street from the majestic Thayer residence was the newly erected Clark University, where Freud would come in 1909 to give his famed *Five Lectures on Psycho-analysis* (Thayer undoubtedly heard about that landmark event, which might have subsequently given him the idea of inviting Freud to the United States for another round of lectures). Scofield's father, Edward Thayer, died of appendicitis in 1907, too early to be dismayed by the way his progeny would spend his fortune. Florence Scofield, his mother, was a stickler for social propriety and her son considered her a philistine, a cardinal sin in his eyes.

The young Scofield Thayer was an aesthete. He loved beauty, in people and in things. Extremely handsome, always well dressed with a slight Bohemian touch (he wore an old hat that had holes in it), he wanted to become a poet or a thinker, he wasn't quite sure which. He went to all the right schools where he met all the right people: Milton Academy, where one of his slightly older schoolmates was T. S. ('Tom') Eliot; Harvard, where he befriended Edward Estlin Cummings (also known as e e cummings), his future partner James Sibley Watson Jr, the philosopher George Santayana and Alan Seeger, the young poet who had a 'Rendezvous with Death' in the trenches of the First World War; and then Magdalen College, Oxford, where he reunited with Santayana and Eliot, who in turn introduced him to Ezra Pound, Bertrand Russell and Raymond Mortimer.

At Oxford, while the war was already raging on the Continent, Thayer dabbled in literature, philosophy and various social activities such as golf and the highly exclusive (and cruel) sport of beagling. Through his cousins Ellen and Lucy Thayer, who lived in London at the time, he met the scintillating and 'nervous' Vivienne Haigh-Wood, with whom he soon engaged in an intensely flirtatious relationship that may or may not have blossomed into a true love affair. But Thayer dabbled in love as he dabbled in everything else and, in a gesture that he was to repeat many times in his life, he bequeathed Vivienne to his friend Eliot who was equally smitten with her. T. S. Eliot and Vivienne Haigh-Wood married the very day Thayer boarded the ship back to the United States without having taken his degree. Vivienne declared that she wouldn't miss Scofield's 'promising-much & fulfilling-little countenance'.

Upon his return, Thayer leased an apartment in the Benedick, a bachelors-only luxury building overlooking Washington Square in New York City. Ever the aesthete, he decorated it himself with Chinese red lacquer furniture, painted the ceilings black, hung his collection of Aubrey Beardsley drawings on gold-papered walls and became engaged to the well-born and stunningly beautiful Elaine Orr. He had met her in 1912 when she was barely fifteen, which was probably part of her appeal to this 'connoisseur of puberty and lilies', as Eliot described him. Thayer called her 'the Lily Maid of Astolat' (a reference to the virgin Elaine who died of love for Lancelot in the Arthurian legend), a 'fairy child', 'a virgin of Ashtaroth'. His friends agreed: to John Dos Passos, Elaine 'seemed the poet's dream', and Cummings, whom Thayer commissioned to write a poem as a wedding gift, instantly fell in love with her: 'I considered EO as a princess, something wonderful, unearthly, ethereal, the like of which I had never seen.'

The wedding took place on 21 June 1916, after which the newly-weds embarked on a long (fifteen-month) honeymoon in California, accompanied by a cook and a butler-chauffeur. What happened then and when exactly remains obscure. Jack Dempsey, Thayer's biographer, points to personal notes in which Thayer refers elliptically to a moment of crisis while Elaine and he stayed at the luxury Potter Hotel in Santa Barbara: 'EO's cry at the Potter was not only the cry of the broken virgin, it was also the cry of the lost soul when,

Elaine Orr, 1919.

driven backwards, without the strength of backbone to withstand the Devil's push – when it feels the earth give way and only air beneath it.' As Thayer later confessed to Cummings, he had had 'a neurotic turning away from Elaine but it was not conscious'. Elaine was not the ethereal virgin any longer. During sex, he wrote, she was a 'hairless Mexican dog', 'a meal worm, or maggot': 'I would no more feel like shooting E.O. than like shooting a mess of shit.' Marriage was a source of disappointment: 'Long girls in bed in coition are like warm snakes. They taste – after a year of marriage – like baked bananas.'

Thayer therefore proposed to Elaine that they live separately and enjoy sex with others. No commitment, free love, only ephemeral encounters. When the two of them finally returned to New York in October 1917, Elaine moved into an apartment across from Thayer's suite at the Benedick. To keep up appearances, the couple explained that Scofield needed his apartment for his work (for all his libertinism, Thayer remained his mother's son, always maintaining a facade of Victorian correctness). Confused, feeling wronged, Elaine soon fell in love with Cummings, who had become a regular at the informal literary salon she maintained in her apartment. From his suite (he could peek into her place across Washington Square), Thayer encouraged the affair, even writing a cheque to Cummings 'for the time, energy and other things you have expended on Elaine'. Cummings cashed the cheque. When Elaine, two years later, gave birth to her lover's child, Thayer liberally assumed legal and financial responsibility for fatherhood. Elaine and Cummings agreed not to tell anyone – appearances had to be saved. (In a twist worthy of Beaumarchais, the little Nancy 'Mopsy' Thayer would learn the truth only much later, when she almost fell in love with Cummings, by then long estranged from Elaine, and he informed her he was her real father.)

In April 1918 Thayer bought $600,000 worth of stock in *The Dial*, a venerable literary magazine whose first editors in the 1840s had been Margaret Fuller and Ralph Waldo Emerson. Thayer, revulsed by a war that had claimed his friend Alan Seeger, was interested in supporting the pacifist line defended within the magazine by one of its editors, the essayist Randolph Bourne, against a pro-war faction led by John Dewey and Thorstein Veblen. He was also looking for employment so as to avoid being drafted and was indeed promptly named associate editor in exchange for his generosity. However, Thayer soon discovered that the position did not give him enough power to dictate the editorial line, so when the money-losing magazine defaulted on its financial obligations in the autumn of 1919, he along with his friend James Sibley Watson Jr decided to purchase it (Watson could afford it, being an heir to the Western Union fortune).

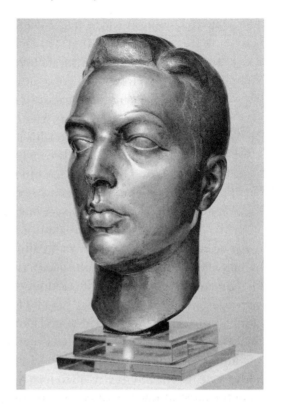

Bronze bust of Scofield
Thayer by Gaston
Lachaise, 1923.

Thayer could now practise generosity on a grand scale, sponsoring his many friends and admirations, and losing up to $50,000
a year in the process. The new owners' editorial line was simple:
they would 'follow their own tastes', and Thayer's in particular
was very sure. In its first year, the new *Dial* published poetry by
e e cummings (of course), Ezra Pound, William Carlos Williams,
William Butler Yeats, H.D., Marianne Moore (who would later join
the magazine's editorial staff) and James Joyce; fiction by D. H.
Lawrence, Marcel Proust, Arthur Schnitzler, Mina Loy and Djuna
Barnes; criticism and philosophy by T. S. Eliot, Bertrand Russell,
John Dewey, Romain Rolland, Edmund Wilson, Edward Sapir,
Kenneth Burke and Gilbert Seldes (two other future editors). The
magazine was printed on paper allowing the reproduction in full
colour of artworks by Odilon Redon, Paul Signac, Henri Matisse,
Pierre Bonnard, Marc Chagall, Edvard Munch and Thayer's dear
Picasso. Thanks essentially to Thayer's tireless networking and
cultural entrepreneurship, *The Dial* almost instantly morphed from
a rather traditional liberal magazine into a highly influential beacon

Alyse Gregory, undated.

of modernism. It is only natural that Thayer would have wanted, that very same year, to enlist Sigmund Freud in his cultural offensive.

Thayer's personal life was more complicated. Behind the icy facade of the highbrow millionaire, Thayer was, as his friend Alyse Gregory put it, 'molten lava'. After his separation from Elaine, he seems to have thrown himself into some pent-up sexual activity: 'I felt after E.O. the need to be in my sexual life messy because of my overlong virginity.' What Thayer meant exactly by 'messy' is unclear (his private notes are as abundant and sex-obsessed as they are reticent and allusive). We know that he had an affair – perforce sporadic – with the feminist writer Alyse Gregory, another advocate of free love (despite her subsequent marriage to the equally 'liberated' novelist Llewelyn Powys). Thayer also had a relationship with the young Doris Beck, a self-described 'school-girl'. In the summer of 1920 he had a brief and intense encounter with the journalist and activist Louise Bryant, who was about to leave for Soviet Russia to join her second husband, the Communist John Reed. Bryant, it seems, got 'seriously' smitten, but as she wrote in one of the many love letters she sent him over a few weeks, 'I know that is a grave fault.' She also sent him a poem that referred cryptically to a 'sad circumstance / On a night in June' that had prevented him from enjoying her 'garden': 'Will you come again?' Before embarking on her journey to Russia, she left him with a nude photograph of herself. The gift must have pleased him, for he would soon become a compulsive collector of erotic art by Gustav Klimt, Egon Schiele and Pablo Picasso, among others. These pieces, he wrote to his unsuspecting mother, were not for *The Dial* but 'for my private pleasure'.

For all this Don Juan-esque cataloguing, something must have been amiss, for this was also the time when Thayer went into analysis with Pierce Clark to clear unspecified 'troubles'. He was indeed 'nervous'. From a young age, he had always been a hypochondriac and an extreme germophobe. Like Proust, he could not stand the slightest noise. Behind his haughty demeanour and literary rakishness, he was almost pathologically shy and inhibited: 'He used to be terribly shy and when he'd come in, he'd break out in sweat, and always wipe off his hands' (Mura Dehn-Thomas). But whatever symptoms he may have wanted to get rid of, the analysis with Clark was getting nowhere. So Thayer decided in the spring of 1921 to call once again on Edward Bernays to intercede with Freud on his behalf. On 31 May 1921 Bernays wrote to his uncle: 'I am writing you this letter in that you may have before you the facts in the case of Scofield Thayer, a colleague of mine, who desires to come to Austria to be treated by you and has asked me to give you such information as may guide him in his plans . . . Mr. Thayer is rather a nervous type, highly intellectual and tells me that he has been treated by psychoanalysts in New York who have, however, done him little good, he says. He is desirous of knowing whether you would care to undertake him as a patient, and is willing to remain in Europe as long as you deem it necessary to have him do so, should you find him acceptable . . . He is willing to travel to the ends of the earth to confer with you.'

Freud answered on 19 June: 'Dear Edward, I see that you provide me not only with dollars, but with patients . . . I intend to leave the town middle of July not to return before Oct. 1st. On this date I expect to find more people claiming my hours than I could accept, most of them doctors from England and America, that is to say: pupils not patients. I will have to make my choice. Your colleague should bring me some advance data if I take him instead of another man. He should pay $20, while doctors only pay $10. If he agrees to these conditions (Oct. 1st and $20), the further decision will depend on the nature of his case. He ought to write me and state what it is. For example, I would not take him if he be a homosexual and desired to be changed, etc.'

Freud's letter arrived on the very day Thayer was to sail for Europe to join Elaine and Cummings in Paris to get a so-called French divorce (divorces were easier – and more discreet – in France than in the USA). Bernays was able to reach him before the departure and confirmed to his uncle that Thayer was agreeable to his conditions: 'He assures me that he is not a homosexual, and that he is writing you in full detail about his case' (5 July 1921). We do not know how Thayer laid his 'troubles' before Freud, but he must have been convincing. To Alyse Gregory he wrote: 'I had in Paris the sweetest letter imaginable from him [Freud] and forgive him for being a Jew' (while in no way a rabid antisemite such as Ezra

Pound, Thayer was, like Eliot, Cummings, Hemingway and so many other American modernists, casually racist).

Freud's 'sweetest letter' ran as follows: 'I am sorry I cannot get you fresh, your having gone through a long, unsuccessful treatment with another man is surely no advantage; yet let us hope that the incompetency of the analyst [Leon Pierce Clark was an early follower of his and a prominent member of the New York Psychoanalytical Society] was for something in the matter, and that I will be able to justify your expectations ... Let me say in concluding that I feel very sympathetic about the determination you express to get out of your inhibitions or whatever it may be. The man who suffers deeply has a good chance to recover by analysis.'

Thayer arrived in Vienna in September 1921 and stayed there for almost two years, going to see Freud five times a week. At first, he kept mum about the analysis. To Alyse Gregory who asked him about it, he wrote: 'News from Vienna you must not expect. I am tapping my way among not wholly unfamiliar but not for that reason the less awful shapes.' Meanwhile, Thayer maintained an active social life and quickly became a fixture of Vienna's cultural life (he spoke German fluently, having had a German tutor when he was young). He continued to direct The Dial from a distance, soliciting contributions from new friends such as Arthur Schnitzler, Thomas Mann and Hugo von Hofmannsthal (the last of whom he commissioned to write a regular 'German Letter' in The Dial).

He was also building an impressive collection of modern art, purchasing throughout Europe and at staggering speed some six hundred works by Picasso, Derain, Braque, Kokoschka, Matisse, Chagall, Munch, Demuth and so on for inclusion in Living Art, a portfolio of reproductions that he planned to publish as a supplement to The Dial (his erotic pieces were by-products of this buying spree). He was helped in this by Adolf Dehn, a young expatriate American artist whom he had befriended and tasked with the logistics of acquiring, shipping and printing the artworks. Dehn, an ebullient Epicurian, was the exact opposite of his shy patron and Thayer used him as a pilot fish in the world of the Viennese süsse Mädel ('sweet girl'). Through his girlfriend and soon-to-be wife, the eighteen-year-old ballerina Mura Ziperovitch, Dehn introduced Thayer to young girls with whom he would have tea and then engage in little 'love affairs' (Mura Dehn-Thomas). In an interview with Kurt Eissler in 1959, Adolf Dehn reminisced: 'At that time . . . he wanted to meet girls . . . And I knew some, and I said: well, I'll introduce you to some . . . If they were very young, he would be interested . . . When I say "very young", I mean *quite* very young; that is, definitely a little over 16 years they were *passées* already. And if they were 14 or 15, it was better, and they *definitely* should be unsoiled, untouched.'

Other sexual forays were more threatening. In an undated note appended to his interview of Adolf Dehn, Kurt Eissler recounts what had happened to a lady of his acquaintance while she was on a visit to Vienna back in the early 1920s. She had gone with Thayer to an art exhibit and he had offered to show her some of the drawings and paintings he had just acquired: 'She went to the apartment with him – unsuspecting. He left her alone with the artworks and after a while came back naked.' She had the presence of mind to jump on the ledge of the open window and threaten to throw herself out if he got closer. 'The next day he sent her the most exquisite perfumes and flowers.' (This may or may not be the enigmatic 'known Vienna events' that Thayer's nemesis, the fellow millionaire and art collector Albert C. Barnes, would threaten a couple of years later to make public, along with Thayer's 'perversion'.)

Whether Thayer's sexual acting-up had anything to do with his daily sessions with Freud is unclear. Three months into the analysis, Thayer was nonplussed. In January 1922 he wrote to Gregory: 'You have expressed interest in my affair with the great Master . . . Firstly, I was reminded by the speed with which he made his diagnosis of my case of your criticism to me of his apparently almost too immediately certain diagnoses of certain cases instanced by him in his most recent book . . . He [Freud] bristles with the most startling and penetrating comments upon apparently superficially meaningless details in dreams, free associations, and daily experience. Therefore a natural sceptic like myself is constantly being jolted . . . And in the essential foundation-lines of Dr. Freud's diagnosis of my neurosis – a diagnosis made during the first weeks of my stay in Vienna – I am not in agreement with him. As I have already been here for three months, this is certainly discouraging. Neither of us budges . . . I cannot honestly accept the diagnosis. So I really do not know whether I shall be staying on in Vienna until the summer . . . or whether either Dr. Freud or I may feel forced to break off things sooner, that is, any time.'

What was Freud's contentious diagnosis? According to Dehn, Freud had told Thayer that he had a 'death complex' (probably some reference to Freud's novel ideas about a 'death drive') and that he was a 'latent homosexual'. The latter was of course Freud's default diagnosis, but in Thayer's case he was stating the obvious, or at least part of it. Thayer's compulsive attraction to young girls did indeed have another side, which he could probably not allow himself to admit. Adolf Dehn: 'I knew he had a terrible problem about girls. And I knew this latent homosexual thing, as he told me. . . At times he would see some young boy of, oh, any age, ten, nine, eleven and twelve . . . rather pre-adolescent boys, and he would just stand there and say: Oh, how beautiful he is! . . . He just absolutely would become overcome, let us say, with the beauty of this boy!' But Thayer does not seem to have ever acted on these pederastic impulses, any more than Gustav von Aschenbach does in Thomas Mann's *Death in Venice*. Thayer was most proud of having printed an English translation of Mann's story in *The Dial*.

Thayer eventually decided to give analysis another chance. To Gregory he wrote: 'Speaking of the doctor, I might mention that he and I . . . are somewhat reconciled to each other . . . he now goes on record as feeling that we are making some advance and is hoping that in time we may get somewhere.' Thayer even obtained from Freud a text for *The Dial*, the essay on 'A Seventeenth-century Demonological Neurosis' (it was turned down by Watson and Kenneth Burke after Freud refused to alter some sexually explicit 'details'). But the 'advance' promised by Freud was not forthcoming. 'The analysis goes on much as always,' Thayer told Gregory. 'As did Henry Adams, so here one in the abstract accepts the tenets of evolution without perceiving much advance from the character of Julius Caesar to that of Ulysses S. Grant.' And in a note to himself: 'I follow Freud's gestures seeking dreams as does a dog who, when his master throws, leaps forward and away from the stone. And in this case (as often with the dog) one does not know but that the hand was empty.'

Tired of leaping at the shiny object, Thayer called it quits in the spring of 1923 and left Vienna for Paris where he intended to buy art (Picassos, notably) before returning to the United States. Freud announced the move to Bernays: 'Mr Thayer is going to leave Vienna, not without much improvement' (8 April 1923). Thayer was less sanguine. He reported to Gregory: 'When I leave Vienna ... I shall, after two years forced compression, be chock full of the Great Man ... I shall, I fear be only dragging myself off to some un-Viennese-as-possible sandbar to get my breath after these two years which have consisted chiefly of disillusionings and grippes [influenzas]. "I could a tale unfold!"' To Watson, Thayer wrote somberly that he was to 'return after two years of imprisonment more criminal, or, if you will, more insane than before'. Cummings, who was in Paris at the time, did indeed notice a sharp change from the charming Thayer he had met in Vienna just six months before. Thayer was tense, agitated, contentious, suspicious of people. (He also had a message for Cummings from Freud: 'Freud tells Thayer I should marry E'; Cummings dutifully married Elaine the next year, only to learn three months later from Elaine that she had fallen in love with another man and wanted to annul the marriage.)

Back in the United States, Thayer resumed his editorial activities and his picking of fresh lilies. Dehn, who returned briefly to New York the next year, introduced him (again) to two young girls just out of high school. Thayer was interested in one of them, but required her to get a medical attestation of virginity before he would touch her. Having obtained what he wanted, he set her up in an apartment, gave her $1,000 and shortly thereafter asked Dehn to date her in order to get rid of her (Dehn declined: 'You see,' he told Eissler, 'he [Thayer] had really a ruthless, sadistic streak in him.'). Thayer then repeated exactly the same intrigue with the second girl, leaving both of them confused and distraught. Dehn later learned that Thayer had touched neither of them: 'They were still virgins after he was done with them. Or let us say, demi-vierges, because he did play with them, fondled them, kissed them.' Thayer was an adept of the 'dry school'.

In parallel with these 'twin romances' (Dehn), Thayer was having an affair with Eleanor Parker, an aspiring writer and office assistant at *The Dial* with whom he escaped 'surreptitiously' to Bermuda at the beginning of 1925. When Dehn, who by then was back in Vienna, asked him about his various adventures, Thayer replied: 'Miss Parker is now in an asylum (or sanatorium if you will) at Bloomingdale, New York . . . I have spent most of this month in New York with lawyers and have spent all my money too.' Something had happened in Bermuda and Eleanor Parker had suffered a breakdown upon returning from the trip. In a strongly worded letter to Thayer, her mother hinted at his responsibility and demanded compensation, threatening legal action: 'Your suspicions as to what she might say to hurt your reputation, shows me how much she had to bear and I agree with others that the wonder is that she did not break down sooner.'

Thayer hired lawyers and detectives to defend himself. He had taken refuge at his Edgartown residence on Martha's Vineyard and felt besieged – by Parker and her family, by Alfred Barnes with whom he had engaged in a bizarre feud, by his collaborators at *The Dial* who he felt were conspiring against him. His 'enemies' were out to get him, so in June 1925 he informally resigned as editor of *The Dial* and fled to Europe. There he went from place to place, trying to elude imaginary pursuers who were bugging his rooms with dictaphones and opening his mail: Paris, Berlin, the Baltic Sea, then Berlin again. He was accompanied by Dehn, who seems to have been the only person he trusted and who tried to soothe his friend's paranoid delusions without contradicting him. In November they arrived in Vienna, the idea being to seek help from Freud. Thayer checked in at the Bristol, where he bumped into an acquaintance of his, the diplomat and fellow millionaire William C. Bullitt Jr, and his new wife – Louise Bryant. Bullitt was on Freud's couch, wanting him to help him become a great writer (they eventually wrote together a psycho-biographical study of President Woodrow Wilson, Bullitt's former boss).

Thayer wrote to Gregory that he had asked Freud to take him in treatment again but that Freud was too busy and that he himself didn't want to 'stick it Freudless in Vienna'. In fact, Freud must have seen him for at least a few sessions, for one day Bullitt excitedly told Dehn that he had discovered that Thayer was in analysis with the great man, which was no news to Dehn. Contradicting himself, Thayer also wrote Gregory: 'I am not well. I am up to my ears in trouble – the same trouble, the Parker trouble. Even Freud was a couple of days ago by my plight moved to *tears*.' But by mid-January Thayer must have felt that Freud could not help him, for he sent Gregory 'the most serious telegram of my life', begging her to come and rescue him. Gregory, sensing the urgency, arrived promptly in Vienna with Powys to bring him back to their place in England.

She consulted Freud, who told her that Thayer had 'a most gentle heart'. He also gave her some modestly helpful advice about how to handle Thayer: 'Freud said it was important that no one should pretend to believe S– [which so far had been Dehn's strategy], because if he found one person to believe him it would fix his obsessions all the more deeply.' Freud sent a note (in German) to Thayer, seconding Gregory's intention of taking him home with her: 'Dear Mr Thayer, I hear with regret that it is not at all possible for your friends to stay here beyond or even until Febr. 14. Under those circumstances, I must advise that you accompany your friends to England and rest there for a while. Anyway, you could come back to Vienna at any time should you hold your presence here necessary or if you wanted to continue the analysis' (23 January 1926, although Freud wrote '1925' by mistake). Thayer promised to leave with Gregory and Powys but then did not show up at the train station, probably to foil his evil pursuers.

Thayer stayed in Vienna for a little while. It is not clear whether the analysis with Freud 'continued' or not. Thayer then moved to Germany, Switzerland and Italy, still trailed by his 'enemies'. He was writing poetry, much of which was published in *The Dial*. His friends and colleagues received bizarre postcards or long cables that remind one of Nietzsche's 'madness letters'. Finally, his mother came to Europe in the spring to retrieve him. Upon his return he was hospitalized in the elite McLean Hospital, where he stayed twice for several months. The diagnosis was paranoid schizophrenia. Then, for almost sixty years, Thayer disappeared from sight, never answering any letters from friends or receiving any visitors (even Elaine's daughter Nancy, who still thought he was her biological father, was barred from seeing him). He spent the rest of his life between his various properties, luxury hotels and occasional sanatoria, attended by two male nurses. He was declared legally insane in 1937 after his mother died. He wrote compulsively in his room, in English, in German, in French, and from time to time he would scream. An undated note states: 'At Mem[orial] Hosp[ital in Worcester] I was a beautiful angel beating his wings in a . . . void in vain.'

Scofield Thayer died in his home in Edgartown on 9 July 1982, at the age of 92. The four people to whom he had bequeathed his fortune in his last valid will (Alyse Gregory being one of them) had all died in the meantime. His vast collection of artworks went to the Met in New York. In three trunks that had been stored during all these years at the Worcester Storage Company, the executors found Thayer's collection of erotica, including *La Douceur*, a long-ignored painting from Picasso's 'blue period' (1903) representing the pubescent artist being fellated by a naked damsel of Aviñón, a street in Barcelona known for its brothels. Before Thayer bought the painting separately, Picasso and his dealer Daniel-Henry Kahnweiler had attached to it a same-sized Cubist still-life, *Guitar, Gas-jet and Bottle* (1913), whose function was to hide its licentious content from sight. When presented in the 1960s with a photograph by Adolf Mas of his youthful self-portrait, Picasso firmly denied being its author. Like Thayer, Picasso had his secrets.

38

CARL LIEBMANN

(c. 1900–1969)

arl Liebmann was born at the beginning of the last century to one of the wealthiest families in New York. His father, Julius Liebmann, had inherited from his own grandfather Samuel Bär Liebmann the venerable Rheingold Beer Brewing Company, which produced one of the most popular beers in the United States ('Rheingold, the DRY beer' was for a long time the official beer of the Brooklyn Dodgers). Carl grew up in the vast and luxurious Julius Liebmann Mansion his father had built on Clinton Avenue in Brooklyn. According to Dr Leopold Stieglitz, the family doctor (and incidentally the brother of photographer and avant-garde artist Alfred Stieglitz, himself a cousin by marriage of Julius Liebmann), Carl had always been 'different': 'He did not readily take part in sports and athletic exercises, was, if anything, afraid of doing things such as climbing trees.' Intellectually precocious, he was not very sociable and did not play with other children. When adolescence came, he showed no interest in girls. From the age of twelve, he was sexually aroused by the sight or thought of a man wearing a pubic sheath. He satisfied himself by masturbating, while reproaching himself obsessively that he was causing genocide by killing the babies who could have been born from his sperm.

His years of study at Yale were hardly happy. Again according to Stieglitz, 'He was called a "fairy" by the boys and acknowledged to me that he enjoyed seeing the nude bodies of the boys in the swimming pool and occasionally had dreams of an erotic nature in connection with these boys. He particularly enjoyed wearing a jock strap and seeing the boys when they wore a jock strap.' When he graduated from college in 1922, he developed paranoid thoughts, and Stieglitz sent him to his colleague the psychoanalyst Leon Pierce Clark, who noted his fetishism.

After a brief analysis with Clark, Carl left for Europe. He wanted to become an artist. Having arrived in Zurich in 1924, he went to consult the pastor-psychoanalyst Oskar Pfister. Aware that he was dealing with a difficult case, Pfister sent him for diagnosis to Eugen Bleuler, the director of the psychiatric Burghölzli hospital. During the interview with Bleuler, Carl spoke agitatedly about his compulsion to wash his hands and his obsessional fear of being watched by passers-by on the street. Noting the disjointed nature of the patient's thoughts, Bleuler ruled out a diagnosis of obsessional neurosis. In his opinion, it was a 'mild schizophrenia' that was likely to respond to psychoanalytic treatment of the directive type: 'He [Carl Liebmann] is at such an early stage, that psychoanalysis could still be useful, if it is conducted less as analysis and more as an education . . . By education I mean primarily the creation of an interest in a certain kind of work and a certain goal-directed regulation of life' (letter to Pfister, 1924).

Pfister did not feel up to the task and asked Freud if he would take Liebmann for treatment. Freud took the opposite view from his ex-ally Bleuler, speaking of obsessional neurosis rather than schizophrenia, and began by passing the buck to Theodor Reik: 'Do not worry about your young American. The man can be helped. Dr Reik here in Vienna has specialized in these severe obsessional neuroses' (letter to Pfister of 21 December 1924). Faced with Pfister's insistence that he himself accept the patient for treatment, Freud agreed on 19 February 1925 to meet Carl with Pfister at Easter. However, Freud clearly set out his conditions: 'My uniform fee is $20 an hour.' This first contact with Carl was followed in May by a visit to Vienna by his parents, Julius and Marie Liebmann, who came especially from the United States. Freud reported to Pfister that they 'seem willing to make sacrifices, which generally points to a bad prognosis. I could promise them nothing definite, but could only indicate my general willingness' (10 May 1925).

Freud evidently hesitated to take charge of this problematic case. In August he wrote to Pfister: 'As for your young hopeful, I think you should let him go to his ruin' (10 August 1925). Then he changed his mind: 'I began to feel sorry for the poor lad,' he explained a little later to Pfister (11 October 1925). Also, Carl was fluent in German, unlike all those other Americans who flocked to his office. Freud sent a letter to Julius and Marie Liebmann to explain that he was willing to take Carl for analysis, but that the treatment would be long and that he could in no way guarantee them a favourable result. They accepted his conditions: $25 an hour (no longer just $20, as Freud had indicated to Pfister), payable to his account at the Anglo-Austrian Bank Ltd., Lombard Street, London. As Freud, exceptionally, had taken Carl Liebmann into analysis as soon as on 15 September, while he was still on holiday in Semmering, he added: 'In terms of treatment while I am on vacation (until 1 October), I propose an honorarium of twice as much' (letter to Julius and Marie Liebmann, 17 September 1925).

The treatment lasted five years, during which time Carl Liebmann pursued graduate studies at the Institute of Art History at the University of Vienna under the direction of Josef Strzygowski, assisted by Fritz Novotny (he never managed to finish his doctorate, much to the chagrin of his parents). Carl's condition deteriorated from the start of treatment, which led Freud to implicitly adopt the diagnosis made by Bleuler: 'My belief as a physician that he is on the verge of a paranoid dementia has increased. I was again very near the point of giving him up, but there is something touching about him which deters me from doing that' (letter to Pfister, 3 January 1926). Freud was also afraid that Carl would commit suicide. As for the patient's psychotic aggravation, this had been caused by an interpretation that Freud seems to have made very early in the treatment. In the same letter to Pfister, Freud wrote: 'The great deterioration ... was connected with my telling him the apparently real secret of his neurosis. The immediate reaction to that revelation was bound to be an enormous increase in the resistance.' Freud wrote a few days later to Carl's parents, telling them that his patient 'shows a tremendous feeling of guilt, the explanation of which I can however not give here' (13 January 1926).

We now know what the 'secret' was: Freud insisted that Carl's troubles dated from the day he realized that his mother had no penis. In 1927 Freud mentioned Carl Liebmann's fetish in his article on fetishism, seeing in it an ambiguous case of the denial/recognition of female castration: 'In very subtle instances both the disavowal and the affirmation of the castration have found their way into the construction of the fetish itself. This was so in the case of a man whose fetish was an athletic support-belt which could also be worn as bathing drawers. This piece of clothing covered up the genitals entirely and concealed the distinction between them. Analysis showed that it signified that women were castrated and that they were not castrated; and it also allowed the hypothesis that men were castrated, for all these possibilities could equally be concealed under the belt – the earliest rudiment of which in his childhood had been the fig-leaf on a statue.'

The revelation of this secret, however, brought no improvement in Carl's condition. For five years, he continued to display the same traits of 'paranoia' and 'schizophrenia' (letters to Pfister, 14 September 1926, 11 April and 22 October 1927). In 1927 Freud tried to force things by forbidding Carl to masturbate, without result: 'The lad is a severe ordeal. I am trying hard to get him to deliberately resist his fetishist masturbation to enable him to corroborate for himself all that I have discerned about the nature of the fetish, but he will not believe that such abstinence will lead him to this and is essential for the progress of the treatment' (letter to Pfister, 11 April 1927).

In addition to his pessimistic discussions with Pfister, Freud regularly kept Julius and Marie Liebmann informed of the progress of the analysis, over which he blew hot and cold. On the one hand, he hid nothing of the difficulty of the task; on the other, he constantly encouraged the parents to hope for a favourable outcome. In July 1928 he wrote to Mary Liebmann: 'I have no right to keep from you that the diagnosis in your son's case is Paranoid Schizophrenia,' while adding in the same breath that 'such a diagnosis means little and does not help penetrate the uncertainty about his future.' The following year, he interpreted a worsening of Carl's compulsive symptoms as a good sign: 'Together with other signs, it proves that the dreaded delusion has not progressed, for the obsessional symptoms tend to return with the development of the delirium . . . I still think that if he manages to bring his studies to an end we will have won the game' (3 November 1929). None of this really reassured Carl's parents, who were also concerned about the length of the treatment. In April 1927 Ferenczi, who was in the United States, reported: 'Herr and Frau Liebmann, the parents of your patient, have already called on me twice to have me explain certain sentences from your letters. I did it to the best of my knowledge and strove to reconcile them, above all, with the long duration of the treatment' (8 April 1927).

Julius and Marie Leibmann travelled frequently to Europe to check on the well-being of their son. On these occasions they would socialize with Freud, visiting him in the Semmering during his summer holidays. In the spring of 1929 they also visited the Sanatorium Schloss Tegel, as Freud had mentioned the possibility of placing Carl there. Founded in 1927 by the psychoanalyst Ernst Simmel and built by the architect Ernst Freud, the son of Sigmund, this private clinic was the first in the world to offer an exclusively psychoanalytic treatment to its patients. Freud, who made frequent stays there to treat his cancer, was very attached to this project, which he had generously aided out of his own funds. However, the economic situation in Germany was bad and Schloss Tegel was struggling to stay afloat financially. On 23 August 1929, two months before the Wall Street Crash, Freud took up his pen to ask Julius Liebmann for help. Reminding him of his visit to the clinic, Freud continued: 'At the time, however, I expected that we would have recourse to it for Carl, which is now very unlikely . . . As a result of a misfortune that hit the main donor, it is beset by debt. Yesterday I suddenly received the news that if help does not come quickly, collapse is imminent in the first days of Sept[ember]. I find the courage to draw your attention to this case because it does not involve a fruitless donation, but an investment that, if the current difficulties are overcome, even promises to bring a profit. The merit of serving a good cause is thereby not reduced.' The Liebmanns therefore made a donation, which temporarily prevented bankruptcy. The Sanatorium Schloss Tegel was however to close definitively in 1931, despite multiple injections of liquidity from other wealthy Freudians such as Dorothy Burlingham, Max Eitingon and Princess Marie Bonaparte.

Carl's treatment resumed shortly after his return from holiday in the United States. In January 1930 Freud reported to his mother that Carl was not doing well; he was depressed and neglected his studies (28 January 1930). In March Freud announced to Julius and Mary that he had finally understood why their son had stopped going to lectures. Carl had decided to start a self-analysis, on the sidelines of his treatment, with the result that he never left his hotel room: 'He has undertaken to complete his analysis himself, to solve all the riddles contained in him, and he tries to do this by speculating about it for hours every day – probably longer than he admits ... The bad news is that nothing can be achieved in this way. No one who has attempted this has yet succeeded, in the manner of [the legendary Baron] von Münchhausen's feat, in pulling himself by his plait out of the swamp.'

At the end of the year, Freud threw in the towel. To Fritz Novotny, Strzygowski's assistant at the Institute of Art History, he confessed: '"I was unable to cure this man." ... After that he [Freud] gave up this treatment that to my knowledge had lasted for years. And that was it.' Freud sent Carl to his disciple Ruth Mack Brunswick, apparently in the hope that a female analyst would be better able to get him to give up his fetishist masturbation. Simultaneously, he reassured the parents: 'Frau B[runswick] is ... the smartest of my female students' (31 November 1930) and 'She applies herself primarily to get [Carl] out of his speculations and push him back to the Institute [of Art History]' (7 December 1930).

The analysis with Mack Brunswick was short-lived. Carl Liebmann did not understand why Freud had terminated the analysis, and withdrew into his psychosis. He stopped all communication with his parents and saw Freud for one last time in March 1932. After this he went to Paris, where he undertook a brief analysis with Otto Rank, Freud's renegade disciple. Rank, as was to be expected, suggested that Carl Liebmann's initial trauma was not the discovery of castration, as Freud thought, but the trauma of birth.

Carl, unpersuaded of this and financially at the end of his tether, decided to sail in a third-class berth to New York, where he arrived with $150 in his pocket. He rented a room at the Mills Hotel, a hostel for impecunious bachelors, and took driving lessons to become a taxi driver while washing cars at night to survive. His parents eventually convinced him to accept a small income for acting as his father's driver. (Journeys with him were chaotic, because he was afraid of killing a child and kept looking over his shoulder all the time to check whether he had hit one.) In 1933 he pierced his rib cage with a hunting knife in his parents' bathroom, missing his heart by barely an inch.

Carl's parents sent him to be analysed again, first by Abraham Brill, then by Hermann Nunberg, a Viennese disciple of Freud who had just emigrated to the United States. Brill, noting that Carl

Liebmann had been analysed six times, concluded that 'analysis gave [him] considerable insight, but has not changed his delusional trend.' Brill illustrated his point by noting that the patient 'imagined that he was followed by detectives'. He did not know that Carl's parents had had him constantly followed ever since he left Vienna.

In desperation, Julius and Marie Liebmann had their son interned at Harvard's McLean psychiatric hospital, where he was to stay until the end of his life. Carl protested vigorously against his internment in a ten-page long letter, but his father replied that there was no other solution: 'It was difficult for us to make this decision and we did not consult you because we knew that we would not get you to agree – since having had analysis for so many years – you did not believe in psychiatry. Even the analysts Doctors Freud, Mack Brunswick, Brill and Nunberg felt that analysis could no longer help you, having tried it for nine years, and the ones consulted here insisted it was only fair to give you medical treatment. Whatever you may think about us, we have considered your welfare above our own.'

Julius Liebmann also explained that the McLean hospital was the best possible for Carl. McLean was indeed the closest American institution to the Binswangers' Bellevue Sanatorium, Switzerland. It had a rich and distinguished clientele, and over the years Carl Liebmann could have come across the poets Robert Lowell, Anne Sexton and Sylvia Plath, the mathematician John Nash and musicians Ray Charles and James Taylor, not to mention fellow analysand Scofield Thayer. In 1935, at the time of Carl Liebmann's admission, McLean was in the process of 'opening up' the asylum by placing patients in as comfortable and reassuring an environment as possible.

Carl wanted to continue psychoanalytic treatment in the hospital, which would have been possible, but his mother objected: 'If Drs Pfister, Freud, Ruth Mack Brunswick, Brill and Nunberg have not helped you by analysis,' she wrote to the psychiatrist who cared for Carl, 'it is pretty well proven that analysis will not help you. Freud had given him up, saying: "I have given you all of which analysis is capable, now you must try to get along by yourself" (which I fear Carl Liebmann has construed as his own written self-analysis of which even Freud told him, I could not cure).'

The different psychiatrists who treated Carl Liebmann over the years noted that he had developed an intense guilt about masturbation because Freud had forbidden him to indulge in it. Whenever he gave in, he would come to the doctor to confess. We also find in Carl's files this note, written by one of his psychiatrists in 1935: 'The patient has the idea that the beginning of his neurosis was due to the shock he received at the time of discovering that a woman does not have a penis. He thinks he must have discovered this from observing his mother . . . When asked about the source of this idea, he said it was Freud. He admitted that he could not remember the shock nor recall anything about it. Nevertheless, he believes it to be absolutely true . . . Claiming that in order to get well one must have a full understanding and knowledge of the beginning of one's troubles, he is still unsatisfied and not well. He feels that he must analyse the situation more, and has been doing this in his writings all year long at this place.'

Over the years, Carl Liebmann underwent all the psychiatric treatments fashionable at the time: lobotomy, topectomy, insulin coma therapy, ECT. He survived valiantly and in the 1950s, when American psychiatry became 100 per cent Freudian, Carl Liebmann had his hour of revenge. Everyone in the business knew that he had been undergoing analysis with Freud, and Boston psychiatric interns scrambled to meet the 'Man Who Knew Freud', as he was called. When he was not mute, Liebmann inexhaustibly regaled them with tales of his meetings with the master of Vienna, how he discussed philosophy with Freud, how the Professor walked up and down past the couch while his chow observed, how he punctuated his interpretations with his cigar while prohibiting the patient from smoking (which annoyed Liebmann, who saw it as a refusal of his masculinity).

For a long time, Carl Liebmann would greet the doctors he met in the corridors with a resounding 'I am my father's penis.' He also continued to analyse himself in writing in an attempt to recover the memory of the day he had seen Marie Liebmann naked, as Freud said he had. He died in 1969 without having succeeded.

SOURCES

BERTHA PAPPENHEIM

Borch-Jacobsen, Mikkel, *Remembering Anna O.: A Century of Mystification* (New York, 1996)

—, and Sonu Shamdasani, *The Freud Files: An Inquiry into the History of Psychoanalysis* (Cambridge, 2012)

Breuer, Josef, and Sigmund Freud, *Studies on Hysteria, Standard Edition of The Complete Psychological Works of Sigmund Freud* [1895] (London, 1953–74) [henceforth referred to as Standard Edition], vol. II

Edinger, Dora, *Bertha Pappenheim, Freud's Anna O.* (Highland Park, IL, 1968)

Eitingon, Max, 'Anna O. (Breuer) in psychoanalytischer Betrachtung', *Jahrbuch der Psychoanalyse*, XL (1998), pp. 14–30

Ellenberger, Henri F., 'The Story of "Anna O.": A Critical Review with New Data', *Journal of the History of the Behavioral Sciences*, VIII/3 (1972), pp. 267–79

Herzog, Max, ed., *Ludwig Binswanger und die Chronik der Klinik 'Bellevue' in Kreuzlingen* (Berlin, 1995)

Hirschmüller, Albrecht, *The Life and Work of Josef Breuer* (New York, 1991)

Homburger, Paul, 'Re: Bertha Pappenheim', letter to the editor, *Aufbau*, 7 June 1954

Jensen, Ellen M., *Streifzüge durch das Leben von Anna O / Bertha Pappenheim. Ein Fall für die Psychiatrie. Ein Leben für die Philanthropie* (Frankfurt am Main, 1984)

Kaplan, Marion A., *The Jewish Feminist Movement in Germany: The Campaigns of the Jüdischer Frauenbund, 1904–1938* (Westport, CT, 1979)

—, *The Making of the Jewish Middle Class: Women, Family, and Identity in Imperial Germany* (New York and Oxford, 1991)

Loentz, Elizabeth, *Let Me Continue to Speak the Truth: Bertha Pappenheim as Author and Activist* (Cincinnati, OH, 2007)

Swales, Peter J., 'Freud, Breuer and the Blessed Virgin', unpublished lecture, Seminars on the History of Psychiatry and the Behavioral Sciences, New York Hospital, Cornell Medical Center, 1986

ERNST FLEISCHL VON MARXOW

Charcot, Jean-Martin, note to Theodor Gomperz re: Fleischl,
    Jean-Martin Charcot Papers, Manuscript Division, Library
    of Congress, Washington, DC, c. 1884

Crews, Frederick, personal communication, 2011

Ewart, Felicie (pen name of Emilie Exner), Zwei Frauenbildnisse.
    Erinnerungen (Vienna, 1907)

Exner, Sigmund, 'Biographische Skizze', in Ernst Fleischl von Marxow,
    Gesammelte Abhandlungen, ed. Otto Fleischl von Marxow (Leipzig,
    1893), pp. v–ix

Fleischl von Marxow, Ernst, letters to Sigmund Freud, Sigmund Freud
    Collection, Box 25, Folder 28, Manuscript Division, Library of
    Congress, Washington, DC, 1884–5

Freud, Sigmund, letter to Professor Josef Meller, 8 November 1934,
    Sigmund Freud Collection, Box 37, Folder 20, Manuscript
    Division, Library of Congress, Washington, DC

—, Cocaine Papers, ed. Robert Byck (New York, 1974)

—, Schriften über Kokain, ed. Albrecht Hirschmüller (Frankfurt
    am Main, 1996)

—, and Martha Bernays, Die Brautbriefe, ed. Gerhard Fichtner,
    Ilse Gubrich-Simitis and Albrecht Hirschmüller, 5 vols
    (Frankfurt am Main, 2011–)

Hirschmüller, Albrecht, The Life and Work of Josef Breuer: Physiology and
    Psychoanalysis (New York, 1989)

Israëls, Han, Het geval Freud. 1. Scheppingsverhalen (Amsterdam, 1993);
    German translation: Der Fall Freud: Die Geburt der Psychoanalyse
    aus der Lüge (Hamburg, 1999)

Kann, Robert A., ed., Theodor Gomperz: Ein Gelehrtenleben im Bürgertum
    der Franz-Josefs-Zeit. Auswahl seiner Briefe und Aufzeichnungen,
    1869–1912, erläutert und zu einer Darstellung seines Lebens verknüpft von
    Heinrich Gomperz (Vienna, 1974)

Karch, Steven B., A Brief History of Cocaine (Boca Raton, FL, 2006)

Medwed, Hans-Peter, Ernst Fleischl von Marxow (1846–1891). Leben und
    Werk (Tübingen, 1997)

MATHILDE SCHLEICHER

Freud, Sigmund, 'Über das chemische Verhalten der Harne nach
    Sulfonal-Intoxikation' (report on the Mathilde Schleicher case
    written at the request of Adolf E. Jolles), Internationale Klinische
    Rundschau, 6 December 1891, col. 1913–14

Hirschmüller, Albrecht, 'Freuds "Mathilde": Ein weiterer Tagesrest zum
    Irma-Traum', Jahrbuch der Psychoanalyse, XXIV (1989), pp. 128–59

—, 'Freud, Meynert et Mathilde: l'hypnose en question', Revue
    Internationale d'Histoire de la Psychanalyse, VI (1993), pp. 271–85

Shorter, Edward, 'Women and Jews in a Private Nervous Clinic in
    Late Nineteenth-century Vienna', Medical History, XXXIII (1989),
    pp. 149–83

Voswinckel, Peter, 'Der Fall Mathilde S. . . .: Bisher unbekannter klinischer Bericht von Sigmund Freud. Zum 100. Geburtstag des Sulfonal-Bayer', *Arzt und Krankenhaus*, LXI (1988), pp. 177–84

ANNA VON LIEBEN

Brentano, John, interview with Kurt Eissler, Sigmund Freud Collection, Box 113, Folder 15, Manuscript Division, Library of Congress, Washington, DC, 1954

Breuer, Josef, and Sigmund Freud, *Studies on Hysteria*, Standard Edition, vol. II

Dupont, Judith, ed., *The Clinical Diary of Sándor Ferenczi* (Cambridge, MA, 1988)

Freud, Sigmund, and Minna Bernays, *Briefwechsel 1882–1938* (Tübingen, 2005)

Fuks, Evi, and Gabrielle Kohlbauer, eds, *Die Liebens: 150 Jahre Geschichte einer Wiener Familie* (Vienna, 2004)

Kobau, Ernst, *Rastlos zieht die Flucht der Jahre . . . Josephine und Franziska von Wertheimstein – Ferdinand von Saar* (Vienna, Cologne and Weimar, 1997)

Lieben, Anna von, *Gedichte. Ihren Freunden zur Erinnerung* (Vienna, 1901)

Lloyd, Jill, *The Undiscovered Expressionist: A Life of Marie-Louise von Motesiczky* (New Haven, CT, and London, 2007)

Masson, Jeffrey Moussaieff, ed., *The Complete Letters of Sigmund Freud to Wilhelm Fliess, 1887–1904* (Cambridge, MA, and London, 1985)

Motesiczky [misspelled 'Motesitzky'], Henriette, and Marie-Louise von Motesiczky, interview with Kurt Eissler, Sigmund Freud Collection, Box 118, Folder 9, Manuscript Division, Library of Congress, Washington, DC, 1972

Rossbacher, Karlheinz, *Literatur und Bürgerturm. Fünf Wiener jüdische Familien von der liberalen Ära zum Fin de Siècle* (Vienna, Cologne and Weimar, 2003)

Swales, Peter J., 'Freud, His Teacher, and the Birth of Psychoanalysis', in *Freud: Appraisals and Reappraisals*, ed. Paul E. Stepansky (Hillsdale, NJ, 1986), vol. I, pp. 2–82

ELISE GOMPERZ

Breuer, Josef, and Sigmund Freud, *Studies on Hysteria*, Standard Edition, vol. II

Freud, Sigmund, *An Autobiographical Study*, Standard Edition, vol. XX

—, correspondence with Heinrich Gomperz, Sigmund Freud Collection, Box 28, Folder 40, Manuscript Division, Library of Congress, Washington, DC (1920–33)

—, 'Lettres à Elise Gomperz', in *Sigmund Freud: L'Hypnose, textes (1886–1893)*, ed. Mikkel Borch-Jacobsen (Paris, 2015)

—, and Martha Bernays, *Die Brautbriefe*, ed. Gerhard Fichtner, Ilse Gubrich-Simitis and Albrecht Hirschmüller, 5 vols (Frankfurt am Main, 2011–)

Holzapfel, Bettina-Gomperz, *Reinerstrasse 13. Meine Jugend in Wien d. Jahrhundertwende* (Vienna, 1980)

Kann, Robert A., ed., *Theodor Gomperz: Ein Gelehrtenleben im Bürgertum der Franz-Josefs-Zeit. Auswahl seiner Briefe und Aufzeichnungen, 1869–1912, erläutert und zu einer Darstellung seines Lebens verknüpft von Heinrich Gomperz* (Vienna, 1974)

Masson, Jeffrey Moussaieff, ed., *The Complete Letters of Sigmund Freud to Wilhelm Fliess, 1887–1904* (Cambridge, MA, and London, 1985)

Medwed, Hans-Peter, *Ernst Fleischl von Marxow (1846–1891). Leben und Werk* (Tübingen, 1997)

Rossbacher, Karlheinz, *Literatur und Bürgerturm. Fünf Wiener jüdische Familien von der liberalen Ära zum Fin de Siècle* (Vienna, Cologne and Weimar, 2003)

Swales, Peter J., 'Freud, His Teacher, and the Birth of Psychoanalysis', in *Freud: Appraisals and Reappraisals*, ed. Paul E. Stepansky (Hillsdale, NJ, 1986), vol. I, pp. 2–82

Van Lier, Reina, personal communication, 27 January 2015

FRANZISKA VON WERTHEIMSTEIN

Breuer, Josef, and Sigmund Freud, *Studies on Hysteria*, Standard Edition, vol. II

Charcot, Jean Martin, letter to Theodor Gomperz, 18 March 1888, Jean-Martin Charcot Papers, Manuscript Division, Library of Congress, Washington, DC

Felicie Ewart (pen name of Emilie Exner), *Zwei Frauenbildnisse. Erinnerungen* (Vienna, 1907)

Kann, Robert A., ed., *Theodor Gomperz: Ein Gelehrtenleben im Bürgertum der Franz-Josefs-Zeit. Auswahl seiner Briefe und Aufzeichnungen, 1869–1912, erläutert und zu einer Darstellung seines Lebens verknüpft von Heinrich Gomperz* (Vienna, 1974)

—, ed., *Briefe an, von und um Josephine von Wertheimstein. Ausgewählt und erläutert von Heinrich Gomperz, 1933* (Vienna, 1981)

Kobau, Ernst, *Rastlos zieht die Flucht der Jahre . . . Josephine und Franziska von Wertheimstein – Ferdinand von Saar* (Vienna, Cologne and Weimar, 1997)

Lloyd, Jill, *The Undiscovered Expressionist: A Life of Marie-Louise von Motesiczky* (New Haven, CT, and London, 2007)

Rossbacher, Karlheinz, *Literatur und Bürgerturm. Fünf Wiener jüdische Familien von der liberalen Ära zum Fin de Siècle* (Vienna, Cologne and Weimar, 2003)

FANNY MOSER

Andersson, Ola, correspondence regarding Frau Emmy von N. (Frau Fanny Moser von Sulzer-Wart), Sigmund Freud Collection, Box 50, Manuscript Division, Library of Congress, Washington, DC, 1960–65, 1977, n.d.

Andersson, Ola, 'A Supplement to Freud's Case History of "Frau Emmy von N." in *Studies on Hysteria* (1895)', *Scandinavian Psychoanalytic Review*, II/5 (1979), pp. 5–16

Bauer, E., 'Ein noch nicht publizierte Brief Sigmund Freuds an Fanny Moser über Okkultismus und Mesmerismus', *Freiburger Universitätsblätter*, 25 (1986), pp. 93–110

Ellenberger, Henri F., 'The Story of "Emmy von N.": A Critical Study with New Documents', in *Beyond the Unconscious: Essays of Henri F. Ellenberger in the History of Psychiatry*, ed. Mark S. Micale (Princeton, NJ, 1993), pp. 273–90

Freud, Sigmund, letter of 3 May 1889 to Josef Breuer, Freud Museum, London

—, letter of 13 July 1918 to Fanny Hoppe-Moser, Sigmund Freud Collection, Box 30, Folder 4, Manuscript Division, Library of Congress, Washington, DC

—, letter of 13 July 1935 to Gerda Walther (actually Fanny Hoppe-Moser), Sigmund Freud Collection, Box 43, Folder 16, Manuscript Division, Library of Congress, Washington, DC

Moser, Mentona, *Ich habe gelebt* (Zürich, 1986)

Swales, Peter J., 'Freud, His Teacher, and the Birth of Psychoanalysis', in *Freud: Appraisals and Reappraisals*, ed. Paul E. Stepansky (Hillsdale, NJ, 1986), vol. I, p. 67, n. 34 and 35

Tögel, Christfried, '"My bad diagnostic error": Once More about Freud and Emmy von N. (Fanny Moser)', *International Journal of Psychoanalysis*, LXXX (1999), pp. 1165–73

Wetterstrand, Otto Georg, 'Om långvarig sömn särskildt vid behandling af hysteriens svårere former', *Hygeia*, LXI/5 (1899), p. 525

MARTHA BERNAYS

Barsis, Mrs Max, interview with Kurt Eissler, Sigmund Freud Collection, Box 112, Folder 9, Manuscript Division, Library of Congress, Washington, DC, 1956

Bernays, Hella, interview with Kurt Eissler, Sigmund Freud Collection, Box 113, Folder 8, Manuscript Division, Library of Congress, Washington, DC, 1952

Billinsky, John, 'Jung and Freud (the End of a Romance)', *Andover Newton Quarterly*, X/2 (1969), pp. 39–43

Borch-Jacobsen, Mikkel, 'Response to Richard Skues', *Psychoanalysis and History*, XX/2 (2018), pp. 241–8

Brabant, Eva, Ernst Falzeder and Patrizia Giamperi-Deutsch, eds, *The Correspondence of Sigmund Freud and Sándor Ferenczi*, vol. I: 1908–1914 (Cambridge, MA, 1993)

Freud, Martin, *Glory Reflected* (London, 1957)

Freud, Sigmund, 'A Case of Successful Treatment by Hypnotism', Standard Edition, vol. I, pp. 115–28

—, and Minna Bernays, *Sigmund Freud/Minna Bernays Briefwechsel 1882–1938*, ed. Albrecht Hirschmüller (Tübingen, 2005)

Freud-Marlé, Lilly, 'Onkel Sigi. Aus den Memoiren einer Freud Nichte', *Luzifer-Amor*, XVII / 34 (2004), pp. 132–53

Goldmann, Stefan, '"Ein Fall von hypnotischer Heilung" in Sigmund Freuds Privatpraxis', *Psychosozial*, XXXVII / 136 (2014), pp. 127–39

Graf, Max, interview with Kurt Eissler, Sigmund Freud Collection, Box 115, Folder 13, Manuscript Division, Library of Congress, Washington, DC, 1952

Hammerschlag, Bertha, interview with Kurt Eissler, Sigmund Freud Collection, Box 115, Folder 16, Manuscript Division, Library of Congress, Washington, DC, 1951

Hammerschlag, Ernst, interview with Kurt Eissler, Sigmund Freud Collection, Box 115, Folder 17, Manuscript Division, Library of Congress, Washington, DC, undated

Heller, Judith Bernays, interview with Kurt Eissler, Sigmund Freud Collection, Box 128, Folder 2, Manuscript Division, Library of Congress, Washington, DC, 1952

Hirst, Albert, interview with Kurt Eissler, Sigmund Freud Collection, Box 116, Folder 2, Manuscript Division, Library of Congress, Washington, DC, 1952

Jekels, Ludwig, interview with Kurt Eissler, Sigmund Freud Collection, Box 116, Folder 8, Manuscript Division, Library of Congress, Washington, DC, 1951

Jung, Carl Gustav, interview with Kurt Eissler, Sigmund Freud Collection, Box 117, Folder 2, Manuscript Division, Library of Congress, Washington, DC, 1953

Maastright, Anna, interview with Kurt Eissler, Sigmund Freud Collection, Box 118, Folder 4, Manuscript Division, Library of Congress, Washington, DC, 1954

McGuire, William, ed., *The Freud / Jung Letters* (Princeton, NJ, 1974)

Maciejewski, Franz, 'Freud, His Wife and His "Wife"', *American Imago*, LXXXIII / 4 (2007), pp. 497–506

Masson, Jeffrey Moussaieff, ed., *The Complete Letters of Sigmund Freud to Wilhelm Fliess, 1887–1904* (Cambridge, MA, and London, 1985)

Rosenfeld, Eva, interview with Kurt Eissler, Sigmund Freud Collection, Box 121, Folders 10–11, Manuscript Division, Library of Congress, Washington, DC, 1953

Schur, Max, interview with Kurt Eissler, Sigmund Freud Collection, Box 132, Folder 16, Manuscript Division, Library of Congress, Washington, DC, 1953

—, letter to Ernest Jones of 30 September 1955, Ernest Jones Papers, Archives of the British Psychoanalytical Society, London

Skues, Richard, 'Who Was the "Heroine" of Freud's First Case History? Problems and Issues in the Identification of Freud's Patients', *Psychoanalysis and History*, XIX / 1 (2017), pp. 7–54

PAULINE SILBERSTEIN

Anonymous, 'Selbstmord im Stiftungshause', *Neue Freie Presse*,
    15 May 1891
—, 'Selbstmord', *Neues Wiener Tagblatt*, 15 May 1891
—, 'Lebensmüde', *Die Presse*, 15 May 1891
—, 'Selbstmord im Stiftungshause', *Illustriertes Wiener Extrablatt*,
    15 May 1891
—, 'Totenbeschauprotokoll', *Polizeidirektion Wien*, 1891
Boehlich, Walter, ed., *The Letters of Sigmund Freud to Eduard Silberstein*
    (Cambridge, MA, 1990)
Brujin, Lucas, personal communication, 3 and 14 July 2020
Freud, Sigmund, and Minna Bernays, *Briefwechsel 1882–1938*
    (Tübingen, 2005)
Hamilton, James W., 'Freud and the Suicide of Pauline Silberstein',
    Psychoanalytic Review, LXXXIX/6 (2002), pp. 889–909
Vieyra, Mia, personal communication and archives, Boulogne-
    Billancourt, 2010

ADELE JEITELES

Freud, Sigmund, 'Ein Wort zum Antisemitismus', *Die Zukunft*,
    25 November 1938
Koestler, Arthur, interview with Kurt Eissler, Sigmund Freud
    Collection, Box 117, Folder 9, Manuscript Division, Library
    of Congress, Washington, DC, 1953
Koestler, Mrs Arthur [Kösztler, Adele], interview with Kurt Eissler,
    Sigmund Freud Collection, Box 117, Folder 10, Manuscript
    Division, Library of Congress, Washington, DC, 1953
Paneth, Marie, interview with Kurt Eissler, Sigmund Freud Collection,
    Box 118, Folder 15, Manuscript Division, Library of Congress,
    Washington, DC, 1955
Scammell, Michael, *Koestler: The Odyssey of a Twentieth-century Sceptic*
    (New York, 2009)
—, personal communication, 2011

ILONA WEISS

Breuer, Josef, and Sigmund Freud, *Studies on Hysteria*, Standard Edition,
    vol. II
Gross, Paula, 'Memorandum for the Sigmund Freud Archives',
    Sigmund Freud Collection, Box 124, Folder 31, Manuscript
    Division, Library of Congress, Washington, DC, 1953
Tögel, Christfried, 'Elisabeth von R.' – Geburtshelferin der freien
    Assoziation. Neues zu Familie und Leben von Helene Weiss, verh.
    Gross', *Luzifer-Amor*, LX (2017), pp. 175–81

AURELIA KRONICH

Breuer, Josef, and Sigmund Freud, *Studies on Hysteria*, Standard Edition, vol. II

Fichtner, Gerhard, and Albrecht Hirschmüller, 'Freuds "Katharina" – Hintergrund, Entstehungsgeschichte und Bedeutung einer frühen psychoanalytischen Krankengeschichte', *Psyche*, XXXIX (1985), pp. 220–40

Swales, Peter J., 'Freud, Katharina, and the First "Wild Analysis"', in *Freud: Appraisals and Reappraisals: Contributions to Freud Studies*, ed. Paul Stepansky (Hillsdale, NJ, 1988), vol. III, pp. 80–163

EMMA ECKSTEIN

Anderson, Harriet, *Utopian Feminism: Women's Movements in Fin-de-siècle Vienna* (New Haven, CT, and London, 1992)

Brücke [Teleky], Dora von, interview with Kurt Eissler, Sigmund Freud Collection, Box 122, Folder 17, Manuscript Division, Library of Congress, Washington, DC, 1953

Eckstein, Friedrich, *'Alte, unnennbare Tage': Erinnerungen aus siebzig Lehr- und Wanderjahren* (Vienna, 1936)

Elias [Hirsch], Ada, interview with Kurt Eissler, Sigmund Freud Collection, Box 114, Folder 9, Manuscript Division, Library of Congress, Washington, DC, 1953

Freud, Sigmund, correspondence with Emma Eckstein, Sigmund Freud Collection, Box 21, Folder 24, Manuscript Division, Library of Congress, Washington, DC, 1895–1910

Hirst [Hirsch], Albert, interview with Kurt Eissler, Sigmund Freud Collection, Box 116, Folder 1, Manuscript Division, Library of Congress, Washington, DC, 1952

Huber, W.J.A., 'Emma Eckstein – Eine Frau in den Anfänge der Psychoanalyse, Freuds Patientin und erste Schülerin', *Studien zur Kinderpsychoanalyse*, 6 (1986), pp. 67–81

Ludwig, Emil, *Doctor Freud, An Analysis and a Warning* (New York, 1947)

Lynn, David J., 'Sigmund Freud's Psychoanalysis of Albert Hirst', *Bulletin of the History of Medicine*, LXXI/1 (1997), pp. 69–93

Masson, Jeffrey Moussaïeff, *The Assault on Truth: Freud's Suppression of the Seduction Theory* (New York, 1984)

—, ed., *The Complete Letters of Sigmund Freud to Wilhelm Fliess, 1887–1904* (Cambridge, MA, and London, 1985)

Roazen, Paul, *How Freud Worked: First-hand Accounts of Patients* (Northvale, NJ, 2005)

Swales, Peter J., interview with Mikkel Borch-Jacobsen and Sonu Shamdasani, Borch-Jacobsen and Shamdasani archives, 1993, 1995

Teleky, Ludwig, interview with Kurt Eissler, Sigmund Freud Collection, Box 133, Folder 10, Manuscript Division, Library of Congress, Washington, DC, 1956

OLGA HÖNIG

Brychta-Graf, Olga, letter to Kurt Eissler, Sigmund Freud Collection, Box 127, Folder 10, Manuscript Division, Library of Congress, Washington, DC, 1953

Graf, Herbert, interview with Kurt Eissler, Sigmund Freud Collection, Box 115, Folder 11, Manuscript Division, Library of Congress, Washington, DC, 1959

Graf, Max, interview with Kurt Eissler, Sigmund Freud Collection, Box 115, Folder 13, Manuscript Division, Library of Congress, Washington, DC, 1952

Graf, Mrs [Liselotte], interview with Kurt Eissler, Sigmund Freud Collection, Box 115, Folder 12, Manuscript Division, Library of Congress, Washington, DC, 1960

Masson, Jeffrey Moussaieff, ed., *The Complete Letters of Sigmund Freud to Wilhelm Fliess, 1887–1904* (Cambridge, MA, and London, 1985)

Praz, Josiane, 'Le "Petit Hans" et sa famille: données historiques et biographiques', in *La sexualité infantile et ses mythes*, ed. J. Bergeret and M. Houser (Paris, 2001), pp. 121–39

Wakefield, Jerome C., 'Max Graf's "Reminiscences of Professor Sigmund Freud" Revisited: New Evidence from the Freud Archives', *Psychoanalytic Quarterly*, LXXVI (2007), pp. 149–92

WILHELM VON GRIENDL

Anonymous, 'Selbstmord eines Irrenarztes (Dr. Wilhem v. Griendl)', *Neue Wiener Tagblatt*, 7 August 1898

—, 'Selbstmord eines Irrenarztes', *Neue Freie Presse*, 8 August 1898

—, 'Selbstmord eines Irrenarztes', *Neues Wiener Journal*, 8 August 1898

—, *Scranton Wochenblatt*, 18 August 1898, p. 5

—, 'Deutsche Lokal-Nachrichten', *Indiana Tribüne*, 22 September 1898

Freud, Sigmund, *The Psychopathology of Everyday Life*, Standard Edition, vol. VI

Maciejewski, Franz, 'Freud, His Wife and His "Wife"', *American Imago*, LXXXIII / 4 (2007), pp. 497–506

Swales, Peter J., 'Freud, Death, and Sexual Pleasures: On the Psychical Mechanism of Dr. Sigm. Freud', *Arc de Cercle*, I (2003), pp. 5–74

Tögel, Christfried, *Unser Herz zeigt nach dem Süden: Reisebriefe 1895–1923* (Berlin, 2003)

—, 'Die 'Nachwirkung einer Nachricht' – Zum Freitod eines Patienten im Jahre 1898', *Kleine Texte zur Freud-Biographik*, 2015, www.freud-biographik.de / kleine-texte-zur-freud-biographik

BARONESS MARIE VON FERSTEL

Anonymous, 'Eduard Thorsch', *Neue Freie Presse*, 27 July 1883

Bachler, Martina, and Miriam Koch, 'Die Treichl-Saga', *Format, Österreichs Magazin für Wirtschaft, Geld und Politik*, 30, 26 July 2013, pp. 1, 6, 24–9

Beckh-Widmanstetter, H. A., 'Erinnerungen an Sigmund Freud und Julius Wagner von Jauregg, wissenschafts-theoretisch erörtert', Sigmund Freud Collection, Box 124, Folder 6, Manuscript Division, Library of Congress, Washington, DC, 1966
Jones, Ernest, The Life and Work of Sigmund Freud (New York, 1953), vol. I
—, The Life and Work of Sigmund Freud (New York, 1955), vol. II
Masson, Jeffrey Moussaieff, ed., The Complete Letters of Sigmund Freud to Wilhelm Fliess, 1887–1904 (Cambridge, MA, and London, 1985)
Swales, Peter J., 'Freud, Filthy Lucre, and Undue Influence', Review of Existential Psychology and Psychiatry, XXIII/1–3 (1997), pp. 115–41
Treichl, Heinrich, Fast ein Jahrhundert: Erinnerungen (Vienna, 2003)
Zehle, Sibylle, 'Die fabelhafte Welt der Treichls', Manager Magazin, 25 April 2008, p. 192

MARGIT KREMZIR

Anonymous, 'Lebensmüde', Neue Freie Presse, 20 April 1900
Masson, Jeffrey Moussaieff, ed., The Complete Letters of Sigmund Freud to Wilhelm Fliess, 1887–1904 (Cambridge, MA, and London, 1985)

IDA BAUER

Binswanger, Ludwig, interview with Kurt Eissler, Sigmund Freud Collection, Box 126, Folder 4, Manuscript Division, Library of Congress, Washington, DC, 1954
Decker, Hannah S., Freud, Dora, and Vienna 1900 (New York, 1991)
Deutsch, Felix, 'A Footnote to Freud's "Fragment of an Analysis of a Case of Hysteria"', Psychoanalytic Quarterly, XXVI (1957), pp. 159–67
Eissler, Kurt, letter to Anna Freud of 20 August 1952, Anna Freud Papers, Box 19, Manuscript Division, Library of Congress, Washington, DC, 1952
Ellis, Andrew W., Oliver Raitmayr and Christian Herbst, 'The Ks: The Other Couple in the Case of Freud's "Dora"', Journal of Austrian Studies, XLVIII/4 (2015), pp. 1–26
Foges, Elsa, interview with Kurt Eissler, Sigmund Freud Collection, Box 114, Folders 15–17, Manuscript Division, Library of Congress, Washington, DC, 1953
Freud, Sigmund, 'Fragment of an Analysis of a Case of Hysteria', Standard Edition, vol. VII, pp. 3–122
Gross, Alfred, interview with Kurt Eissler, Sigmund Freud Collection, Box 115, Folder 15, Manuscript Division, Library of Congress, Washington, DC, 1954
Leichter, Otto, interview with Kurt Eissler, Sigmund Freud Collection, Box 129, Folder 11, Manuscript Division, Library of Congress, Washington, DC, 1954
Mahony, Patrick J., Freud's Dora: A Psychoanalytic, Historical, and Textual Study (New Haven, CT, 1996)
Roazen, Paul, 'Freud's Dora and Felix Deutsch', Psychologist/ Psychoanalyst, 15 (1994), pp. 34–6

Stadlen, Anthony, 'Was Dora Ill?', in *Sigmund Freud: Critical Assessments*, ed. Laurence Spurling (London, 1989), vol. I, pp. 196–203

—, '"Just how interesting psychoanalysis really is"', *Arc de Cercle: An International Journal of the History of the Mind-sciences*, 1/1 (2003), pp. 143–73

Zellenka, Otto, interview with Kurt Eissler, Sigmund Freud Collection, Box 129, Folder 9, Manuscript Division, Library of Congress, Washington, DC, 1954

ANNA VON VEST

Anonymous, 'Bericht von [Anna von Vests] Nichte', Sigmund Freud Collection, Box 43, Folder 2, Manuscript Division, Library of Congress, Washington, DC, undated

Freud, Sigmund, 'Analysis Terminable and Interminable', Standard Edition, vol. XXIII, pp. 216–54

—, correspondence with Anna von Vest, Sigmund Freud Collection, Box 43, Folder 2, Manuscript Division, Library of Congress, Washington, DC, 1903–26

Goldmann, Stefan, 'Eine Kur aus der Frühzeit der Psychoanalyse: Kommentar zu Freuds Briefe an Anna v. Vest', *Jahrbuch der Psychoanalyse*, 17 (1985), pp. 296–337

May, Ulrike, and Daniela Haller, 'Nineteen Patients in Analysis with Freud (1910–1920)', *American Imago*, LXV/1 (2008), pp. 41–105

Molnar, Michael, ed., *The Diary of Sigmund Freud, 1929–1939* (New York, 1992)

BRUNO WALTER

Sterba, Richard, 'A Case of Brief Psychotherapy by Freud', *Psychoanalytic Review*, XXXVIII/1 (1951), pp. 75–80

Walter, Bruno, *Themes and Variations: An Autobiography* (New York, 1946)

HERBERT GRAF

Blum, Harold P., personal communication, 2011

Graf, Colin, personal communication, 2011

Graf, Herbert, interview with Kurt Eissler, Sigmund Freud Collection, Box 115, Folder 11, Manuscript Division, Library of Congress, Washington, DC, 1959

Graf, Max, interview with Kurt Eissler, Sigmund Freud Collection, Box 115, Folder 13, Manuscript Division, Library of Congress, Washington, DC, 1952

Graf, Mrs [Liselotte], interview with Kurt Eissler, Sigmund Freud Collection, Box 115, Folder 12, Manuscript Division, Library of Congress, Washington, DC, 1960

Praz, Josiane, 'Le "Petit Hans" et sa famille: données historiques et biographiques', in *La sexualité infantile et ses mythes*, ed. J. Bergeret and M. Houser (Paris, 2001), pp. 121–39

Rizzo, Francis, 'Memoirs of an Invisible Man: Herbert Graf Recalls
a Half-century in the Theater: A Dialogue with Francis Rizzo,
Interview', *Opera News*, 36, 5 February 1972, pp. 24–8; 12 February
1972, pp. 26–9; 19 February 1972, pp. 26–9; 26 February 1972,
pp. 26–9
Ross, John Munder, 'Trauma and Abuse in the Case of Little Hans:
A Contemporary Perspective', *Journal of the American
Psychoanalytic Association*, LV / 3 (2007), pp. 779–97
Wakefield, Jerome C., 'Max Graf's "Reminiscences of Professor
Sigmund Freud" Revisited: New Evidence from the Freud
Archives', *Psychoanalytic Quarterly*, LXXVI (2007), pp. 149–92

ALOIS JEITTELES

Marie Paneth Papers, Sigmund Freud Collection, Manuscript Division,
Library of Congress, Washington, DC, 1938–68
Paneth, Marie, Memorandum, Sigmund Freud Collection, Box 125,
Folder 10, Manuscript Division, Library of Congress, Washington,
DC, undated
—, interview with Kurt Eissler, Sigmund Freud Collection, Box 118,
Folder 15, Manuscript Division, Library of Congress, Washington,
DC, 1955
Ulrich, Tom, personal communication, 25–27 August 2020
Yivo Institute, *Yivo Encyclopedia of Jews in Eastern Europe*, undated,
https:// yivoencyclopedia.org/ article.aspx / Jeitteles_Family

ERNST LANZER

Borch-Jacobsen, Mikkel, 'Un citoyen au-dessus de tout soupçon',
in *Le livre noir de la psychanalyse*, ed. Catherine Meyer
(Paris, 2005)
—, and Sonu Shamdasani, *The Freud Files: An Inquiry into the
History of Psychoanalysis* (Cambridge, 2012), pp. 209–223
Freud, Sigmund, 'Original Record of the [Ratman] Case [1907–8]',
Standard Edition, vol. X, pp. 253–318
—, 'Notes upon a Case of Obsessional Neurosis [1909]', Standard
Edition, vol. X, pp. 1–56
Hawelka, Elsa Ribeiro, ed., *L'Homme aux rats. Journal d'une analyse*,
4th edn (Paris, 1994)
Mahony, Patrick, *Freud and the Rat Man* (New Haven, CT, 1986)
Stadlen, Anthony, '"Just how interesting psychoanalysis really is"',
*Arc de Cercle: An International Journal of the History of the Mind-
sciences*, 1/ 1 (2003), pp. 143–73

ELFRIEDE HIRSCHFELD

Binswanger, Ludwig, interview with Kurt Eissler, Sigmund Freud
Collection, Box 126, Folder 4, Manuscript Division, Library
of Congress, Washington, DC, 1954

Falzeder, Ernst, '"My grand-patient, my chief tormentor": A Hitherto Unnoticed Case of Freud's and the Consequences', *Psychoanalytic Quarterly*, LXIII (1994), pp. 297–331

Fichtner, Gerhard, ed., *The Sigmund Freud–Ludwig Binswanger Correspondence, 1908–1938* (London, 2003)

Fiori, René, *Elfriede H, La femme aux épingles. Rencontre avec un cas de Freud, de la névrose obsessionnelle à la mélancolie* (CreateSpace Independent Publishing Platform, 2015)

Freud, Sigmund, correspondence with Oskar Pfister, Sigmund Freud Collection, Box 38, Folders 23–8, Manuscript Division, Library of Congress, Washington, DC, 1909–40

McGuire, William, ed., *The Freud / Jung Letters* (Princeton, NJ, 1974)

May, Ulrike, and Daniela Haller, 'Nineteen Patients in Analysis with Freud (1910–1920)', *American Imago*, LXV / 1 (2008), pp. 41–105

Pfister, Oskar, interview with Kurt Eissler, Sigmund Freud Collection, Box 120, Folder 6, Manuscript Division, Library of Congress, Washington, DC, 1953

KURT RIE

Dehning, Sonja, *Tanz der Feder: künstlerische Produktivität in Romanen von Autorinnen vom 1900* (Würzburg, 2000), pp. 146–8

Krafft, Margarete, 'Recollections', Sigmund Freud Collection, Box 124, Folder 47, Manuscript Division, Library of Congress, Washington, DC, undated

—, interview with Kurt Eissler, Sigmund Freud Collection, Box 124, Folder 47, Manuscript Division, Library of Congress, Washington, DC, 1954

Rie, Bella, interview with Kurt Eissler, Sigmund Freud Collection, Box 132, Folder 3, Manuscript Division, Library of Congress, Washington, DC, 1953

Rie, Robert, interview with Kurt Eissler, Sigmund Freud Collection, Box 132, Folder 4, Manuscript Division, Library of Congress, Washington, DC, 1953

ALBERT HIRST

Anonymous, 'Albert Hirst, 87, Lawyer, Is Dead: Specialist in Life Insurance Wrote Exemption Law', *New York Times*, 2 March 1974

Elias [née Hirsch], Ada, interview with Kurt Eissler, Sigmund Freud Collection, Box 114, Folder 9, Manuscript Division, Library of Congress, Washington, DC, 1953

Hirst, Albert, interview with Kurt Eissler, Sigmund Freud Collection, Box 116, Folder 2, Manuscript Division, Library of Congress, Washington, DC, 1952

—, correspondence with Anna Freud and Ernest Jones, Ernest Jones Papers, Institute of Psychoanalysis, London, 1953

—, *Analyzed and Reeducated by Freud Himself*, Sigmund Freud Collection, Box 60, Manuscript Division, Library of Congress, Washington, DC, 1972

Lynn, David J., 'Sigmund Freud's Psychoanalysis of Albert Hirst', *Bulletin of the History of Medicine*, LXXI/1 (1997), pp. 69–93

Roazen, Paul, *How Freud Worked: First-hand Accounts of Patients* (Northvale, NJ, 2005), chap. 1

BARON VICTOR VON DIRSZTAY

Broch, Hermann, *Das Teesdorfer Tagebuch für Ea von Allesch* (Berlin, 1995)

Eissler, Kurt R., note joined to a letter from Sigmund Freud to Victor von Dirsztay of 10 June 1920, Sigmund Freud Collection, Box 21, Folder 13, Manuscript Division, Library of Congress, Washington, DC, 1959

Kratzer, Hertha, *Die unschicklichen Töchter. Frauenporträts der Wiener Moderne* (Vienna, 2003)

May, Ulrike, 'Fourteen Hundred Hours of Analysis with Freud: Viktor von Dirsztay: A Biographical Sketch', *Psychoanalysis and History*, XIII/1 (2011), pp. 91–137

Obholzer, Karin, *The Wolf-man: Conversations with Freud's Patient – Sixty Years Later* (New York, 1982)

Reik, Theodor, 'The Characteristics of Masochism', *American Imago*, 1 (1939), pp. 26–59

—, *Masochism in Modern Man* (New York and Toronto, 1941)

—, interview with Kurt Eissler, 5 March 1954, Sigmund Freud Collection, Box 121, Folder 4, Manuscript Division, Library of Congress, Washington, DC

Timms, Edward, 'The "Child-woman": Kraus, Freud, Wittels, and Irma Karcewska', *Austrian Studies*, 1 (1990), pp. 87–107

SERGIUS PANKEJEFF

Berthelsen, Detlef, *Alltag bei Familie Freud: Die Erinnerungen der Paula Fichtl* (Hamburg, 1987)

Eissler, Kurt, note on three visits to Sergius Pankejeff at the Steinhof hospital, Sigmund Freud Collection, Box 125, Folder 11, Manuscript Division, Library of Congress, Washington, DC, 1978

—, *Freud and the Seduction Theory: A Brief Love Affair* (Madison, CT, 2001), pp. 387–406

Freud, Sigmund, correspondence with Sergius Pankejeff, Sigmund Freud Collection, Box 38, Folder 11, Manuscript Division, Library of Congress, Washington, DC, 1912, 1919, 1926, 1930

—, 'From the History of an Infantile Neurosis [1918]', Standard Edition, vol. XVII, pp. 1–124

Gardiner, Muriel, ed., *The Wolf-man by the Wolf-man, with The Case of the Wolf-man by Sigmund Freud* (New York, 1971)

—, 'The Wolf Man's Last Years', *Journal of the American Psychoanalytic Association*, XXXI (1983), pp. 867–97

May, Ulrike, and Daniela Haller, 'Nineteen Patients in Analysis with Freud (1910–1920)', *American Imago*, LXV/1 (2008), pp. 41–105

Muriel Gardiner Papers, Sigmund Freud Collection, Manuscript Division, Library of Congress, Washington, DC, 1890–1986

Obholzer, Karin, *The Wolf-man Sixty Years Later: Conversations with Freud's Controversial Patient* (New York, 1982)

—, interview with Mikkel Borch-Jacobsen, Vienna, 15 March 1994, Borch-Jacobsen private archive

Pankejeff, Sergius, interviews with Kurt Eissler, Sigmund Freud Collection, Box 119, Manuscript Division, Library of Congress, Washington, DC, 1952, 1954–5

—, interviews with Kurt Eissler, Sigmund Freud Collection, Box 130 and 131, Manuscript Division, Library of Congress, Washington, DC, 1953, 1957–60

—, letters to Ernest Jones, Ernest Jones Papers, Institute of Psychoanalysis, London, 1953–4

—, letters pertaining to Freud's 'History of an Infantile Neurosis', *Psychoanalytic Quarterly*, XXVI (1957), pp. 449–60

Ruth Mack Brunswick Papers, Sigmund Freud Collection, Manuscript Division, Library of Congress, Washington, DC, 1921–43

Sergius Pankejeff Papers, Sigmund Freud Collection, Manuscript Division, Library of Congress, Washington, DC, 1901–79

Weil, Frederick, interview with Kurt Eissler regarding Sergius Pankejeff, Sigmund Freud Collection, Box 123, Folder 1, Manuscript Division, Library of Congress, Washington, DC, 1955

Wulff, Moshe, interview with Kurt Eissler, Sigmund Freud Collection, Box 123, Folder 8, Manuscript Division, Library of Congress, Washington, DC, 1962

BRUNO VENEZIANI

Accerboni Pavanello, Anna Maria, 'La sfida di Italo Svevo alla psicoanalisi: Guarire dalla cura', in *Guarire dalla cura. Italo Svevo e la medicina*, ed. Riccardo Cepach (Trieste, 2008)

Anzellotti, Fulvio, *Il segreto di Svevo* (Pordenone, 1985)

—, *La villa di Zeno* (Pordenone, 1991)

Amouroux, Rémy, 'Marie Bonaparte, Her First Two Patients and the Literary World', *International Journal of Psychoanalysis*, XCI (2010), pp. 879–94

Fallend, Karl, *Sonderlinge, Träumer, Sensitive; Psychoanalyse auf dem Weg zur Institution und Profession; Protokolle der Wiener Psychoanalytischen Vereinigung und biographische Studien* (Vienna, 1995)

Falzeder, Ernst, ed., *The Complete Correspondence of Sigmund Freud and Karl Abraham* (London, 2002)

Freud, Sigmund, correspondence with Edoardo Weiss, Sigmund Freud Collection, Box 43, Folder 22, Manuscript Division, Library of Congress, Washington, DC, 1919–23

Ghidetti, Enrico, *Italo Svevo: la coscienza di un borghese Triestino* (Roma, 1980)

Groddeck, Georg, *The Meaning of Illness: Selected Psychoanalytic Writings* (London, 1977)

—, *Das Buch vom Es. Psychoanalytische Briefe an eine Freundin* (Berlin, 2016)

Jahier, Alice, 'Quelques lettres d'Italo Svevo', *Preuves*, v/48 (1955), pp. 26–32

May, Ulrike, and Daniela Haller, 'Nineteen Patients in Analysis with Freud (1910–1920)', *American Imago*, LXV/1 (2008), pp. 41–105

Palmieri, Giovanni, *Schmitz, Svevo, Zeno. Storia di due 'biblioteche'* (Milan, 1994)

Roazen, Paul, *Edoardo Weiss: The House That Freud Built* (New Brunswick, NJ, 2005)

Svevo, Italo, *Opera Omnia*, I (Trieste, 1966)

—, *La coscienza di Zeno*, in *Romanzi e 'continuazioni'* [1923] (Milan, 2004), pp. 625–1085

—, *Soggiorno londinese*, in *Teatro e saggi* [1927] (Milan, 2004), pp. 893–910

—, *Conferenza su James Joyce*, in *Teatro e saggi* [1927] (Milan, 2004), pp. 911–36

Veneziani Svevo, Livia, *Vita di mio marito* [1950] (Trieste, 1976)

Voghera, Giorgio, 'Gli anni della psicanalisi', in *Quassù Trieste*, ed. L. Mazzi (Bologne, 1968)

Weiss, Edoardo, interview with Kurt R. Eissler, Sigmund Freud Collection, Box 123, Folders 3 and 4, Manuscript Division, Library of Congress, Washington, DC, 1954, undated

—, *Sigmund Freud As A Consultant: Recollections of a Pioneer in Psycho-analysis* (New York, 1970)

ELMA PÁLOS

Berman, Emanuel, 'Sándor, Gizella, Elma: A Biographical Journey', *International Journal of Psychoanalysis*, LXXXV/2 (August 2003), pp. 489–520

Borch-Jacobsen, Mikkel, and Sonu Shamdasani, *The Freud Files: An Inquiry into the History of Psychoanalysis* (Cambridge, 2006), pp. 280–82

Brabant, Eva, Ernst Falzeder and Patrizia Giampieri-Deutsch, eds, *The Correspondence of Sigmund Freud and Sándor Ferenczi*, vol. I: 1908–1914 (Cambridge, MA, and London, 1993)

Laurvik [née Pálos], Elma, interview with Kurt Eissler, Sigmund Freud Collection, Box 117, Folder 18, Manuscript Division, Library of Congress, Washington, DC, 1952

Laurvik, J. Nilsen, *Is It Art? Post-Impressionism, Futurism, Cubism* (New York, 1913)

May, Ulrike, and Daniela Haller, 'Nineteen Patients in Analysis with Freud (1910–1920)', *American Imago*, LXV/1 (2008), pp. 41–105

LOE KANN

Appignanesi, Lisa, and John Forrester, *Freud's Women* (New York, 1992)

Brabant, Eva, Ernst Falzeder and Patrizia Giampieri-Deutsch, eds,

The Correspondence of Sigmund Freud and Sándor Ferenczi, vol. 1:
1908–1914 (Cambridge, MA, and London, 1993)

Maddox, Brenda, *Freud's Wizard: The Enigma of Ernest Jones* (London,
2006)

May, Ulrike, and Daniela Haller, 'Nineteen Patients in Analysis with
Freud (1910–1920)', *American Imago*, LXV/1 (2008), pp. 41–105

Paskauskas, R. Andrew, ed., *The Complete Correspondence of Sigmund
Freud and Ernest Jones*, 1908–1939 (Cambridge, MA, 1995)

Wilsey, John, H. *Jones VC: The Life and Death of an Unusual Hero*
(London, 2003)

KARL MEYREDER

Anderson, Harriet, ed., *Tagebücher 1873–1937 / Rosa Mayreder*
(Frankfurt am Main, 1988)

—, *Utopian Feminism: Women's Movements in Fin-de-siècle Vienna*
(New Haven, CT, 1992)

May, Ulrike, and Daniela Haller, 'Nineteen Patients in Analysis with
Freud (1910–1920)', *American Imago*, LXV/1 (2008), pp. 41–105

Mayreder, Rosa, 'Review of S. Freud, *Three Essays on Sexual Theory*',
Wiener Klinische Rundschau, X (1906), pp. 189–90

MARGARETHE CSONKA

Eissler, Kurt, *Freud and the Seduction Theory: A Brief Love Affair*
(Madison, CT, 2001), pp. 370–71

Rieder, Ines, and Diana Voigt, *Heimliches Begehren. Die Geschichte der
Sidonie C.* (Vienna, 2000)

Ruhs, August, 'Freud 1919: Ein Fall von weiblicher Homosexualität
und gewisse Folgen . . .', in *Sigmund Freud Vorlesungen 2006. Die
grossen Krankengeschichten*, ed. Christine Diercks and Sabine
Schlüter (Vienna, 2008), pp. 135–44

Trautenegg [née Csonka], Margarethe von, correspondence and
interview with Kurt Eissler, Kurt R. Eissler Papers, Box 2,
Manuscript Division, Library of Congress, Washington, DC,
1969–88

ANNA FREUD

Anna Freud Papers, Manuscript Division, Library of Congress,
Washington, DC

Burlingham, Michael John, *The Last Tiffany* (New York, 1989)

Fichtner, Gerhard, ed., *The Sigmund Freud–Ludwig Binswanger
Correspondence*, 1908–1938 (London, 2003)

Freud, Anna, 'Beating Fantasies and Daydreams [1922]', in *Introduction
to Psychoanalysis: Lectures for Child Analysts and Teachers*, 1922–1935.
Writings (New York, 1974), vol. 1

Freud, Sigmund, '"A child is being beaten": A Contribution to the
Study of the Origin of Sexual Perversion', Standard Edition,
vol. XVII, pp. 175–204

—, 'Some Psychological Consequences of the Anatomical
    Difference between the Sexes', Standard Edition, vol. xix,
    pp. 248–58
Gay, Peter, *Freud: A Life for Our Time* (New York, 1988)
Heller, Peter, and Günther Bittner, *Eine Kinderanalyse bei Anna Freud
    (1929–1932)* (Würzburg, 1983)
—, ed., *Anna Freud's Letters to Eva Rosenfeld* (Madison, CT, 1992)
Mahony, Patrick, 'Freud as Family Therapist: Reflections',
    in *Freud and the History of Psychoanalysis*, ed. Toby Gelfand
    and John Kerr (Hillsdale, NJ, 1992), pp. 307–17
Paskauskas, R. Andrew, ed., *The Complete Correspondence
    of Sigmund Freud and Ernest Jones, 1908–1939* (Cambridge,
    MA, 1995)
Peter Heller Papers, Manuscript Division, Library of Congress,
    Washington, DC
Young-Bruehl, Elisabeth, *Anna Freud: A Biography* (New York, 1988)

HORACE FRINK

Ames, Thaddeus H., interview with Kurt Eissler, Freud Collection,
    Box 112, Folder 15, Manuscript Division, Library of Congress,
    Washington, DC, 1952
Blumgart, Leonard, interview with Kurt Eissler, Freud Collection,
    Box 113, Folder 13, Manuscript Division, Library of Congress,
    Washington, DC, 1952
Edmunds, Lavinia, 'His Master's Choice', *Johns Hopkins Magazine*
    (April 1988), pp. 40–49
Eissler, Kurt, *Freud and the Seduction Theory: A Brief Love Affair*
    (Madison, CT, 2001), pp. 29–32
Fredric Wertham Papers, Box 1, Manuscript Division, Library of
    Congress, Washington, DC, 1911–80
Freud, Sigmund, correspondence with Horace and Angelika Bijur
    Frink, Freud Collection, Box 28, Folder 27, Manuscript Division,
    Library of Congress, Washington, DC, 1921–3
Frink, Angelika Bijur, interview with Kurt Eissler, Freud Collection,
    Box 115, Folder 7, Manuscript Division, Library of Congress,
    Washington, DC, 1952
Frink Family Collection, Alan Mason Chesney Medical Archives,
    Johns Hopkins Medical Institutions
Kardiner, Abraham, Clarence Oberndorf and Monroe Meyer,
    'In Memoriam, Horace Westlake Frink, MD (1883–1936)',
    Psychoanalytic Quarterly, v (1936), pp. 601–3
—, *My Analysis with Freud: Reminiscences* (New York, 1977)
Oberndorf, Clarence, interview with Kurt Eissler, Freud Collection,
    Box 118, Folders 13–14, Manuscript Division, Library of
    Congress, Washington, DC, 1952
Roazen, Paul, *Freud and His Followers* (New York, 1975), pp. 378–80
—, *How Freud Worked: First-hand Accounts of Patients* (Northvale, NJ,
    2005), pp. 68–9

Viola Wertheim Bernard Papers, 1918–2000, Box 32, Folders 2–9,
    Augustus C. Long Health Sciences Library, Archives and Special
    Collections, Columbia University, New York
Zitrin, Arthur, 'Freud-Frink-Brill: A Puzzling Episode in the History of
    Psychoanalysis', *Bulletin of the Association for Psychoanalytic Medicine
    of the Columbia University Psychoanalytic Center*, 13 January 1998

MONROE MEYER

Anonymous, 'In Memoriam', *Psychoanalytic Quarterly*, VIII / 2 (1939),
    pp. 138–40
Blumgart, Leonard, interview with Kurt Eissler, Freud Collection,
    Box 113, Folder 13, Manuscript Division, Library of Congress,
    Washington, DC, 1952
Fredric Wertham Papers, Box 1, Manuscript Division, Library of
    Congress, Washington, DC, 1911–80
Freud, Sigmund, correspondence with Horace and Angelika Bijur
    Frink, Freud Collection, Box 28, Folder 27, Manuscript Division,
    Library of Congress, Washington, DC, 1921–3
Kardiner, Abraham, *My Analysis with Freud: Reminiscences* (New York,
    1977)
Oberndorf, Clarence, interview with Kurt Eissler, Freud Collection,
    Box 118, Folders 13–14, Manuscript Division, Library of Congress,
    Washington, DC, 1952
Stern, Adolph, 'Monroe A. Meyer, MD', *Psychoanalytic Review*, XXVI / 4
    (1939), p. 599
—, interview with Kurt Eissler, Freud Collection, Box 122, Folder 10,
    Manuscript Division, Library of Congress, Washington, DC, 1952

SCOFIELD THAYER

Beam, Alex, *Gracefully Insane: Life and Death Inside America's Premier
    Mental Hospital* (New York, 2001)
Bernays, Edward L., *Biography of an Idea: Memoirs of a Public Relations
    Counsel* (New York, 1965)
Cox, Richard W., 'Adolf Dehn: The Life', in *The Prints of Adolf Dehn:
    A Catalogue Raisonné*, ed. Joscelyn Lumsdaine and Thomas
    O'Sullivan (St Paul, MN, 1987)
Dehn, Adolf, interview with Kurt Eissler, Sigmund Freud Collection,
    Box 114, Folder 1, Manuscript Division, Library of Congress,
    Washington, DC, 1959
—, interview with Kurt Eissler, Sigmund Freud Collection, Box 124,
    Folder 14, Manuscript Division, Library of Congress, Washington,
    DC, undated
Dehn-Thomas, Mura, interview with Kurt Eissler, Sigmund Freud
    Collection, Box 114, Folder 2, Manuscript Division, Library of
    Congress, Washington, DC, 1960
Dempsey, James, *The Tortured Life of Scofield Thayer* (Gainesville, FL,
    2014)

Dial/Scofield Thayer Papers, Beinecke Rare Book and Manuscript
    Library, Yale University, New Haven, CT, 1879–1982
Ducharme, Diane J., Guide to the Dial/Scofield Thayer Papers,
    Beinecke Rare Book and Manuscript Library, 1988: https://
    archives.yale.edu/repositories/11/resources/1531
Freud, Sigmund, correspondence with Scofield Thayer, Sigmund Freud
    Collection, Box 42, Folder 38, Manuscript Division, Library of
    Congress, Washington, DC, 1925
—, correspondence with Edward Bernays, Sigmund Freud Collection,
    Box 1, Folders 3–4, Manuscript Division, Library of Congress,
    Washington, DC, 1919–24
Hollevoet-Force, Christel, 'Les Picasso de Soler ou la découverte d'un
    tableau caché', Colloque Revoir Picasso, Paris, Musée Picasso,
    26 March 2015: http://revoirpicasso.fr
Sawyer-Lauçanno, Christopher, E. E. Cummings: A Biography
    (Naperville, IL, 2004)

CARL LIEBMANN

Beam, Alex, Gracefully Insane: Life and Death Inside America's Premier
    Mental Hospital (New York, 2001)
Brabant, Eva, Ernst Falzeder and Patrizia Giampieri-Deutsch, eds,
    The Correspondence of Sigmund Freud and Sándor Ferenczi, vol. III:
    1920–1933 (Cambridge, MA, and London, 1993)
Freud, Sigmund, correspondence with Oskar Pfister, Sigmund Freud
    Collection, Box 38, Folders 23–8, Manuscript Division, Library
    of Congress, Washington, DC, 1909–39
—, correspondence with Julius [and Marie] Liebmann [misspelled
    'Liebman'], Sigmund Freud Collection, Box 36, Folder 30,
    Manuscript Division, Library of Congress, Washington, DC,
    1925–32
—, 'Fetishism', Standard Edition, vol. XXI, pp. 149–58
Hofmann, Rolf, 'The Originators of Rheingold Beer: From
    Ludwigsburg to Brooklyn – A Dynasty of German-Jewish Brewers',
    Aufbau, 21 June 2001
Liebmann [misspelled 'Liebman'], Julius, interview with Kurt Eissler,
    Sigmund Freud Collection, Box 118, Folder 2, Manuscript
    Division, Library of Congress, Washington, DC, 1954
Lynn, David J., 'Freud's Analysis of A. B., a Psychotic Man', Journal
    of the American Academy of Psychoanalysis, XXI/1 (1993), pp. 63–78

ACKNOWLEDGEMENTS

I would like to express my debt to all those who, for the past forty years, have revolutionized our understanding of psychoanalysis by patiently reconstructing the fate of these anonymous or pseudonymous patients on whom Freud claimed to have based his theories: Ola Andersson, Lavinia Edmunds, Henri F. Ellenberger, Ernst Falzeder, John Forrester, Helen Frink Kraft, Stefan Goldmann, Albrecht Hirschmüller, Han Israëls, David J. Lynn, Patrick J. Mahony, Ulrike May, Karin Obholzer, Inès Rieder, Paul Roazen, Anthony Stadlen, Peter J. Swales, Christfried Tögel, Diana Voigt and Elisabeth Young-Bruehl. I have drawn heavily on their work, without which my own would simply not have been possible.

I also wish to thank all of those – sometimes the same people – who have helped me during the writing of this little book and, more generally, during my own research on Freud's patients over the past 25 years: Harold P. Blum, Lucas Brujin, Riccardo Cepach, Frederick Crews, Kurt R. Eissler†, Ernst Falzeder, John Forrester†, Lucy Freeman†, Toby Gelfand, Stefan Goldmann, Ann-Kathryn Graf, Colin Graf, Albrecht Hirschmüller, Han Israëls, Reina van Lier, Patrick J. Mahony, Karin Obholzer, Josiane Praz, Paul Roazen†, Karlheinz Rossbacher, Michael Scammell, E. Randol ('Randy') Schoenberg, Sonu Shamdasani, Richard Skues, Peter J. Swales, Andreas Treichl, Tom Ulrich, Mia Vieyra and Jerome C. Wakefield. It goes without saying that I bear sole responsibility for the assertions and any errors contained in this book.

PHOTO ACKNOWLEDGEMENTS

The author and publishers wish to express their thanks to the below sources of illustrative material and/or permission to reproduce it. Every effort has been made to contact copyright holders; should there be any we have been unable to reach or to whom inaccurate acknowledgements have been made, please contact the publishers, and full adjustments will be made to subsequent printings.

A. C. Long Health Sciences Library, Columbia University Medical Center: p. 241; Roger Nicholas Balsiger: p. 57; Gesellschaft für eine Gesamtkultur, Bern: pp. 42, 43; Jewish Museum, Merano: p. 112; Koestler Archive, University of Edinburgh: p. 77; Library of Congress: pp. 25, 150, 166, 167, 230, 231, 242; property of Museo Sveviano, Trieste: p. 180; National Gallery of Art, Washington: p. 199; Sigmund Freud Museum, Vienna: pp. 213, 216; Andreas Treichl: p. 106; Mia Vieyra: p. 73.